SELECTED LETTERS OF
Charles Baudelaire

SELECTED LETTERS OF
Charles Baudelaire
The Conquest of Solitude

Translated and Edited by
ROSEMARY LLOYD

WEIDENFELD AND NICOLSON
London

ROSEMARY LLOYD is university lecturer in the French
department at the University of Cambridge. She is the author
of *Baudelaire et Hoffmann, Baudelaire's Literary Criticism,*
and *Mallarmé: Poésies.*

The translations in this volume are based on the text of
La Correspondance de Baudelaire, edited by Claude Pichois,
© 1982 by Editions Gallimard.

For my colleagues at New Hall,
who taught me the true meaning of Fellowship

Contents

Translator's Note

In selecting Baudelaire's letters I have sought to include those reflecting major developments in the poet's life that have a bearing on his creative and critical writing; those that refer in any detail to works he was producing or planning; those that reveal his relationships with other writers of the time; and those that evoke the emotional atmosphere and physical conditions in which he was living.

Because of the differences between the French legal system, and those of Britain and the United States, there is no exact equivalent for the terms *conseil de famille* (literally, family council), *conseil judiciaire* (lit. judiciary council), or *tuteur* (lit. tutor, guardian). I have therefore left those terms in French. To avoid ambiguity I have also left in French the titles of Baudelaire's translations of works by Poe, when it is clear that it is the translation and not the original that is at issue.

My thanks are due to my colleague, Zara Steiner, whose enthusiasm for this project never waned; to Mme A. Chevallier, of Gallimard, for her help in obtaining translator's rights; and above all to M. Claude Pichois, to whose erudite edition of the letters for the Pléiade collection and to whose warm interest in their translation this work is profoundly indebted.

Introduction

Baudelaire was born in Paris on 9 April 1821, less than a month before the death of Napoleon, twenty-two years after Balzac was born, nineteen after Victor Hugo.[1] It was the year that saw the birth of Flaubert, whose novel *Madame Bovary* was to go on trial in the same year as *The Flowers of Evil*; the death of the German Romantic writer, E. T. A. Hoffmann, whose works Baudelaire admired; and the publication of De Quincey's *Confessions of an English Opium Eater*, which Baudelaire was to translate and adapt as part of his study of intoxicants.

In the biographical and bibliographical notes that he assembled at the request of a journalist friend, Watripon, in 1852, Baudelaire indicates three phases in his childhood. The first of these, brought to an abrupt end by his father's death and his mother's subsequent remarriage to Jacques Aupick, were years when his mother was both an idol and a comrade to him (letter 131), and when the seeds were sown for that permanent love of art that he himself stressed and that dominates his articles of art criticism: "old furniture in the style of Louis XVI, antiques, the consulate, pastels, the society of the eighteenth century."[2] In 1832, Baudelaire and his mother moved to Lyon, where Aupick was stationed. They remained there for four years, returning to Paris in 1836. In both cities, Baudelaire, in accordance with contemporary middle-class custom, attended boarding schools, whose spartan conditions and harsh regulations intensified his sense of separation from his mother. The letters dating from his school days indicate a complex character already settling into the mold that would determine his future development and behavior: a love of color, a restless energy, a sense of revolt, a feeling of failure created both by his parents' demands and by his own longing to obtain the marked and ticketed success of school prizes. The letter to Watripon mentions the "heavy melancholy" of this period, and elsewhere he notes a "sense of *solitude*, beginning in childhood. Despite my family—and particularly among my schoolmates—a sense of an eternally solitary destiny. And yet a very intense taste for life

1. For a detailed biography, see Enid Starkie, *Baudelaire* (Harmondsworth: Penguin, 1971).
2. Baudelaire, *Œuvres complètes*, 2 vols. (Paris: Pléiade, 1975–76), 1:784.

and pleasure."[3] It is typical of the multifaceted nature of Baudelaire's mind that he should attempt to find something positive in this despairing sense of solitude: "there is an invincible taste for prostitution in man's heart and it's this that creates his horror of solitude. —He wants to be *two*. The man of genius wants to be *one*, and therefore solitary."[4] The childhood letters, with their descriptions of Baudelaire's search for congenial companions, his disgust with modern literature, his countless confessions that yet again his leave of absence had been suspended, testify clearly to this sense of solitude, but his love of dancing and skating, his early fascination with Delacroix's paintings, and his excitement in finding (albeit briefly) in M. J. W. Rinn a teacher who seemed to appreciate him, show also that the "horror of life" already had as its inextricable counterpart the "ecstasy of life."[5]

Expelled from his high school in 1839 for the last in a series of minor acts of disobedience, Baudelaire prepared the *Baccalauréat* himself and passed it on 12 August, thus earning, at least in his own eyes, the right to embark on what he describes to Watripon as "free life in Paris." It was around this stage that Baudelaire contracted the syphilis that was to recur at various intervals throughout his life and from which he eventually died. No doubt the disease and it side effects contributed in large measure to the bouts of despair and lethargy that mark the poet's life and of which he so frequently complains in his letters.

This was a time of close friendships with other budding writers and artists, but it was also at this stage that Baudelaire began to contract debts at such a rate that his stepfather, fearing that he would fritter away his fortune even before he came of age to inherit it, sent him on a sea voyage, which, he mendaciously declares to Watripon, took him to India.

Aupick had a further motive for taking this course of action and one that indicates an uncanny intuition of the central themes of *The Flowers of Evil*: as he claims in a letter written in April or May 1841, he hoped that the experience, if it failed to prevent Baudelaire from becoming a poet, would at least encourage him to draw his inspiration from "better sources than the sewers of Paris."[6] Much has been made of Baudelaire's relationship with his stepfather. Although the seven-year-old boy may well have been jealous, at least initially, at having to share his mother with a stranger, the letters indicate that the two were on fairly good terms until the 1840s, when Baudelaire's determination to be a poet, his refusal to be

3. Ibid., 1:680.
4. Ibid., 1:700.
5. Ibid., 1:703.
6. Published in *Mercure de France*, 15 March 1937, p. 631.

a "useful" member of society, and his rejection of the values Aupick held dear, led to angry altercations. Later, it is clear that Baudelaire held his stepfather to blame for the imposition of the *conseil de famille*, and all subsequent references to him, until the time of the General's death, are marked by varying degrees of hostility.

However homesick Baudelaire may have been, and although he seems not to have gone further than the Pacific islands of Mauritius and Reunion, this voyage was to have a profound impact on his imagination, stocking it with the treasure trove of images, rhythms, and exotic sensations that inform much of his poetry. Only two letters dating from the voyage seem to have survived: a hasty note to his mother, including, interestingly, a request that she give his nephew his copy of *Robinson Crusoe* (one of the "sailors forgotten on an island" that he later invoked in his famous poem "The Swan" ["Le Cygne"]); and the curiously formal letter accompanying the sonnet "To a Creole Lady" ("A une dame créole"). This stilted, courtly formality recurs in the letters Baudelaire later wrote Apollonie Sabatier.

With his return to Paris in 1842, Baudelaire again threw himself into his former bohemian existence, cultivating the friendship of artists and writers, and incurring so many debts for clothes, furniture, and works of art that his family subjected him, in 1844, to what he was to consider for the rest of his life as the unforgivable and unforgettable humiliation of a *conseil de famille*, in which control over his fortune was taken out of his hands and placed in those of a legal adviser, the lawyer Narcisse Ancelle, who was to administer Baudelaire's funds for the rest of the poet's life. The letters dating from this traumatic period, as well as obsessive attempts in later life to regain control of his funds, show that even if the attempted suicide of 1845, when he tried to stab himself, was no more than a histrionic scream of protest, Baudelaire always felt this judgment as an ineradicable blot on his honor. More tangibly, in their desire to safeguard the young man's capital, the *conseil*, as Baudelaire's biographer, Enid Starkie, expresses it, "left him owing more than a thousand pounds, with only a diminished income of seventy-five pounds a year to live on and from which to pay his debts." [7] Thus began the endless rounds of borrowing small sums for partial payments of debts, the constant search for credit, and the increasingly impossible attempts to pay off the interest on the accumulating loans. Baudelaire's letters bear acrimonious witness to the debilitating drain on his time and energy that his well-meaning *conseil* inflicted on him. Nevertheless, he eventually came to respect and even like Ancelle, and the correspondence between them is both rich and

7. Starkie, *Baudelaire*, p. 138.

revealing in the light that it sheds on Baudelaire's character; the mixture of frustration and courtesy; the longing to convince Ancelle (representative here of the French public in general) of his poetic genius and to instill in him a sense of true beauty, combined with the conviction that such a task was impossible; and finally gratitude for Ancelle's desire to help him find a publisher, yoked to the unshakable belief that Ancelle's bungling attempts would only worsen matters. Much later, in a letter to his publisher and staunch friend Auguste Poulet-Malassis, he was to sum up the financial situation caused by the *conseil* in tones of resigned dignity:

> when you find a man who, free at the age of 17, with an excessive taste for pleasure, and with no family, sets out on his literary career owing 30,000 francs and after almost 20 years has increased that debt by a mere 10,000, and, what's more, is far from feeling the intelligence crushed out of him, introduce him to me, and I'll salute him as my equal.[8]

Although the biographical notes speak of his "long-lasting difficulty in being understood by the editor of any magazine," Baudelaire did manage to publish poems, the novella *La Fanfarlo*, and literary and artistic reviews during the 1840s, and it was at this stage, too, that he first came across the writings of Edgar Allan Poe, to which he was to devote so much attention as translator and critic. His letters reveal his attempts to find congenial editors, his enthusiasm at the thought of being put in charge of a periodical (to the extent that he even asked his mother to get her friends to subscribe), his growing friendships with such leading literary figures as Banville and Sainte-Beuve, and his plans for future literary projects. But they also reveal the degree to which Baudelaire, however busy or harassed, sought to help his friends, urging Chennevières, for instance, to take advantage of Baudelaire's relationship with the editor Lepoitevin Saint-Alme to get his own short stories published in *Le Corsaire-Satan*. Later we will find him providing a key to Champfleury's novel *Mademoiselle Mariette*, trying to arrange for Poulet-Malassis to publish Gautier's *Le Roman de la momie*, and devoting hours of his time to helping the young Léon Cladel polish his novel *Les Martyrs ridicules*.

Few letters have been found from the period immediately before and after the Revolution of 1848, and Baudelaire's intellectual and physical involvement is a subject of dispute among critics. A note in *My Heart Laid Bare* (*Mon cœur mis à nu*) speaks of his "intoxication of 1848,"

8. Baudelaire, *Correspondance* (Paris: Pléiade, 1973), 2:94.

attributing it partly to a taste for vengeance, and a "*natural* pleasure in demolition," and partly to the effect of his reading,[9] a reference, no doubt, to the kind of books mentioned in the prose poem "Let's Beat Up the Poor," ("Assommons les pauvres"), books that "deal with the art of making populations happy, wise, and rich, in 24 hours."[10] The letters to the economic theorist Proudhon hint darkly at intrigue, while that to Ancelle about the politician Madier de Montjau reveals a clear-sighted realism concerning the peasants' "inescapable socialism, ferocious, stupid, as bestial as the socialism of the brand and sickle" (letter 31). Whatever political enthusiasms he may have had, however, were crushed into disgust at the coup d'état when Louis-Napoleon declared himself emperor and hopes for a republican France were yet again quashed. Yet, however "depoliticized" (letter 38 [6 March 1852]) he might claim to be, however sharply aware of what a heartless science politics is, references in his letters nevertheless reflect the way in which "every time a serious matter arises, [he is] seized yet again with passion and curiosity" (letter 106): Orsini's attempted assassination of Napoléon III, the tension between France and Italy, or the change of attitude toward the Belgian king Léopold I over the period of mourning for him.

The years between the coup d'état and the publication of *The Flowers of Evil* were a time of great hardship for Baudelaire, who, dunned by creditors, frequently changing lodgings, suffering physical and mental anguish through his tormented but necessary relationship with Jeanne Duval, still managed to publish reviews of artistic exhibitions and literature, to work on his translations and studies of Poe, and to produce the poems for the first edition of the work on which his fame rests. His determination not to be bracketed with movements of the time, such as Paganism or the pantheist poetry of the last wave of Romantics, is underscored not just in his critical articles (his virulent attack on the Pagan poets, for instance, pummeled them with a series of ironic questions: "Do you expect all these marble statues to turn into devoted women when you're on your death bed, in the days when you're tormented by remorse, at times when you're powerless? Can you drink ambrosia broth? Or eat Paros cutlets? How much do you get for a lyre at the pawnbrokers?")[11] but also in his letters, notably the famous response to Desnoyers's request for "poems on Nature": "you know very well that the vegetable kingdom fails to move me and that my soul rebels at that strange new religion which will always be, so it seems to me, rather

9. *Œuvres complètes*, 1:679.
10. Ibid., 1:357.
11. Ibid., 2:47.

shocking to any *spiritual* being. I'll never believe that the souls of the gods inhabit plants, and even if they did, I really couldn't work up much enthusiasm for the fact, and would consider my own soul as of much more importance than that of the sanctified vegetables" (letter 48).[12] What excited him more was "our amazing cities" and the possibility of evoking them in such a way as to give expression to the "lamentations of mankind" (letter 48) through the power of that "most scientific of faculties" (letter 63), the imagination, with its ability to discern allegories and correspondences between the eternal world and the human soul. And because he believed that regularity and symmetry on the one hand, and complication and harmony on the other, were "primordial needs of the human mind,"[13] we see him already grouping his poems to form that "secret architecture" which becomes even more important in the second edition of the poems. Thus we find the pairing of poems on twilight, and the insistence that he and his publisher should work out together, "for the question is of importance" (letter 70), the order of the pieces to be printed. As the proofs come in Baudelaire reveals that unending search for perfection, more calculated to delight his readers than his editors; a search that ranged from the hunt for the ideal expression, through the far from purely conventional importance of punctuation, to the appearance of the poem on the page—his dislike of Poulet-Malassis's "strangely hooked inverted commas" (letter 75), his wish for slimmer print in the dedication and to have the word *Flowers* in italics (letter 73). Despite the reception given *The Flowers of Evil* by the critics, who, according to Baudelaire, denied him everything "from the ability to invent, to knowledge of [his] own language," he remained unshaken in his conviction that "this volume, with all its qualities and faults, [would] make its way into the memory of the literate public, along with the best poetry of Victor Hugo, Théophile Gautier, and even Byron" (letter 79). Even the humiliation and frustration of the trial served merely to sharpen his long-standing belief that beauty was the sole aim of art, and that any art that pursued a moral goal as its prime aim was thereby necessarily debased.

Moreover, the need to replace, for a second edition, the works censored by the court spurred the habitual procrastinator, through a blend of anger and that sense of challenge that often produced his greatest works, into creating far more poems than had been excised and allowed a rearrangement that stressed the architectural patterning of groups and

12. For a more balanced view, see F. Leakey, *Baudelaire and Nature* (New York: Barnes & Noble, 1969).
13. *Œuvres complètes*, 1:663.

symmetries. The years between the two editions also seem to have taut-
ened Baudelaire's awareness of the creative potential of the city: although
his dream of writing poetical responses to Méryon's drawings of Paris
foundered against the astonishingly pedantic line taken by the artist (see
letter 115), the poems sent to Victor Hugo ("The Seven Old Men" ["Les
Sept Vieillards"], "The Little Old Ladies" ["Les Petites Vieilles"], and
above all "The Swan" ["Le Cygne"] show him working the rich vein of
the constantly changing spectacle of a great city. Above all, the letters
written during this period cast light on numerous aspects of Baudelaire's
poetry: the desire to explore different responses to a single theme by
transposing a statue into a poem (letter 100); the keen awareness of the
mot juste that made him describe death as the great camp follower at the
heels of the army of mankind; the famous evocation of the sonnet, in
whose very restrictions lies the secret of success: "because the form is
constricting, the idea bursts forth all the more intensely" (letter 117).
And in these years, too, he sought an "allegorical frontispiece" for each of
three works: the studies on Poe, *Opium and Hashish*, and the poems. He
dreamed of prefacing the new *Flowers of Evil* with the picture of "a
skeleton turning into a tree, with legs and ribs forming the trunk, the
arms stretched out to make a cross and bursting into leaves and buds,
protecting several rows of poisonous plants in little pots, lined up as in a
gardener's hothouse" (letter 106).

It was not just *The Flowers of Evil* that occupied Baudelaire's attention
at this time: he produced some of his finest articles of literary criticism,
on Poe and on his French contemporaries, and his adaptation of De
Quincey's confessions created a work he saw as "brilliant and dramatic"
(letter 104), more "free-wheeling and abrupt" (letter 97) than the earlier
studies of those other stimulants, wine and hashish. For this work, too,
he sought "an allegorical frontispiece expressing the main pleasures and
torments [he'd] related" (letter 106), again underlining the important
link he discerned between the printed word and visual images. The
letters referring to this work show him justifying the lengthy biographical section as "essential in providing a key to the utterly individual
phantasmagoria of *Opium*" (letter 97); his awareness of the importance of
publicity—"let's hope that Mr. de Quincey will send the paper a fine
letter of thanks" (letter 97)—and the extraordinary insensitivity of some
of his publishers: "At last I found an opening whose solemnity resembles
the opening bars of an orchestra. But smack! You think it would be more
judicious to introduce as an opening the obituary notice" (letter 113).

The years 1861–62 also saw him embark on what he later termed "a
horrible odyssey [. . .] with neither sirens nor lotus" (letter 138), his ill-
starred attempt to secure nomination to the French Academy. Whether

this was a bid to save himself and his works from plunging into the abyss created by the collapse of Poulet-Malassis's publishing concern, a despairing endeavor to gain his mother's approval, or a defiant gesture flung at an uncomprehending and frequently shocked public, Baudelaire threw himself into his candidacy with characteristic determination and, equally characteristically, dreamed of salvaging the hours thus lost and assuaging the insults that resulted by writing a book about his experience, just as later he contemplated wreaking revenge on Belgium through a vitriolic analysis of its character and morals.

However painful and frustrating they might have been, the years leading up to the publication of the second edition of *The Flowers of Evil* were marked by three important and fruitful encounters: the friendship with the poet de Vigny, whose support Baudelaire had sought in his bid for the Academy; the discovery of Wagner's music, to which he devoted one of his most revealing critical articles; and his growing friendship with the artist Manet, whom Baudelaire supported, encouraged, and cajoled throughout his remaining years.

With the publication of the new *Flowers of Evil* behind him, Baudelaire devoted much of his attention to a form of expression in which he had been experimenting for several years, the prose poem. His letter to Houssaye announcing the project speaks of his "embarking on a long-term experiment with this genre" (letter 138). The prose poems, however, posed problems Baudelaire was never able to solve completely: from Brussels he described them in a letter to Sainte-Beuve as "laborious little nothings that demand constant good humor [. . .] and a bizarre elation that demands spectacles, crowds, music, even street lights" (letter 174). And later still, again in a letter to the famous critic that alludes to the latter's early pieces of creative writing, he made the following lament: "At last I hope that one of these days I'll be able to show a new Joseph Delorme fixing his rhapsodic poetry on everything that occurs during his wanderings and drawing from each object an unpleasant moral lesson. But these little things, when one wants to express them with both penetration and lightness of touch, are so difficult to perform!" (letter 188). Worse still, completed prose poems ran the risk of being mauled by publishers, as an angry letter to Charpentier reveals: "suppress a *whole piece*, if a single *comma* displeases you, but don't suppress the comma—it's there for a reason" (letter 153).

It was a time of increasing solitude for Baudelaire, who was torn between the long-nourished plan to live with his mother in the small Normandy town of Honfleur and a conviction that his presence in Paris was essential, not merely for financial reasons but also to establish a lasting literary reputation. His letters reveal, too, a continual, if irregular, oscillation between idle lethargy and furious action: the increasing attempts to understand this aspect of his nature, an analysis that has its counterpart in the many poems and prose poems that try to discover the root cause of habitual vices, act as a constant, painful refrain to the letters of this period:

> I'm attacked by a frightful illness, which has never played such havoc with me as in this year—I mean my reveries, my depression, my discouragement, my indecision. Truly, I consider the man who succeeds in healing himself of a vice as infinitely braver than a soldier or a man who defends his honor in a duel. But how to heal myself? How transform despair into hope, weakness into will-power? Is this illness imaginary or real? Has it become real after being imaginary?" [letter 158]

Certainly the physical did play a role in this procrastination, for the symptoms of the syphilis contracted in youth were beginning to recur with disturbing violence.[14] Yet, even weighed down by this sense of physical and psychological debility and further oppressed by a growing conviction of the horror and deterioration of contemporary life (see particularly letter 147), Baudelaire could still find the time and summon up the energy to thank Judith Gautier for her review of *Eureka* in a letter quintessentially typical of his epistolary style: self-analysis, enthusiasm, and spontaneity fuse to create an explosive response that may well have left his recipient unsure of whether to be delighted or offended: "you proved to me something that I would readily have judged impossible, and that is that a young girl could find in books serious amusement, a sort of amusement utterly different from the highly stupid and common-place amusements that generally fill the lives of women" (letter 159). Moreover, the death of Delacroix moved him to produce his last great artistic review, a study of the life and aesthetics of the painter whose works Baudelaire had admired since adolescence and whose sayings he had been so fond of quoting. And finally he formed in these years one final project: a lecture tour of Belgium, where Poulet-Malassis talked of establishing himself as a printer of obscene books—the kind of work, need it be added, that Baudelaire despised (letter 180).

Although initially his letters to his mother indicated that he planned only a brief stay, Baudelaire remained in Brussels (apart from fleeting visits to Paris) until the attack that left him lucid but paralyzed and all

---

14. For an account of the prevalence of syphilis in Baudelaire's day, see T. Zeldin, *France 1848–1940* (Oxford: University Press, 1979), 1:304–6; and R. L. Williams, *The Horror of Life* (Chicago: University of Chicago Press, 1980).

but speechless made it essential that his mother and friends bring him back to Paris, where he died on 31 August 1867, at the age of forty-six. That he had had premonitions of the kind of illness that awaited him is shown by a note in his private diaries:

> morally as well as physically I've always had the sensation of an abyss, not merely the abyss of sleep, but that of action, dream, memory, desire, regret, remorse, beauty, numbers, etc. I cultivated my hysteria with pleasure and terror. Now I suffer constantly from vertigo and today, 23 January 1862, I experienced a remarkable warning, for I felt pass over me the wind from the wing of imbecility.[15]

The letters written from Brussels are shaped by four major threads. First, in the wake of the failure of the lectures (at least in financial terms) he dreamed of taking revenge on the Belgians, with the additional aim of sharpening his claws for a subsequent attack on France. As with his plans for avenging himself on the Academy, he planned a book so humiliating for the Belgians that it would be impossible to publish it while he was still in Brussels, for fear that, like Proudhon, he would be driven out "under a rain of stones" (letter 162). As with many of Baudelaire's works, he considered it a wager made with fate, where the very difficulty of writing an interesting work on a boring subject would guarantee its creation. Nevertheless, one might well need the genius of a Baudelaire to see how the repetitive, vitriolic notes that are all that were written could be forged into a work of creative value. Second, the letters chart the ill-starred attempt to find a literary agent who could act on his behalf in Paris: his choice, Julien Lemer, could hardly have been more disastrous, for Lemer, a former publisher, was clearly loath to find outlets for Baudelaire's works, for which he himself hoped to secure publishing rights at a later date. Eventually Baudelaire saw through Lemer's complaisant pleas for "patience, if that's possible; by not appearing too eager, we'll reach our goal."[16] The resulting despair, together with his rapidly worsening physical state, the pain of the headaches, the fear of attacks that threw him helpless to the ground, and the pervasive and corrosive hatred of everything to do with Belgium, form the third leitmotiv of this section. But even in these dark days, Baudelaire continued to give advice and support to friends: Michel Lévy is urged to consider a new translation of Maturin's *Melmoth the Wanderer*; Manet and the young poet Catulle Mendès are given encouragement, albeit in teasing tones; and Flaubert's novel

15. *Œuvres complètes*, 1:668.
16. *Lettres à Charles Baudelaire*, comp. Claude Pichois (Neuchatel: A la Baconnière, 1973) p. 223.

Salammbô receives tactfully expressed support in a letter to Sainte-Beuve, delicately, courteously, but firmly suggesting that the critic "laughed too much" at Flaubert's high seriousness (letter 179). And despite all his physical and financial difficulties, he still elaborates plans for further works: *Poor Belgium!* [*Pauvre Belgique!*], the prose poems; and a long-nurtured study of Chateaubriand, the focus of which was to be an evocation of Chateaubriand as dandy, a focus revealing yet again the way in which critical articles were, for Baudelaire, not merely analyses of other minds but also explorations of himself.

Indeed, throughout the letters runs a tracery of projects sketching out a vast and tantalizing array of the "ever more about to be": short stories "neither in Balzac's manner, nor in that of Hoffmann, or Gautier, or even Poe, who is the best of them all" (letter 99); novels (but Balzac, however stupid and gauche in his youth, had always possessed willpower and, adds Baudelaire self-mockingly, all he and Balzac had in common were plans and debts [see letter 35]); the "great book" that would gather all Baudelaire's rage, *My Heart Laid Bare*, of which only fragments were completed; and the "two plays" (letter 130), the outline of one of which is contained in various letters, although Baudelaire seems never to have put much flesh on this seductive skeleton.

Three women dominate the correspondence: Jeanne Duval, Mme Sabatier, and Baudelaire's mother.[17] There survives only one letter from Baudelaire to Jeanne Duval, a mulatto woman whose image recurs in many of the love poems of *The Flowers of Evil*. Baudelaire had become involved with her in the 1840s, and the suffering she caused him, but also the depth of his need for her, can be gauged from several letters, notably that of March 1852 (40), where he claims that Jeanne "has become an impediment not merely to [his] happiness, [. . .] but also to the improvement of [his] mental faculties," and above all in the letter of 11 September 1856, in which he laments that his "fourteen-year-old relationship with Jeanne has broken up," and in which, with moving lucidity, he evokes the eternal image of separation: "whenever I see a beautiful object, a lovely painting of a country scene, anything pleasant at all, I find myself thinking: why isn't she at my side to admire this with me, to buy that with me?" (letter 68). Nevertheless, he continued to see her and to support her financially, when he could, for the rest of his life, and her tormenting, exotic presence remains "caught within the cadences"[18] not only of *The Flowers of Evil* but also of the letters.

His letters to Apollonie Sabatier, a famous Second Empire beauty who

17. There were many other women in Baudelaire's life, but it is these three whose memory is most closely associated with the letters.

18. *The Flowers of Evil*, trans. R. Howard (Brighton: Harvester, 1982), p. 45.

gathered around her a lively circle of artists and writers, seem determined to preserve "the silent fiction of [her] eyes."[19] From the end of 1852 to the spring of 1855 he wrote to her anonymously, enclosing poems inspired by her and adopting a style so formal as to appear to preclude both emotion and sincerity. No doubt what Baudelaire wanted of her primarily was an idol on which he could place a cloak of metaphors and illusions; but in the heightened emotional torment of the *Flowers of Evil* trial, Baudelaire asked her to intervene to help him. Whether she used her influence in the trial or not, she does seem to have offered him a consolation that made her the "happiest of women," but that seems to have disturbed and distanced Baudelaire. As she herself wrote:

> Look, my dear, do you want me to tell you my thoughts on the matter, thoughts that are very cruel and cause me much suffering? I think you don't love me. That's what's causing your fears, your hesitations at embarking on an affair which, in those conditions, would become a source of boredom for you and a constant torment for me.[20]

The relationship ended gently, on terms of distant friendship.

Similar tendencies of idolization of the distant beloved, and frustration in her presence, of a need whose obverse is incompatibility, can be seen in Baudelaire's relationship with his mother. The childhood letters clearly reveal an intense love of her physical being—her clothes, her perfume, her voice, the texture of skin and hair—combined with a mixture of fear and subconscious rebellion at her moral being. His longing to please her in winning prizes at school and the constant fear of not doing well enough so shaped his adult personality that an undeniable parallel exists between the child putting off letterwriting in the hope that soon there will be a better result to announce, and the adult waiting to write until there was news of a successful publication or a favorable review. "My mother," he jotted down in his diaries, "is fantastic: you have to fear her and please her."[21] Nevertheless, many of his letters contain childhood memories that stand out as peaceful, happy moments of calm in the dark storm of his youth. The child, he insists to Poulet-Malassis, "loves his mother, his sister, his nurse for the pleasant tickling of her satin and furs, for the perfume of her breast and hair, for the sound of her jewels, the play of her ribbons" (letter 123). Elsewhere, he gives a more personal note to the image of "maternal tenderness": "in my childhood I went through a stage when I loved you passionately. [. . .] I

19. Ibid., p. 46.
20. *Lettres à Baudelaire*, pp. 322–23.
21. *Œuvres complètes*, 1 : 662.

remember an outing in a coach. You'd just come out of a clinic you'd been sent to, and to prove that you'd given some thought to your son, you showed me some pencil sketches you'd done for me" (letter 131). The liaison with Jeanne and the imposition of the *conseil de famille* led to a break in the relationship between mother and son. Indeed, in 1847 she wrote the following lines to Ancelle:

> I can't hear you say that my son has no clothes and no food without my heart bleeding. But I don't intend to make up my differences with him, for I can't, and won't, forgive so quickly the wounding things he dared to write to me, his mother, and I shall give him back my affection only when he's proved himself worthy of it.[22]

Gradually, however, the relationship was patched up, and with the letter of 1856 announcing the break with Jeanne, Baudelaire's correspondence to his mother assumes an increasingly confessional, self-analytical tone and reflects a degree of affection capable—provided he was not obliged to spend too much time in her company—of withstanding not only her incomprehension of his poetic genius, but even her desire for him to be like "ordinary men." Whereas the clearest image of Jeanne the letters provide is, perhaps, of her awakening the poet to physical reality after the dream he describes to Asselineau (letter 64), and that of Mme Sabatier is of her transfixing him merely by wishing him good evening (letter 82), that of his mother is marked by a blend of humor, love, and fear: "my thoughts are always turning to you. I see you in your bedroom or living room working, walking, moving about, complaining and reproaching me from afar" (letter 183).

However sharply focused such images might be, and however moving some of the accounts of his suffering, it is clear that Baudelaire was not one of those who enjoy letter writing. He is not like Flaubert, who seized on the opportunity to relax after a day's creative writing in those wonderfully rich and varied letters to friends; unlike Mme de Sévigné, it is not through letters but through poetry that he expresses the depths of affection or soothes the pain of separation; and neither the amusing pirouettes nor the professional analyses of Berlioz find a real equivalent in the letters of Baudelaire. Indeed, from a very early stage that "mind that gives birth only with the aid of forceps" (letter 98) sought to understand its constant prevarication of letter writing, which, he noted wistfully, should be both a duty and a pleasure. Yet that procrastination itself provokes those passages of clear-sighted and unpitying analysis that are among the most revealing and moving of any letters:

22. Quoted in Starkie, *Baudelaire*, p. 184.

when a man's nerves are greatly weakened by a morass of worries and sufferings, the Devil, despite all resolutions, slips into his brain every morning in the form of this thought: "Why shouldn't I take a day off and forget about everything? Tonight I'll do in a single burst of activity everything that's urgent." And then night falls, the mind is horrified at all the things that are overdue; a crushing sense of sorrow renders you powerless to do anything and the following day it's the same palaver—all in good faith—with the same trust and the same conscience. [letter 89]

Echoes of these analyses can be found in his creative writing: in his intimate diaries, for instance, with the assertion that "there is in every man, at every moment, two simultaneous instincts, one toward God, the other toward Satan"[23]; or in the *Artificial Paradises* [*Les Paradis artificiels*]:

Alas, human vices, however horrible one might imagine them to be, contain the proof (were it only in their infinite expansion) of man's longing for the infinite; but it is a longing that often takes the wrong route. [. . .] It is my belief that the reason behind all culpable excesses lies in this depravation of the sense of the infinite.[24]

And it is, at least in part, because of his delays that the letters, when they do come, appear all the more explosive and intense, the raw material of the human responses and relationships that assume poetic guise in *The Flowers of Evil* and *The Spleen of Paris*. Perhaps what makes the letters moving and memorable is precisely the sense of raw immediacy they evoke, their stark delineation of the abyss between the ideal and real, between the beauty of the imagined world and the grinding, inescapable, banal horror of the real world. It is in the letters that we find the base materials that Baudelaire's alchemy transforms into the gold of artistic creation.

23. *Œuvres complètes*, 1:682.
24. Ibid., 1:402–3.

Suggested Reading

There are numerous translations of Baudelaire's poetry. Two recent attempts are by Joanna Richardson (Harmondsworth: Penguin, 1975) and Richard Howard (Brighton: Harvester, 1982). His diaries have been translated by Christopher Isherwood (San Francisco: City Lights Books, 1983). The art criticism has been translated by Jonathon Mayne in two volumes: *The Mirror of Art* (London: Phaidon Press, 1955) and *The Painter of Modern Life and Other Essays* (London: Phaidon Press, 1955). A translation of the studies of intoxicants, together with writings on the same subject by Gautier, has been done by M. Strong, *Hashish, Wine, Opium* (London: Calder and Boyars, 1972).

There is a vast range of studies on Baudelaire. The following works in English would provide a starting point.

W. Benjamin, *Charles Baudelaire: A Lyric Poet in the Era of High Capitalism*, translated by H. Zohn. (London: NLB, 1973).

T. S. Eliot, "Baudelaire," in *Selected Essays* (London: Faber and Faber, 1972).

Alison Fairlie, *Baudelaire: 'Les Fleurs du mal'* (London: Edward Arnold, 1960).

P. Mansell Jones, *Baudelaire* (Cambridge: Bowes and Bowes, 1952).

F. Leakey, *Baudelaire and Nature* (Manchester: University of Manchester Press; and New York: Barnes and Noble, 1969).

D. Mossop, *Baudelaire's Tragic Hero* (Oxford: Oxford University Press, 1961).

J. P. Sartre, *Baudelaire*, translated by M. Turnell (London: Hamish Hamilton, 1964).

E. Starkie, *Baudelaire* (Harmondsworth: Penguin, 1971).

R. L. Williams, *The Horror of Life* (Chicago: University of Chicago Press, 1980)

For historical background to the period in which Baudelaire lived, see J. and M. Lough, *An Introduction to Nineteenth Century French Studies* (London: Longman, 1978) and T. Zeldin, *France 1848–1945* (Oxford: Oxford University Press, 1979). For introductory studies of French verse forms see P. Broome and G. Chesters, *The Appreciation of Modern French Poetry* (Cambridge: Cambridge University Press, 1976), R. Lewis, *On Reading French Verse* (Oxford: Clarendon Press, 1982), and C. Scott, *French Verse Art: A Study* (Cambridge: Cambridge University Press, 1979).

Chronology

1759 Birth at La Neuville-au-Pont of Joseph-François Baudelaire, father of C. B.

1793 Birth in London of Caroline Archenbaut Defayis, C. B.'s mother. Her name is also spelled Dufaÿs or Dufays, and in the 1840s C. B. occasionally uses it as a pseudonym.

1797 Marriage of Joseph-François Baudelaire and Jeanne-Justine-Rosalie Janin.

1805 Birth of Claude-Alphonse Baudelaire, C. B.'s half-brother.

1814 Death of Jeanne-Justine-Rosalie Janin.

1819 Marriage of Joseph-François Baudelaire and Caroline Dufaÿs.

1821 9 April: Birth of Charles-Pierre Baudelaire.

1827 10 February: Death of C. B.'s father.

1828 Caroline Baudelaire marries Lieutenant-Colonel Jacques Aupick.

1832 C. B. and his mother go to Lyon, where Aupick is stationed.

1836 Return to Paris. C. B. attends the College Louis-le-Grand.

1839 Expelled from Louis-le-Grand.

1840 Begins to mix with young writers and artists of the time.

1841 C. B. sent on a voyage, meant to take him to Calcutta. Stops at Reunion and Mauritius, then refuses to travel any further. Returns to France, arriving 15 February 1842.

1842 Inherits 100,000 francs from his father on attaining his majority.

1843 Collaborates with Prarond on a project for a play.

1844 *Conseil de famille* takes control of C. B.'s fortune. Narcisse Ancelle appointed trustee.

1845 Publications of C. B.'s *Salon* of 1845 and his poem "To a Creole Lady" ("A une dame créole"). First translations of the works of Poe begin to appear in the French press.
30 June: C. B. attempts suicide by stabbing himself.

1846 C. B.'s *Salon* published. Back page announces forthcoming publication of a collection of his poems, *Les Lesbiennes*.

1847 Publication of his short story *La Fanfarlo*.

1848 February Revolution and uprisings of the June Days. Baudelaire participates on the side of the revolutionaries. Collaborates with Champfleury and Toubin on a newspaper *Le Salut public*, only two numbers of which appeared. 15 July: publication of C. B.'s first translation of Poe, *Magnetic Revelation*.

1849   Beginning of friendship with publisher Auguste Poulet-Malassis.

1850   June: publication of "Pride's Punishment" ("Châtiment de l'orgueil") and "The Wine Honest Folk Drink" ("Le Vin des honnêtes gens").

13 July: publication of the poem "Lesbos."

1851   Publication of *Concerning Wine and Hashish* (*Du vin et du haschisch*).

9 April: *Le Messager de l'assemblée* publishes eleven poems under the title *Les Limbes* (*Limbo*).

August: publication of C. B.'s review of Pierre Dupont.

27 September: publication of "The Soul of Wine" ("L'Ame du vin").

2 December: coup d'état, in which Louis-Napoleon declares himself emperor, bringing the short-lived Republic to an end.

1852   22 January: C. B.'s article "The Pagan School" ("L'Ecole païenne") published.

1 February: publication of "The Two Twilights" ("Les deux crépuscules").

March and April: publication in the *Revue de Paris* of C. B.'s study of Poe.

Various translations by C. B. of Poe stories published.

1853   Various publications of poems and translations.

1854   July–April 1855: *Le Pays* publishes translations of Poe by C. B.

1855   May–August: C. B.'s review of the World Fair published in *Le Pays*.

June: *La Revue des deux mondes* publishes eighteen poems under the title *The Flowers of Evil*.

June: publication of the first of C. B.'s prose poems, "Twilight: Evening" ("Le Crépuscule du soir") and "Solitude."

July: "Of the Essence of Laughter" ("De l'essence du rire") published in *Le Portefeuille*.

3 August: contract with Michel Lévy brothers to publish *Histoires extraordinaires* and *Nouvelles Histoires extraordinaires*.

1856   March: publication of *Histoires extraordinaires*. Contract with Poulet-Malassis and de Broise for *The Flowers of Evil* and collected articles on art.

1857   29 January and 7 February: trial of Flaubert's novel *Madame Bovary*. Acquitted.

8 March: publication of *Nouvelles Histoires extraordinaires*.

27 April: death of General Aupick.

25 June: publication of *The Flowers of Evil*.
5 July: the critic G. Bourdin, in an article in *Le Figaro*, stresses the so-called immorality of the poems.
7 July: *The Flowers of Evil* accused of being an outrage to public decency.
20 August: C. B. condemned to pay a fine of 300 francs and suppress six of the poems.
24 August: publication in *Le Présent*, under the title *Nocturnal Poems* (*Poèmes nocturnes*), of six prose poems.
October: publication of studies on caricature in *Le Présent*.

1858 13 May: publication of C. B.'s translation of Poe's novel *Arthur Gordon Pym*.
19 September: publication in *L'Artiste* of "Duellum."
30 September: *La Revue contemporaine* publishes C. B.'s study of hashish.

1859 First notes for *My Heart Laid Bare*.
20 January: *La Revue française* publishes "Longing for Oblivion" ("Le Goût du néant") and "The Possessed" ("Le Possédé").
13 March: *L'Artiste* publishes *Théophile Gautier*.
15 March: "Dance of Death" ("Danse macabre") appears in *La Revue contemporaine*.
10 April: "Sisina," "The Voyage," ("Le Voyage"), and "The Albatross" ("L'Albatros") in *La Revue française*.
15 September: "Parisian Fantoms" ("Fantômes parisiens"): (1) "The Seven Old Men" (2) "The Little Old Ladies" appear in the *Revue contemporaine*.
30 November: "Sonnet of Autumn" ("Sonnet d'automne"), "Autumn Song" ("Chanson d'automne"), and "The Mask" ("Le Masque") in the *Revue contemporaine*.

1860 1 January: Baudelaire sells Poulet-Malassis and de Broise the second edition of *Flowers of Evil*, *Artificial Paradises*, and his articles of literary and art criticism.
13 January: first attack.
15 and 31 January: *La Revue contemporaine* publishes C. B.'s adaptation of De Quincey's *Confessions*.
22 January: *La Causerie* publishes "Skeleton at Work" ("Le Squelette laboureur"), "To a Madonna" ("A une madone"), and "The Swan" ("Le Cygne").
15 May: *La Revue contemporaine* publishes five poems: "Parisian Dream" ("Rêve parisien"), "The Love of Deceit" ("L'Amour du mensonge"), "The Dream of a Curious Man" ("Le Rêve du curieux"), "Semper eadem" and "Obsession."

May: publication of *Artificial Paradises*.

15 October: publication in *L'Artiste* of "Sympathetic Horror" ("Horreur sympathique"), "The Blind Men" ("Les Aveugles"), "Alchemy of Suffering" ("L'Alchimie de la douleur"), "To a Woman Passing By" ("A une passante"), "A Fantom" ("Une fantôme"), "Afternoon Song" ("Chanson d'après-midi"), "Hymn to Beauty" ("Hymne à la beauté"), "The Clock" ("L'Horloge").

15 January: publication of "The Seven Old Men" in *L'Artiste*.

February: second edition of *Flowers of Evil* goes on sale.

1 April: *La Revue européenne* publishes C. B.'s study of Wagner.

15 May: "Sad Madrigal" ("Madrigal triste") appears in *La Revue fantaisiste*.

15 June–15 August: *La Revue fantaisiste* publishes nine of the ten articles that make up *Reflections on Some of My Contemporaries*.

15 September: *La Revue européenne* publishes "The Pagan's Prayer" ("La Prière d'un paien"), "The Rebel" ("Le rebelle"), "The Warning" ("L'Avertisseur"), "Epigraph for a Condemned Book" ("Epigraphe pour un livre condamné"). Article on the Delacroix murals appears in *La Revue fantaisiste*.

1 November: *La Revue fantaisiste* publishes nine prose poems. *La Revue européenne* publishes "Self-Communion" ("Recueillement").

11 December: C. B. presents his candidature for the Academy.

1862   12 January: *Le Boulevard* publishes seven poems by C. B.

10 February: C. B. withdraws his application to the Academy.

1 March: *L'Artiste* publishes "The Voice" ("La Voix"), "The Abyss" ("Le Gouffre"), "The Offended Moon" ("La Lune offensée").

20 April: *Le Boulevard* publishes C. B.'s review of Hugo's *Les Misérables*.

2 August: publication of Crépet's anthology, *French Poets* (*Les Poètes français*), with seven articles by Baudelaire and an article on C. B. by Gautier.

26–27 August: *La Presse* publishes the first fourteen prose poems.

24 September: *La Presse* publishes the prose poems 15–20.

12 November: Poulet-Malassis imprisoned for debt.

28 December: *Le Boulevard* publishes "The Lament of Icarus" ("Les Plaintes d'un Icare").

25 January: "The Unforseen" ("L'Imprévu") appears in *Le Boulevard*.

1 February: *Le Boulevard* publishes "The Scrutiny at Midnight" ("L'Examen de minuit").

10 June: *La Revue nationale et étrangère* publishes two prose poems (numbers 21 and 25).

14 June: *Le Boulevard* publishes two prose poems (numbers 37 and 38).

2 and 14 September, 22 November: *L'Opinion nationale* publishes "The Work and Life of Eugène Delacroix" ("L'Œuvre et La Vie d'Eugène Delacroix").

10 October: *La Revue nationale et étrangère* publishes two prose poems (numbers 27 and 36).

1863   25 November: Michel Lévy publishes *Eureka*.

26 and 29 November, 3 December: *Le Figaro* publishes C. B.'s study of Constantin Guys, "The Painter of Modern Life."

10 December: *La Revue nationale et étrangère* publishes three prose poems (numbers 32, 36, 34).

1864   7 February: under the title "The Spleen of Paris" (Le Spleen de Paris") *Le Figaro* publishes four prose poems (numbers 30, 22, 29, 33).

14 February: *Le Figaro* publishes two prose poems (numbers 31 and 39).

1 March: *La Revue nouvelle* publishes "Bertha's Eyes" ("Les Yeux de Berthe"), "The Abyss" ("Le Gouffre"), "On Delacroix" 'Tasso in prison'" ("Sur 'Le Tasse en prison' d'Eugène Delacroix"), "Far from Here" ("Bien loin d'ici").

24 April: C. B. arrives in Brussels.

2 May: Lecture on Delacroix.

11 May: Lecture on Gautier.

12, 23 May and 3 June: Lectures on stimulants.

13 June: C. B. gives a reading from his works.

2 July: *La Vie parisienne* publishes prose poem 26.

13 August: *La Vie parisienne* publishes prose poem 14.

1 November: *L'Artiste* publishes three prose poems (numbers 27, 28, and 30).

25 December: under the title "The Spleen of Paris," *La Revue de Paris* publishes six prose poems (26, 24, 41, 40, 23, and 28).

1865   16 March: publication of *Histoires grotesques et sérieuses*.

21 June: *L'Indépendance belge* publishes prose poem 50.

8 July: "The Fountain" ("Le Jet d'eau") published in *La Petite Revue*.

14 October: "To a Malabaraise Woman" ("A une Malabaraise") published in *La Petite Revue*.

16 December: *La Petite Revue* publishes "Ransom" ("La Rançon") and "Hymn" ("Hymne").

1866　10–15 March: about this time C. B. writes his notes on Hugo's *Laborers of the Sea* (*Les Travailleurs de la mer*).

22–23 March: C. B.'s condition worsens.

30 March: Paralysis of the right side.

31 March: *Le Parnasse contemporain* publishes *New Flowers of Evil*.

1 June: *La Revue du XIXe siècle* publishes two prose poems (28 and 29).

2 July: C. B. brought back to Paris.

1867　31 August: Death of C. B.

2 September: C. B. buried at the Montparnasse cemetery.

1868　December: Michel Lévy begins publishing C. B.'s complete works.

SELECTED LETTERS OF
Charles Baudelaire

When I have inspired universal disgust and horror,
I will have conquered solitude.

BAUDELAIRE
Fusées, XI

—for I am one
Whom men love not,—and yet regret . . .

SHELLEY
"Stanzas Written in Dejection, Near Naples"

1 · *Childhood: 1832–1839*

1   To Alphonse Baudelaire

1 February 1832

Dear Brother,

You told me to write to you on the first day of each month, so here I am carrying out my duty. I'm going to tell you about my journey.[1]

Mother's first oversight: as she was getting our things loaded on the coach, she realized she'd mislaid her muff and shouted out, turning it all into a great drama: "My muff!" But I answered coolly: "I know where it is. I'll get it." She'd left it on a bench in the office.

We got into the coach and left at last. I myself began by feeling very bad-tempered because of all the muffs, waterbags, footwarmers, men's hats, women's hats, cloaks, earmuffs, blankets, hundreds of them, all kinds of bonnets, shoes, lined slippers, boots, baskets, jams, beans, bread, towels, enormous fowls, spoons, forks, knives, scissors, thread, needles, pins, combs, dresses, skirts, hundreds and hundreds of skirts, woollen stockings, cotton stockings, corsets piled one on top of the other, biscuits—and I can't remember what else! You know how I'm always jiggling about, hopping from one foot to the other, so you'll realize that not only was it impossible for me to move, but I could barely find room to sit near the window.

But I was soon my usual cheerful self. We changed horses at Charenton and continued our journey. I can hardly remember the changes anymore, so I'll move on to the evening. Day had fallen and I saw a really fine sight, the sunset; that reddish color formed a remarkable contrast with the mountains which were as blue as the deepest pair of trousers. After I'd put on my little silk bonnet, I stretched out in the back of the coach and it seemed to me that traveling all the time would be a marvelous life for me. I'd like to tell you more about it, but a darn translation forces me to close my letter here.

---

1. The three-and-a-half day journey from Paris to Lyon.

[3 March 1832]

Dear Brother,

I'd got up to Villeneuve la guerre [*sic*: Baudelaire means Villeneuve-la-Guyard, between Montereau and Sens] and now I'm going to tell you more about my journey.

When we left Villeneuve we traveled for a long time on a highroad, which was very monotonous to look at and was planted with two rows of dry trees, with no greenery. I don't remember our journey very clearly, but I know that after that we had a lot of uphill climbs and once they harnessed 10 or 11 horses to the coach; since I don't remember it very well, as I said above, I'll go on to the moment when we came into Chalon.

At the approach to this town there was a climb, and mother, the maid, and I got out. As I like to be jiggling about all the time, hopping or running about, I went on ahead both of mother and of the coach. Soon I lost both of them from sight. I must confess here that I was very pleased, because I looked like a *gentleman* alone on the highway between Chalon and Lyon.

Mother wanted to get back into the coach and I wasn't around. At last I heard her voice telling me to come back as she wanted to get back into the coach and when I arrived I heard one of the travelers saying about me: "Here's the little gentleman who runs ahead, all on his own, on the highway!" I couldn't help feeling pleased at being referred to as a *gentleman*. The rest is too pretty and too hard to describe so I'll have to think it over until I write to you again. [. . .]

3   To Alphonse Baudelaire

[12 March 1833]

Dear Brother,

I'm sending you your present: I was second in Greek. I can't send you any proof of this, because that piece of paper is worth 300 lines, and as I'm always getting impositions, I'm sure to need it.[2] We've just been examined. I knew the subject well. The evening before, I didn't know a thing. I've got a good memory, I went over everything quickly, luck was on my side, and it went off well. I think that I'll get the fourth or fifth prize at the Easter prize-giving. Nevertheless, we're to be examined from

2. As a reward for good results, teachers would provide pupils with a certificate that allowed them remission for punishments.

now until the end of the year for the prize for excellence. I'll have to work a bit harder. Perhaps I'll get a better place.

I don't know if you'll be able to read my letter, for it's written during the history lesson, a very boring class. I've just been questioned on the character of the Pelasgic people. I was so wrapped up in my letter I didn't even know what I was being asked. I don't know if I'll answer as well in the history exam as in the Greek and Latin exams, since I don't know a word of it, and I've lost half the homework I did on it.

Write and tell me what you're doing at Fontainebleau. Tell me every detail of your hunting expeditions, whether Théodore is enjoying himself, what the town is like, what walks it has etc. etc.—everything you can about it.

You ask if Mother is well? Unfortunately not. She's just had a violent attack of sore throat, which is still preventing her from going out.

There are lots of fires in Lyon. There was a stage when not a night went by without someone shouting 'Fire!' The worst fire was the last one. That happened at Perrache, which is the favorite promenade from Lyon. An entire cafe burnt. The Saint-Simonians went to help out, all wearing their costumes.

Mother and Father ask to be reminded to you. My love to you, my sister, Théodore, and everyone.

4   To Alphonse Baudelaire

[25 March 1833]

Dear Brother,

Uproar at the college. A master struck a pupil so hard that he gave him pains in the chest. He is very ill and can't get up. I'll tell you all about it. This pupil, after half an hour's study, couldn't understand the work he had to do, so he passed a note to find out. The supervisor, having caught him, came out with his usual silly speeches. The pupil sent yet another note and was given a beating to which the pupil responded by aiming a few kicks at the supervisor. The supervisor, wanting to end the struggle once and for all, kicked him in the back. The drum roll went for supper. The pupil took his usual place but the supervisor made him line up, saying he wasn't worthy of going with the others. Coming back from supper he put him in the coal bin for the same reason. From time to time he'd go and give him a slap; the pupil's back was so sore he couldn't put up any resistance. Bedtime came. Two days later, there was an *exeat*. I got back in the evening to hear that the pupil was in the sick bay, unable to stand up anymore, and that he'd fallen, unconscious, in the lineup. The nurse is determined to do everything possible to get rid of the supervisor, but it's not yet sure that he'll go because he's one of the headmaster's pets.

We kicked up such a rumpus in the yard that the headmaster heard it in his rooms. The supervisor laughed at our protest, but it was a pretty hollow laugh. I'm one of the rebels. I don't want to be one of those bootlickers who are afraid to anger the supervisors.

Revenge on those who have abused their positions. That was an inscription on the Paris barricades. If he doesn't leave, we're going to put an article in the *Courrier de Lyon*.[3] Farewell. [. . .]

5   TO ALPHONSE BAUDELAIRE

17 May [1833]

Dear Brother,

I think I have more right to scold you than you have to scold me. For I'm only two days late, and *you* never answer my letters. Moreover, I've an excuse for not writing: I was waiting to get a good mark that I could tell you about. At last I have one: I was 4th in French. I think I told you that I'd come 2nd in Greek.

In all my letters I ask for an answer. There's a scandal for you! The younger son showing the older his duty! You can see that I'm working on your feelings. I think that's the best course.

As a Parisian I'm filled with indignation at the way they treated Louis-Philippe's name day in Lyon. A few little fairy lights here and there, and that was it. In Paris I bet there were great celebrations. Although you're at Fontainebleau you must have read the descriptions of them in the newspaper. Tell me about it. [. . .]

We've been threatened with great disturbances in Lyon. At the Célestins (the theater in Lyon), on the square, there was a large gathering (or so it was reported); all the young men wore a red cravat, a sign more of their silliness than of their political persuasion. They sang (very softly); whenever a police sergeant so much as came into sight they fell silent. The Saint-Simonians had joined the republicans and had announced that there would be dancing on Bellecour Square (the promenade). On the day that had been fixed for it, no ball, nothing. It had been reported that two leagues from Lyon there was a great uprising. General Aymard sent four gendarmes. They found fifty armed men. They asked them what they planned to do: they answered that they were going to hunt a she-wolf. From these two pieces of information you can imagine what the rest of the revolt was like—in a word, nothing. [. . .]

3. No such article has been found in this conservative newspaper.

22 November 1833

I've got a lot of things to tell you, but first my excuses. There was a degree of vanity in my laziness; as you didn't reply, I thought honor demanded that I shouldn't write twice running. But I realized that that was preposterous, and moreover you're my elder, so I respect you, and my brother, so I love you. Lots of things to tell you, I promise from the very outset of my letter, and I'm going to carry that promise out. I've just sprained my foot, and that means plaster after plaster, and I hate the plasters as much as I hate the doctors.

In Lyon they're building a suspension bridge over the Saône, made entirely of iron wire. All the shops are to have gas lighting: they're digging up all the streets. The Rhône, that fast-flowing river with its sudden rises in level, has flooded yet again. For just now there's a lot of rain in Lyon. There's a glassworks situated on a peninsula close to the city (we collegians used to go there on walks) and the Rhône is constantly eating away at the isthmus; it wears it away, devours it. Tonight it finally managed to destroy the isthmus. Things like that are common occurrences on the Rhône. A cleft becomes an abyss, a spit of land an island, for the river runs very fast. My letter is scrawled awfully badly, but my pen's very poor and besides, I don't care a fig about that. I'm eager to make up for my laziness in a long letter. But you can imagine what torment I'm suffering, for this little sprain prevents me from dancing and I never miss a single quadrille if I can help it. What else? During the holidays I performed a comedy and now I'm going to act out a proverb.

There may be some blunders in my letter: perhaps my ideas are as irregular as my handwriting. Thank goodness our correspondence was interrupted for such a long time that it's not hard to find things to say in our epistolary chat. Moreover it's better to chatter away in friendly fashion than to go in for rubbish and pathos.

But what's this I hear? Théodore won some prizes and . . . Charles got none? 'Od's blood! I'll get some. Tell Théodore thanks to him I'll be crowned victor. A second prize for excellence (my 4th) and one for translation (my 5th)! That's really shameful: but I want prizes and I'll get them. All the same congratulations to Théodore and to me—shame! Tell him he can jeer at me long distance. [. . .]

Carlos

25 February [1834]

Father and Mother,

I'm writing this letter to try to persuade you that there is still some hope of pulling me out of the state that causes you such suffering. I know that as soon as Mother reads the beginning of this letter, she'll say: "I don't believe it's still possible," and Father will say the same. But I'm not going to let that discourage me; you want to punish me for my follies by not coming to see me at the college, but come one last time to give me some good advice and to encourage me. All these follies stem from my thoughtlessness and my dilly-dallying. Last time I promised you once again not to cause you any more grief, I did so in all good faith, I'd resolved to work, and work hard, so that you'd be able to say: "We have a son who is grateful for what we do for him." But my thoughtlessness and my laziness made me forget the feelings I'd had when I made those promises. It's not my heart that needs correction, for I'm good at heart, it's my mind that needs fixing—it needs to be made to reflect solidly enough for the reflections to remain engraved upon it. You're beginning to believe that I'm ungrateful; indeed you're convinced of it, perhaps. How can I make you believe the very opposite? I know how to do it: by getting down to work straightaway. But whatever I do, the time I've spent in laziness, forgetful of what I owed you, will always be a blot. How can I make you forget in a single moment the bad way I've behaved for three months? I don't know, and yet that's just what I want to do. Give me back your confidence and your friendship straightaway, come and see me at college to tell me that I have them again. That will be the best way to make me change immediately.

You've despaired of me as one would despair of a son whose evil was beyond cure, to whom everything was indifferent, who spent his time in laziness, who was weak, cowardly, lazy and lacked the courage to pull himself together. I have been weak, cowardly, lazy, for a while I thought of nothing. But as nothing can alter the heart, my heart, which for all its faults has its good points, has remained unaffected. My heart made me feel I shouldn't despair of myself. I thought I could write to you, and let you know my thoughts, the thoughts inspired by the boredom of a life spent in laziness and punishments. And the very idea that you could regard me as an ingrate gave me a degree of courage. If you don't have the courage to come to the college, at least answer me, and give me the advice and encouragement in your letter that you would have given me in the parlor had you come yourselves. The places for Natural History are being given out on Thursday morning, and I'm hoping for a good one. Can that hope suffice to make you listen to me? Recently I had yet again a bad place, a very bad place, but the desire to make up for that affront made me really work on my exam this morning. If you've really made up your minds not to come to college until a change in my behavior proves to you that I've undergone a total alteration, at least write to me, I'll keep your letters, I'll read them often to fight against my heedlessness, to make me shed tears of repentance, to make sure my laziness and thoughtlessness don't allow me to forget the faults I have to make up for. Finally, as I told you at the start of this letter, my heart's not at fault at all. A careless nature, an invincible tendency toward laziness—it's this that has made me commit so many faults. Do believe this. I'm sure you won't forget that you have a son at college, but don't forget either that this son has a heart. That's what I wanted to write to you. The aim of my letter is very simple. I want to persuade you that there's no reason to give up hope in me. Besides, what boy, thinking his parents didn't want to come and see him any more, wouldn't write as soon as possible to put matters straight? It's not the harsh methods that affect me. It's the shame at having forced you to use them. It's not the house I'm attached to, nor to the comforts I find there when I am permitted to go out, but the pleasure of talking to you for a whole day and the praise you may give me about my work. I promise you I will change, but don't lose faith in me and please go on believing in my promises.

Charles

8   To Caroline Aupick

[23 April 1837?]

My dear Mother,

I'd like to know how Father is, whether he is in much pain, if they're thinking of closing the wound soon, if he mentions me, anything at all, in fact, that you can tell me about him. When I left on Sunday evening, he was beginning to feel some pain: were there any repercussions from this? Is it M. Choquet who's caring for him now? For you told me that Father particularly wanted to be cared for by him. And now I must also ask how you are; when I left you, you were suffering from toothache, and feared you'd spend a bad night. If you've been at the dentist continually since then, it may have passed completely, but I want to know all this. Write to me, or else send Joseph to the college. If you do, he could, if possible, bring me two volumes (Noël's *Literature Course*, second shelf). Would you be so kind as to cover each book firmly in paper, or sew a fabric cover onto them? Moreover, you may perhaps not have the time to do this, for Father must come first in your thinking. And since when he is well he spends such a lot of time amusing us, when he's ill, we should devote ourselves to him. Recently I felt very ashamed that he should have heard me answer you in a rather offhanded way—so, Mother, I do apologize to you. If you'd like to know why I'm asking for the *Literature Course* again this is the reason: you know I felt I was much less good this year than last in writing verse and that I felt discouraged: well, to tell the truth, I wasn't doing very much in that particular exercise. Every time, my teacher would criticize me. Even the headmaster spoke to me about it. The teacher even went so far as to say to me, in his own inimitable style: "For goodness' sake, work at your Latin verse; you're breaking a link with the future." That made me laugh. Finally, thinking there wasn't much time until the competitive exams, I got back to work again, and tried so hard that he's enchanted with my pieces of verse. He's less enchanted for my sake than for his, of course, for I've noticed that if I write bad verse he's very displeased, and if I neglect my Greek, or anything else, he hardly points it out to me. Apart from the tutors that college provides, a former pupil of the college, who was successful in the past and who is now the tutor of M. Rothschild's children, I think, suggested to the headmaster that he would be willing to give us some tutorials specifically on verse. This young man asked me this morning if the tutorials he gave were enjoyable. I was really surprised and of course I insisted that I did enjoy them. Then he wanted to chat with me for a moment, and talked to me about the exams, offered to lend me whatever books I wanted, provided that they had some connection with my stud-ies. He only said he wouldn't lend me novels or anything else of that type because that would risk getting me into trouble. I thanked him very warmly. It may be that he's just being polite in making this offer, and that at heart he doesn't really want to do so, so I'll be careful not to take him up on it. So that's how things stand. I'm not very sure what all this means. Now I'm going to cram. Hugs to both of you.

If this bad weather continues, it would almost be cruel to send Joseph just on my account. If he does come, however, I hope he'll bring me a lot of news from you.

9   To Caroline Aupick

[late June? 1837]

Dear Mother,

Yesterday, everyone in our group who usually goes to the evening session said they didn't want to go anymore: the headmaster flew into a fury because, with the exams coming on, we didn't want to go to the evening preparation and he's forbidden all of us to go out at all until further notice. This gives me yet another reason to work, in everything if I can, to avoid falling foul of the headmaster in any way; for he was really enraged by our request. He shouted in a thunderous voice that this wretched class had been the bane of his life from the outset and that it would never bring him any honor in the examination. It seems we may well wait for quite some time before he allows us any leave of absence. I haven't yet told M. Gros about it. My teacher, however, is pleased with me. I'm 7th in history and 2nd in English.

M. Massoni told me he saw father recently and that he'd spent a bad night. Please tell me how he is when you write. Tell me if he's more comfortable and if they're thinking about closing the wound. Give him a hug for me. So now I'm prevented from seeing him for goodness knows how long because of this M. Pierrot[4] who thinks it's strange that anyone should want to sleep for an extra hour rather than devoting all their attention to bringing him good results in the exam.

Farewell. I'm going to work to try to forget that my *exeats* have been taken away.

I'm now reading *Simple Story*[5] in English during break. Farewell. Hug Father for me. I hope he'll get better.

10   TO CAROLINE AUPICK

[6 November 1837]

Dear Mother,

This is just to let you know that everything has been perfect. I'll tell you all about it from the moment I left you, since I've nothing particular to do at present. Scarcely had I got back with the vice-principal and was, as it happens, taking my hat off, than one of the secretaries began saying: "look, it's that very impolite pupil, the one who treated you so badly." So he said: "It appears, Mr. Vice-Principal, that you cured M. Baudelaire's cold very suddenly. Now you're here he takes off his hat; he kept it on just now for the whole time that I was the only one here." The vice-principal looked at me, laughing, which shows clearly that he didn't want to criticize me for that. I didn't condescend to say anything in reply; sunk in my chair I sent him a look which said that he himself was very insolent in lodging such a complaint.

The vice-principal didn't dare take matters into his own hands and install me definitely in sickbay; but later the Head confirmed every-

4. The headmaster of Louis-le-Grand college.
5. A sentimental novel by Mrs. Elizabeth Inchbald, published in 1791.

thing. He spoke to me in a kindly way about my class, how I fitted into it; and then I went to undress and move into sickbay. When I went into our quarters, my friends seemed really taken aback to see me limping. Then I almost fell over in an unlit corridor. Afterwards I filled my pockets with all my toiletries and all the books I need in sickbay. Several of my classmates thought I was leaving the college for good when they saw me with all my books. Imagine the problems I had! Thirty odd books under my arms, an immense distance to cover, from my quarters to sickbay, stairs to go up and down, and all that, loaded down and limping. I really don't know how I'd have managed if one of the Head's servants, whom I met by chance, hadn't carried my books for me. So this is what my life is like now: I get up when I please, during the day the only walking I do is to go to my class twice, and I'll do all my work here. Although I'm using M. Choquet's liniment, I'll talk to the college surgeon about it. You left a handkerchief with me: if you come to get it, or indeed whenever you come, don't come to the sickbay because you'd have to cross the courtyard and some pupils running through could— quite without wanting to—knock you over: you'd kill yourself. Please have me called to the parlor, don't come to sickbay. At the porters' lodge insist on having someone bring me from sickbay, and tell him very clearly, otherwise he could send no one at all, or send someone to my old quarters. When you send for me on Sunday, don't let Joseph forget to say, if he wants me to come, that I've got to be summoned from sickbay. Please remember all that. Farewell, I truly promise you and Father that I'll work.

11   TO CAROLINE AUPICK

[about 10 June 1838]

My dear Mother,

   I've just received your letter: if you knew how much pleasure it gives me to hear you tell me you're always thinking of me, that I'm always on your mind, that I must work well, that I've got to become a man of distinction! You call that your refrain; I've heard you say it must weary me to hear you constantly repeat the same thing. Not a bit of it! I felt the deepest pleasure in reading your advice. Perhaps it's because you haven't given me any advice for some time that it seemed pleasant and fresh; or is it that mothers, in their continual care, have a talent for expressing the same thoughts in a new style, to enliven them? This may seem a joke. But after all, why shouldn't that be the case? You want to know my results. I've got some bad news: I'm 14th in Latin translation. It was taken from a very obscure author who writes very badly. M. Rinn said to me with a laugh, as if to cheer me up, that one could almost be proud of not understanding these writers, so ridiculous are they. He is always kind and understanding. I'm delighted and pat myself on the back for having *at last* found a teacher I like. Recently, annoyed at seeing me chatting, he punished me, and said after the class: "Baudelaire, you must be cross with me. Your work was bad today and I've put you in detention!" I told him it wasn't for me to be cross when he punished me, because of his kindness. And when he said to me: "Believe me, it's painful to punish a friend," I replied: "When you say things like that, punishments can't hurt." M. Rinn is the only teacher to whom I'd say such things without blushing. If it were anyone else, I'd be ashamed at having stooped to such base flattery, but there's no shame in saying what you think to those you like. And that's why, whatever *you* may say, I'm not afraid to kiss my mother in front of the crowd in the parlor.

This is what my life is like at present. I read books I'm allowed to borrow from the library, I work, I write poems, but at present they're dreadful. In spite of all that, I'm bored. The main reason is that I don't see you anymore. There are other reasons. Our conversations in collège are often extremely useless and boring; that's why I often abandon the schoolmates I'm friendly with, sometimes going on solitary walks, sometimes seeing what other groups and conversations are like; these frequent absences have shocked my friends and in order not to make them any angrier I've come back to them; but their conversations are never anything but chatter; I prefer our long silences, from six to nine, while you work and Father reads.

One of the things I most often think about is what I'll do in the vacation, the promises I've made Father, English, walking, riding and exercise—all these thoughts fill my head. I want to read etc. etc.

I often think about the exams, too, and, as I know how important you consider them, I feel a kind of fear. I feel I'm so weak that I'm convinced I won't do any good, and there'll be tears. So I'm suffering in advance. Tell Father that the last conversation we had in the parlor gave me lots of pleasure. Of course I'll love it in the vacation because we can have conversations like that every day.

Charles

Mme d'Abrantès has just died.[6] MM. Dumas and Hugo went to the funeral. M. Hugo gave a short speech. Or so it says in the newspaper. Even in college we know all the news.

6. The duchess of Abrantès died on 7 June 1838. Her husband had been one of Napoleon's generals. She herself is remembered for her *Memoires*.

[27 June 1838]

My dear Mother,

I'm really longing to get a letter from you. It seems a very long time since I last received one. My days go by, one after the other, very sadly. I can feel the end of the year coming, and that frightens me, because of the competitive exam, in which, I'm afraid, I've really very little hope.[7] I feel my life outside school approaching, and that causes me even more fear. All the people you have to get to know, all the effort you have to put in to find an empty place in the midst of the crowd, all that frightens me. But I've been put into this world to live and I'll do my best. Then it seems to me that in this knowledge one has to acquire, in this struggle with others, even in this difficulty itself there must be a degree of pleasure.

We've had our exams in French discourse and in Latin discourse. We're not going to do any more exams in Latin discourse except for the prizes. We still don't know what places we've been given.

Mme Jaquotot wrote to me asking about you, and wondering if I could spend a day with her. To avoid going out and to offer a perfect excuse, I claimed I'd been forbidden to leave school until the end of the year.

I do beg you to write to me, tell me what you see, and give me news of Father above all. You've doubtless now reached Barèges. I want to have news of you all the time and to follow his cure as if I were with you.

I'm always thinking of the vacations, less for the pleasures they bring than for the work I plan to do in them. I want to fill my days. And to tell the truth if I carried out all the things I'm promising myself that I'll do, I really think I'd run out of time. I know very well what you say when I speak of such plans. But you also know how much courage I have and even how quickly I can do things when it's absolutely necessary. Well, the necessity of living in the outside world is fast approaching, and who knows that I won't suddenly change course for ever, as I suddenly change from time to time where my college work is concerned, and who knows that necessity won't give me memory and energy?

Nevertheless something else frightens me, too. When I begin to think of the enormous number of benefits I owe you, I see that the only way to repay you is by satisfying your vanity, by my successes.

But my poor mother, if nature failed to make me capable of satisfying you, if I'm of too limited intelligence to please your ambitions, you'll die before I've been able to repay you even to a small extent for all the trouble

7. As he feared, Charles did not do well in these exams.

you've given yourself. I assure you I'm saying this in all good faith. For as far as a few college successes are concerned, I, who know how they are obtained, look on them as empty and insignificant, barely finding in them any proof of my intelligence. But I will work. Give Father a good hug for me, and tell me how he is. Tell me if I should put on each letter I send to you: "I request M. Coppenhague to send etc." or whether I should simply send an envelope.

Hitherto I've just put the address to M. Coppenhague and asked him to send the letters on to Mme Aupick, and as I didn't indicate that these letters were from me, I'm afraid he hasn't sent them on.

13   To Jacques Aupick

[17 July 1838]

Dear Father,

Please forgive me for not answering earlier but I wanted to give you my results. They all came out at once. I was 6th in French, 4th in Latin, first in Latin verse. Now we're busy with prize essays and we spend our days walking. There's no homework. Now the days of freedom are coming and they'll continue for the rest of the year. I spend all my time reading. I'm not giving any thought to the essays; I'm not worried about them at all, but when the day comes I'll give them all I've got. Only the exams frighten me; I know mother is so eager for me to do well that if I don't she'll never forgive me; and yet no one can be sure of anything; in any case, in the exams, as at college, I'll do my very best. A few days ago the whole college with all the masters and a group of day pupils attached to the college went to Versailles. The king invites all the royal colleges to visit him, one after the other. The Polytechnic went there before us. So we wandered about in all the rooms and in the chapel. We dined in a low-ceilinged room. Then the king came. We walked about again, following him; finally he led us into the theater where sets were being prepared. He apologized for not putting on a show for us to bring our day to a suitable end, and he thanked us for receiving him so warmly. He had with him the duc d'Aumale, M. Salvandy, and some aides de camp. We set off. All along our route the passersby stopped to stare at our *hundred* hired carriages going by.

I don't know if I'm right, since I know nothing of painting, but it seemed to me that there were very few good pictures there; perhaps what I'm saying is stupid but apart from some paintings by Horace Vernet, two or three by Scheffer, and Delacroix's *Battle of Taillebourg* I don't remember any of them, except, too, a canvas by Regnault on some marriage or other of the emperor Joseph, but this painting stands out for an entirely different reason. All the paintings made during the Empire which are supposed to be very beautiful often seem so regular, so cold. The people in them are frequently arranged like trees, or minor characters in an opera. It's probably very silly of me to talk in this way of paintings that have been so highly praised; perhaps I'm speaking nonsense, but I'm only giving my own impressions—perhaps it's also the result of reading *La Presse* which praises Delacroix to the skies?[8]

The next day, in a newspaper called *Le Charivari*, it was reported that after dinner we were fed on *crusts*.

My cousin Levaillant came to see me and gave me his address, which I've forgotten. M. de Viterne was also kind enough to come. M. Morin came one morning. He told me that when he asked you if he could take me out, you refused, fearing that other people might be hurt to see him preferred to them; nevertheless he told me that if there was anything I really needed I had only to let you know and he'd be delighted to take me out and your friends need know nothing about it. I was overjoyed at this suggestion for the following reason: I very often go and chat with M. Rinn, my teacher, about the books I'm reading, about literary ideas, Latin writers, what's being done at present, what one should do with one's life, and so on. As he realized how much I like modern authors, he told me he'd be pleased to analyze a modern work with me at length, show me its good and bad sides, and that for this purpose I should visit him at home one Thursday. M. Rinn is an oracle in my eyes, and I was delighted. But unfortunately the Head has refused to let me go out: before she left, Mother begged him to let me do so. So I'd be grateful if you'd agree to send me a letter for the Head, certifying that you allow me to go out occasionally with M. Morin. I'd only use that permission to visit M. Rinn, stay in my room, and chat with M. Morin when he had enough time on his hands. Moreover, I'd only barely make use of it, for now I'm no longer with you and don't chat with M. Rinn any more, it's at college that I'm least bored. [. . .]

14   To Caroline Aupick

3 August [1838]

Dear Mother,

We've done all our exams. As far as the competitive exams are concerned we're in the dark. I can only tell you that apart from verse composition I'm not holding out any hopes. I asked my teacher about the

8. Gautier reviewed the Salon of 1838 in *La Presse* and took the opportunity of including an assessment of Delacroix's paintings on 23 March 1838.

class and he told me my verse composition and my Latin speech were terrible. So that's what a year's work leads to, and what success at school really is. If by any chance you're back for the prize giving I'll ask the Head if I have a prize, and if not of course I won't go to the ceremony. But I don't really hope that you will be back because when I told M. Zinse that you'd be coming home in two weeks he said that would be unwise, that you should benefit from the waters as long as possible and stay until the very last moment. M. Morin also finds it very odd that you should return so early. Since you are there, please get the best out of the cure you've chosen so that you're certain to get the full benefit. You're surely not going on such a long journey in order to stay for so little time. So before you come back, give it a lot of thought, and if you think the waters can go on improving matters, do everything you can to keep Father there.

M. Zinse told me he'd seen you out riding, that you were enjoying yourself and were very happy. Oh, how lucky you are to be able to enjoy yourself! As for me, it's the exact opposite. I'm so bored I cry for no reason. Don't be surprised that I tell you to stay in one breath and in the next I tell you my sorrows as if I were summoning you back. I want you to stay if that's the best solution, and I'm only writing about me because that keeps my mind off things and gives me something to think about. So, I'm very cross with myself: it looks as if I'm not going to have any success; I admit my self-esteem is deeply affronted; I try to react philosophically and tell myself that success at college isn't worth a jot, that it proves very little, etc. It's still true that such successes bring great pleasure. So I'm cross with myself and others make me even crosser. You'll tell me: read a book. Well, goodness me, I've done nothing but read since I last saw you, that is, since we've been left to our own devices at school. You know that at the end of the year there are two empty months, and that then anyone who hasn't enough money to buy books is really unhappy: they spend their time sleeping. I myself spent almost all my money on getting books because I had to pay for a 4-volume work that had been confiscated from one of my classmates. I only read modern books. As for those works that are the talk of the town, highly valued, read by all and sundry, the best in fact: well, all that's false, exaggerated, puffed up. Above all I've got it in for Eugène Sue. I've read only one of his books and that bored me to death. I'm disgusted with all that: only Victor Hugo's theater and poetry, and a book by Sainte-Beuve (*Volupté*) gave me any pleasure. I'm absolutely fed up with literature: I can truly say that ever since I've been able to read I've not yet found a book that entirely pleased me, that I could like from first page to last page; so I don't read anymore. I'm stuffed with literature. I don't talk to anyone. I think of you: you at least are a perpetual book, one can chat with you, one can busy oneself loving you: that doesn't pall as other pleasures do. Truly it's perhaps for the best that we've been separated; I've learned to feel disgust for modern literature, I've learned to love my mother more than ever because I felt she was far from me, so you'll see when you get back that you'll be overwhelmed with kisses, care, attention, and although you already know I love you, you'll still be amazed at just how much I love you. Farewell—we'll see who loves best. [. . .]

15   TO JACQUES AUPICK

26 February [1839]

I'm going to make a request that will greatly surprise you. You've promised me lessons in fencing and riding, and instead of that I'm going to ask you, if you're willing and the thing is possible and won't cause you any problems, to let me have a coach. We've very often said to each other that a coach serves no purpose and is sometimes even harmful to the pupil. That's true if the pupil is lazy and just chats to his coach, getting the latter to do his homework for him.

But I have no need of assistance to follow the class as such, and what I'd want from a coach would be an extra serving of philosophy and subjects that aren't done in class, namely: *religion*, the study of which is not included in the university's program, and Æsthetics, or the philosophy of the arts, which our professor is certainly not going to have the time to tell us about.

What I'd also want him for is Greek—yes, to teach me Greek, which I'm totally ignorant about, like everyone who learns it at college, and which I'd find so hard to learn on my own at a time when so many other things would be overwhelming me.

You know that I've acquired a taste for the languages of antiquity, and I'm very curious about Greek. Despite what people say about it nowadays, I'm convinced that it brings not only a great deal of pleasure, but also tangible advantages. Why should such tastes be stifled? Isn't that essential to what I want to become—science, history, philosophy—who knows? The study of Greek may also make German easier for me.

I think a coach costs 30 francs a month. The pupil needs an authorization from his father first. Then he asks the headmaster and chooses a coach. It's half an hour a day or an hour every second day. I'd choose a young master, who is highly distinguished, has recently graduated from the *Ecole normale* and known at Louis-le-Grand, M. Lasègue. If he were unable to give me lessons, I'd rather go without a coach. This is no vain whim. I've changed my mind so many times, and abandoned so many fine projects that I'm always afraid I won't be trusted. Greek has always been something I've wanted to know. I think this young teacher is able to teach it and *to do so very quickly*. As for the dogmatic side of religion, that's also something that has tormented me since the beginning of the year.— Recently I examined myself, asking myself what I knew—a pretty large number of things on all subjects, but it's all vague, confused, lacking order, and mutually harmful. Nothing is clear, sharp and systematized. What it all amounts to is that I know nothing—and yet I'm about to embark on life—for that you need some sort of package of clearly formed bits of knowledge. What could serve me better at the moment than the study of language that would let me read in the original some very useful books? And what could be better than the study of the finest part of philosophy, religion?

I don't know if my letter is eloquent.—At least I'm acting in all good faith, and I firmly believe in the usefulness of my request.

Moreover, you know so well what my faults have been, what my needs are, and you've told me such true things about education that I'll receive with great respect your advice on this matter.

All good wishes to my dear mother. She'll be greatly astonished at my letter. M. Massoni told me you were improving, and that gives me much pleasure.

As usual, M. Massoni heaped upon me distressing compliments. For, between you and me, we know what I am. As M. Massoni is very fond of me, and as he's older than I am, I'm obliged to respect his flattery, and I think it's better manners to accept them in silence than to protest. But that often causes me acute embarrassment, especially in front of others. Farewell. I hope you'll steal a few moments to answer me. I send you a hug, as I'd like to hug you occasionally in the college parlor.

2 · *Vie de bohème: 1840–1847*

16   To Victor Hugo

[25 February 1840]

Dear Sir,

Recently I saw a performance of *Marion de Lorme*:[1] the beauty of the play filled me with such delight and happiness that I long with all my heart to meet the author and thank him personally. I'm still a schoolboy and it may be that I'm committing an unprecedented piece of impertinence, but I'm completely ignorant of social niceties and I thought that you'd be indulgent towards me. A schoolboy's praise and thanks can't affect you deeply, in comparison with the praise and thanks that have been heaped upon you by so many men of taste. You've probably received so many people that you're not likely to be very eager to attract yet another irksome individual. Still, if you only knew how sincere and how true is the love of the young! It seems to me (perhaps this is just my pride) that I understand all your works. I love you as I love your books; I believe that you are good and openhearted, because you've undertaken to rehabilitate several people; because, far from yielding to general opinion, you've often reshaped it, with pride and dignity. I imagine that by your side, sir, I'd learn numerous good and great things; I love you as one loves a hero, a book, as one loves all beautiful things, purely and without self-interest. Perhaps I'm very bold to send you, willy-nilly, these praises through the post, but I wanted to tell you intensely and simply how deeply I love and admire you, and how I tremble to think that I may be making a fool of myself. And yet, sir, since you've been young yourself, you surely understand this love for an author that a book sparks off within us, and that imperious need to thank him face to face and to kiss his hands in all humility. At 19, would you have hesitated to write as much to a writer who had fired your soul, to M. de Chateaubriand[2] for instance? All this is not well enough expressed—I think better than I write. But I hope that as you too have been young you'll guess what I leave unspoken, and that a step so new, so unusual, won't shock you too

---

1. A play by Victor Hugo, written in 1829 and first performed in 1831.
2. Hugo had dedicated one of his *Odes And Ballads* to Chateaubriand, whom he greatly admired.

much; and that you'll deign to honor me with a reply. I confess that I await it with the utmost impatience.

Whether or not you are so kind as to reply, please accept my everlasting gratitude.

18   To Alphonse Baudelaire
[20 January 1841]

My dear brother,

Herewith a very exact account of my debts. It adds up to a lot more than I'd thought—but they're not all equally urgent.

200 F still to be paid for a long-standing debt I owe my tailor, *very urgent*. I think this man needs the money and this debt distresses me. It's already long overdue.

100 F to a cobbler.

60 F to another cobbler.

215 F to M. Ducessois. *I want to pay this debt myself*—at a later date— I want him to think it's me who has paid him. I gave him my promise and I don't want the humiliation of not sticking to my word.

200 F to *Delagenevraye*, one of my friends (a long-standing debt), used to buy clothes for a prostitute whom I'd taken away from a *brothel*.

180 F to the same, doubtless to pay another urgent debt.

50 F to Songeon, one of my friends—for the same reason—urgent.

300 F to the capmaker, shirtmaker and glovemaker.

Now here is the account of what I owe my tailor:

2 suits,	one casual,	125F
	one formal	110F
	1 quilted cardigan	170F
	1 quilted dressing gown	110F
	4 pairs of pants	200F
	3 waistcoats	120F
	1 little coat	———

In the whole time he's been working for me I've given him only *200 francs*, to be deducted from the account above. All those figures are merely approximations.

In all these accounts there is not a single lie, nor have I deliberately made any of the figures too high. I'd be very relieved if I could give something to my tailor. I suspect him of being rather negligent toward me.

However little you give me, I'm so hard up I'll be infinitely delighted. If you can help me, I beg and beseech you not to let the faintest hint reach my parents. If Mother has to be tormented, let it at least be about something that can benefit me.

I swear to you that once I've got out of this mess, I'll be *reasonable* in the fullest meaning of the word. If you're a little distrustful of me, I'll show you the bills as you send the money. Farewell. I send all my love to you and to my dear sister, whom you've no doubt told all about this and who must bear me a terrible grudge.

18   TO ADOLPHE AUTARD DE BRAGARD

20 October 1841

Dear M. Autard,

In Mauritius you asked me for some lines for your wife and I've not forgotten your request. As it's good, decent, and proper that poetry written to a lady by a young man should pass through the hands of her husband before reaching her, I'm sending these lines to you, so that you can decide whether or not to show them to her. Since leaving you I've often thought about you and your wonderful friends. I'll certainly not forget the marvelous time I've spent with you, Mme Autard, and M. B . . .[3]

If I didn't love Paris so much and miss it so bitterly I'd stay with you as long as possible and I'd force you to like me and to find me a little less *baroque* than I seem. It's not likely that I'll return to Mauritius, unless the ship I take for Bordeaux goes there to collect passengers. Here's my sonnet.[4]

So I'll await your arrival in Paris. My most respectful greetings to Mme Autard.

19   TO JACQUES AUPICK

16 February [1842]

I'm back from my long outing. I arrived yesterday evening, having left Bourbon on 4 November. I haven't brought a cent back with me and I've *often had to go without essentials.*

You know what happened to us on the way out.[5] The return journey, although less remarkable, was much more wearying; it was always either stormy or dead calm. If I wrote down everything I've thought and imagined when I was far from you, I'd run out of paper. So I'll tell you when I see you.

I think I'm returning with a fund of good sense.

3. The identity of M. B. is not known. It is believed that this letter's first publisher substituted the initial for the name.

4. "To a Creole Lady" ("Au pays parfumé," later entitled "A une dame créole").

5. A violent storm, described by the captain as one of the worst he had encountered.

I think I'll leave tomorrow, so I'll be able to hug you in two or three days' time.

20   To Caroline Aupick

16 November 1843

Two days ago I had a long meeting with the director of the *Bulletin de l'ami des arts*. My short story will appear in the first number for January.[6] From that date I'll officially be a member of the editorial staff and I've promised lots of short stories. —I've also promised to get people to subscribe. It's in my interests that this man should feel obliged to me; so I'm counting on you to take out a subscription and even more to encourage the people you know to do so—Paul, Mme Edmond Blanc, etc. The subscription fee (20 francs at present) will be 36 francs from January, given that the paper will come out every week. Another interest I have in this is that the chief editor of the *Bulletin* is a friend of Jules Janin who'll probably be asked to reorganize the staff of *L'Artiste*,[7] which is changing hands this week, and Janin has expressly promised to get me appointed to the staff. I'm counting on you—once you've taken out a subscription and *asked for the back numbers*, send me as they occur to you the names of people likely to subscribe, so I can show these gentlemen my worth.

21   To Caroline Aupick

[late 1843?]

Dearest Mother,

Thanks for all your kindness and generosity. When we drink your tea we'll think of you. Do me the pleasure of reading this manuscript I've finished and where there are a few corrections to make.[8] I took it back this morning from a newspaper (*La Démocratie*) which rejected it because they found it *immoral*, but the really good thing is that it astonished everyone so much that they've done me the honor of asking for another one as soon as possible and were very kind and complimentary about it. You don't know it ends; read it and tell me sincerely what *effect it has on you*.

6. It is not certain what this was, since it was not accepted, but Baudelaire may be referring to his novella, *La Fanfarlo*.

7. Janin was a patron of *Le Bulletin*, but it was Arsène Houssaye who took over control of the prestigious review *L'Artiste*. The first of Baudelaire's works to appear there with his signature was in May 1845, but he may have published earlier works under the pseudonym Privat d'Anglemont.

8. Possibly *La Fanfarlo*, or a piece of satirical writing. *La Démocratie pacifique* was a Fourierist paper.

[summer 1844]

Please read this letter very carefully because it's extremely serious, and makes a final appeal to your good sense and to that very deep tenderness you claim to feel for me. —First and foremost I'm writing this letter to you under the seal of secrecy and I beg you not to show it to anyone. Second I beg you most insistently not to see in it any intention to try to appear an object of sympathy or to move you other than by a few good reasons. The strange way in which our conversations now habitually become acrimonious (though often there's not a grain of truth in the bitter things I say) together with my tendency to become agitated and your determination not to hear me out anymore, have forced me to take the form of a letter in my attempt to persuade you how wrong you can be in spite of all the love you feel for me.

I'm writing this in a thoroughly rested frame of mind, and when I think of how ill my anger and amazement have made me over the last few days I wonder how on earth I could support such a state of affairs if your plans were actually carried out! —To make me swallow the pill you repeat over and over again that it's all completely natural and in no way a stain on one's honor. That's possible and I'm willing to believe what you say, but the truth is that it doesn't matter how the mass of men see a certain thing if I see it *entirely differently*. —You've told me you see my anger and grief as passing moods; you're assuming that you're just giving me a little pain as one might hurt a child for its own good. But for heaven's sake convince yourself of this one truth, that is, in very truth and to my own sorrow, I'm not like other men. —What you consider a necessary and fleeting pain, I cannot, I really cannot bear. —There's an easy explanation for that. When we're alone you can treat me as you like—but I furiously reject anything that encroaches on my freedom. — Isn't it unbelievably cruel to make me submit to the judgment of a handful of men who are bored by the whole matter and who don't even know me? —Between ourselves, who can claim to know me, and to know where I want to go, what I want to do and what degree of patience I'm capable of? In all sincerity, I'm convinced you're committing a grave error. —I'm telling you this coldly because I consider you've condemned me, and I'm sure you won't listen to me; but first take good note of this, that you're knowingly and willingly causing me infinite pain, the extent of which is beyond your comprehension.

You've broken your word in two ways. —When you were kind enough to lend me 8,000 francs, we agreed that at the end of a given time you'd have the right to take a certain amount from all my work. —I got into debt again and when I told you the debts were tiny you promised me you'd wait a little longer. Indeed, a few small monetary advances, together with my earnings, could rapidly cover them. Now you've made your decision in a furious fashion; you set to work with such alacrity that I for my part have no idea what to do—and I'm forced to abandon my plans. I'd thought that my first piece of work—since it's almost a work of science and would come to the attention of several people[9]—would result in your getting a few compliments and that when you saw that money was coming in you'd not have refused me some new loans. This would have meant that after a few months I could have paid off all my debts—that is, got back to the point I'd reached when you lent me the 8,000 francs. Not a bit of it, you weren't willing to wait—you wouldn't even wait two weeks.

Let's see, then, just how false this reasoning is and how illogical your conduct. You cause me enormous suffering and you take a highly offensive step, on what might well be the eve of the beginnings of my success, the eve of the day I'd so looked forward to. That's the very moment you seize on to pull the carpet from under my feet—for, as I've said, I have no wish at all to accept a *conseil* as if it were something anodyne and harmless—I can already feel what effect it would have. And on this score you've fallen into an error that is even worse—which consists in believing that this will spur me on. You can't imagine what I felt yesterday, how my legs felt heavy with despair, when I saw that the affair was becoming serious. I felt something akin to a sudden desire to abandon everything, not to bother with anything anymore, not even to go and get my letter from M. Edmond Blanc—I just kept thinking calmly—I don't need it anymore. My only job now is to swallow like an idiot whatever she chooses to force down my throat.

It's such a bad mistake on your part that M. Ancelle said to me when I was at Neuilly: "I told your mother that if allowing you to spend your entire fortune would lead you to work and to a job, my advice would be to let you go ahead; but she'll never allow that to happen." I cannot believe it possible to say anything more insolent and more stupid. I've never dared go as far as that, and think coldly that I'd blow the lot. I presume that you're not as indulgent as he is. For my own part, I'm too fond of my freedom to do anything so stupid. Now, although I'm your son, you ought to hold me in enough respect not to abandon me to the judgment of strangers when you know how deeply that wounds me. And you ought to bear in mind the difficulty of what I've undertaken. It's absolutely certain—and believe me, my dear mother, this isn't just a threat to make

9. Probably a study of painting, a project Baudelaire planned over a long period but never completed.

you go back on your decision, but the sincere expression of my feelings—the result will be exactly the opposite of what you predict—to be quite precise, it'll lead to a complete collapse.

Now I want to turn to another matter that will no doubt seem more important to you than any kind of promise, and more important, too, than all my hopes. You tell me you're guided by unwavering tenderness and concern. You want to enable me to keep what I possess, despite myself. I'm perfectly willing for that to happen. I've never intended to devour it completely. I'm ready to hand over to you any means of keeping it for me—but with one exception, the very method you've chosen. What does it matter to you what method is chosen provided you succeed? Why do you want to use the sole method that causes me intense suffering? The very one that is most repugnant to a man of my character? Mediators, judges, strangers—what need do we have of them?

Finally, not knowing a thing about the law, I spoke idly to you of a donation, the terms of which would mean the money would come back to me in case of death. I don't know if such a thing is possible; but what is certain is that you won't make me believe that in all the tricks of the lawyers' trade there is no method that can satisfy you apart from the one you want to use. So what are your reasons? Look, can anyone be more loyal, more sincere, than I am—can I give you a more remarkable proof of my good faith, and of the harmony that exists between what you want and what I want? I prefer not to have a fortune anymore and to put myself completely in your hands, rather than subject myself to any judgment whatsoever: the first is still an act of freedom, the other is an attack on my freedom.

To conclude, I beg you on my knees, with utter humility, to spare yourself this terrible pain, and me this frightful humiliation. For the love of God, don't bring in judges and strangers—no conferences. I'd like a moratorium until I've had a lengthy discussion with you and M. Ancelle. I'm going to see him this evening. I hope I'll be able to bring him to see you. But I'm convinced, utterly convinced, that once I've had my first success it will be easy, provided you help a little, to find a good position quickly. I earnestly renew my prayers to you. I'm convinced you're wrong—after that—if I haven't explained to you properly how much more pleasant and sensible it would be to reach an amicable agreement, do what you choose, I don't care what happens.

M. Edmond Blanc has given me an excellent letter with which I'm going to try to straighten things out with the *Revue*[10] this morning. — One last time, I beg you to bear in mind that I'm not asking for any favors other than that you alter the method you've selected.

10. The *Revue de Paris*, which was on the point of collapse.

23   To Charles-Augustin Sainte-Beuve

[late 1844 or early 1845]

Dear Sir,

Stendhal says somewhere or other the following words—or an expression close to it—"I write for a handful of souls whom perhaps I'll never see, but whom I love without ever having seen them."[11] These words provide the importunate with a perfect excuse, for isn't it obvious that every writer is responsible for the sympathies he arouses?

The following lines were written for you—and with such naïveté— that when they were finished I found myself wondering whether they didn't seem impertinent—and whether the person praised wouldn't be perfectly entitled to take offense at such praise. I hope you'll deign to let me know what you think of them.[12]

24   To Narcisse Ancelle

30 June 1845

By the time Mlle Jeanne Lemer gives you this letter I'll be dead. She doesn't know this. You know my will. Apart from the portion reserved for my mother, Mlle Lemer is to inherit everything I have, after the payment of certain debts, a list of which I enclose. I'm dying in a terrible state of anxiety. Remember the conversation we had yesterday. I desire, indeed I insist, that my last wishes be strictly carried out by my executors. Two people can contest my will: my mother and my brother—and their sole cause for contesting it would be that I was not of sound mind. My suicide, together with the various upheavals that there have been in my life, can only aid them in depriving Mlle Lemer of what I want to leave her. I'm obliged therefore to explain to you my suicide and my behavior insofar as it concerns Mlle Lemer—so that this letter addressed to you and that you'll be kind enough to read to her, can serve as her defense, should my will be contested by the above-named people.

I am killing myself without any sense of *sorrow*. I feel none of the agitation that men call *sorrow*. My debts have never been a cause of *sorrow*. It's perfectly simple to rise above such matters. I'm killing myself because I can no longer go on living, because the weariness of falling asleep and the weariness of waking up have become unbearable to me. I'm killing myself because I believe I'm of no use to others—and because I'm a *danger to myself*. I'm *killing* myself because I believe I'm immortal and because I *hope*. At the time of writing these lines I am so lucid that

11. The idea expressed is certainly part of Stendhal's philosophy, but the formula Baudelaire uses has not been found in Stendhal's texts.

12. The poem "In the Days When Our Cheeks Were Unshaven" ("Tous imberbes alors").

27

I'm still copying out a few notes for M. Théodore de Banville[13] and have the necessary strength to busy myself with my manuscripts.

I give and bestow all I possess to Mlle Lemer, including my little stock of furniture and my portrait—because she's the only creature who offers me solace. Can anyone blame me for wanting to repay her for the rare pleasures I've enjoyed in this horrendous world?

I do not know my brother very well—he has neither lived *in me* nor *with me*—he has no need of me.

My mother, who has so frequently and always unwittingly poisoned my life, has no need of money either. —She has her *husband*; she has a *human being*, some one who provides her with affection and *friendship*.

I have no one but Jeanne Lemer. It's only in her that I've found rest, and I *will* not, *can* not bear the thought that people want to strip her of what I'm giving her, on the pretext that my mind is wandering. You've heard me talking to you these last few days. Was I mad?

If I thought that by begging my mother directly and revealing to her how deeply humiliated I am, I could persuade her not to overthrow my last wishes, I'd do it immediately—so sure am I that as she's a woman she'll understand me better than anyone else—and she alone perhaps could talk my brother out of adopting an *unintelligent* position.

Jeanne Lemer is the only woman I've loved—she owns nothing. And it's you, M. Ancelle, one of the few men whom I've found to possess a gentle and lofty mind, whom I charge with my last wishes concerning her. Read this to her—tell her the reasons for my bequest, and explain to her her defense should my last wishes be questioned. You, who are prudent, make her understand the value of money. Try to find some reasonable means of aiding her and making my last wishes useful to her. Guide her, advise her—dare I say—love her—for my sake at least. Set my terrible example before her—and show her how a disordered mind and life lead to dark despair and to complete destruction. *Reason and usefulness, I beg you.*

Do you really think this will can be contested, and could I be prevented from performing a good and reasonable action before dying? You see clearly now how this will is an act neither of bravado, nor of defiance of social and family values, but simply the expression of what is still human in me: love, and the sincere longing to help a being who has sometimes been my delight and consolation. Farewell!

Read this letter to her—I believe in your loyalty and I know you won't destroy my letter. Give her some money forthwith (500). She knows nothing of my final intentions—and expects to see me come and rescue her from some problems she's experiencing.

13. See this letter, no. 25.

Even in the case where a dead man's will is sure to be contested, he has the right to make a few gifts. The other letter she'll give you, and which is for your eyes only, contains the list of those who will have to be paid on my behalf, if my memory is to be preserved with honor.

25   To Théodore de Banville

[6 July 1845]

The attached sonnet shows I'm thinking of you. In return, pluck up courage and write to me forthwith, and at some length. If you can, it will be a distraction for me—but don't play around with my public bum-wipers—by that I mean don't show them to a single soul. This morning I had the strangest of surprises; it's a kind of journal published in Abbe-ville—with an article on me—*delightful*—entirely kind, delicious, and comical as well—it's obviously by *Levavasseur*. He lives in the rue de Beaune but as I don't know the number I can't write to him. If you see him, thank him for me. I've good reason to be devilish scared of Privat; try to close his mouth; he'll know what that means. [Letter concludes with the sonnet entitled "To Théodore de Banville."]

26   To Charles-Philippe de Chennevières

[5 November 1845]

My review of your opus came out yesterday. I hope you'll be pleased with it. M. Lepoitevin Saint-Alme, who has read some of your stories [. . .] is delighted with you. He'd like you to write a few for him. Give some thought to whether you'd like to dash off some reviews at a sou and half per line, which I think gives a grand total of barely 20 francs for the nine columns!! But the real advantage of this is that when the good old chap takes a shine to someone, he finds a real pleasure in helping him in all manner of ways.

If that appeals to you, go and see him, telling him you're *Chen-nevières*.[14] Have you sent copies to Labitte? Has he sent them to all the papers? And the posters?

27   To Caroline Aupick

Saturday 4 December 1847

In spite of the cruel letter you wrote in reply to my last request, I thought I could turn to you once again, not because I'm not perfectly aware of what a bad mood I'm going to put you in, and how hard it'll be

14. Chennevières published under the name Jean de Falaise.

to make you understand that my request is entirely legitimate, but because I feel so convinced that such an action can be infinitely and indisputably helpful to me, and I'm hoping to make you share that conviction. You'll note that I say *once again*, by which I mean in complete sincerity: *for the last time*. Of course I owe you my thanks for being good enough to provide me with the means to obtain some of the things essential to a more sensible life than the one I've been forced to lead for such a long time. I'm referring to the furniture you've given me. But now that the furniture has been acquired I'm penniless, and I'm lacking some of the equally essential things—you can easily guess what sort of things I mean—lamps, a cistern, etc. I'll give you just one example: I had to put up with a lengthy discussion with M. Ancelle merely to extract some wood and coal from his clutches. If you only knew what an effort I've had to make just to take up a pen and write to you again, in no hope of explaining to someone whose life is easy and well regulated how it is possible for me to be in such a mess! Imagine a chronic inability to work caused by a perpetual illness, suffered by someone with a deep hatred for that inability to work, and completely incapable of getting out of it because of the constant lack of money. In such cases it's certainly better, however humiliating, to turn again to you, rather than to outsiders in whom I wouldn't find the same sympathy. Here's what's happening to me now. Overjoyed at having somewhere to live and some furniture, but deprived of money, I'd spent the last two or three days trying to get hold of some cash, when last Monday evening, worn out with weariness, worry, and hunger, I went into the first hotel I came across and since that time I've stayed put, with good cause. I'd given the address of this hotel to a friend whom I'd lent money 4 years ago, in the days when I had money, but he hasn't kept his word to me. Moreover the sum I had in mind wasn't large—30 to 35 francs a week; but that's not the whole problem. For even if, with your usual generosity (alas it's never sufficient), you're willing to get me out of this mess, what shall I do *tomorrow*? For this idleness is killing me, it devours and corrodes me. I really don't know how I have the strength to overcome the disastrous effects of this idleness and have absolute clarity in my thinking and a constant faith in fortune, happiness, and calm. And that's why I beg on *bended knees*, so close I feel to the end not only of other people's patience but of my own. Send me, even if it costs you great suffering and even if you don't believe in the real usefulness of this final service, not merely the sum in question but enough to let me survive for three weeks. Arrange things as you think best. I believe so firmly in my timetable and in the strength of my willpower that I *know for a fact* that if I could succeed in leading a regular life for two or three weeks, *my intelligence would be saved*. This is a final attempt, *a gamble*. Take a chance on the outsider, my dear mother, I do beg of you. The explanation for these 6 years, spent in a way that would have been so strange and so disastrous did I not enjoy a physical and intellectual health that nothing can destroy—is very simple. You could sum it up in the following way: thoughtlessness, procrastination of the most easily realizable plans, resulting in poverty, unending poverty. Do you want a sample? On occasion I've had to spend up to three days in bed, sometimes because I had no clean linen, sometimes because there was no wood. To be honest, laudanum and wine are of little help against sorrow. They make the time pass but they don't change one's life. Moreover, even to sink into brutishness you need money. The last time you were kind enough to give me 15 francs I hadn't eaten for *two days*—48 hours. I was constantly traveling to Neuilly, I didn't dare confess to M. Ancelle, and the only way I kept awake and on my feet was through the brandy I'd been given and I hate liquors because they burn my stomach. May such confessions—for your sake or mine—never be known to living men or to posterity! For I still believe that posterity concerns me. No one could ever believe that a rational being born of a good kind mother could have fallen into such a state. So never let this letter, which is addressed to you alone, to the first person to whom I've ever made such a confession— never let it out of your keeping. You must have in your heart sufficient reasons to understand that such complaints can be addressed only to you and cannot go beyond you. Besides, before writing to you, I thought of everything and resolved not to see M. Ancelle anymore—I've already had two unpleasant interviews with him. If you were to make the mistake of judging this final attempt as commonplace and no different from the others and were to send him this letter or even some advice! I've just reread these two pages and even to me they seem extraordinary. I've never dared to complain so intensely before. I hope you'll attribute this excitement to the sufferings I'm undergoing and of which you know nothing. The absolute idleness of my life as it appears to others, contrasting with the perpetual activity of my ideas, throws me into extraordinary fits of rage. I'm angered by my faults, and I'm angry at you for believing I'm not sincere in my intentions. The fact is that for the last few months I've been living in a supernatural state of mind. Now—to return to the central part of the proof I'm trying to give you, the absurdity of my existence can be explained, generally speaking, in the following way: thoughtless spending of money that should be devoted to work. Time rushes by, but my needs continue. *One last time*, in my longing to be finished with this situation and in my belief in my willpower, I'm turning to you, to make an attempt, a final throw of the dice, as I was saying a moment ago, even if this should seem to you exorbitant yet again, and even if it causes you financial difficulties. I can guess and understand very well how any irregularity in expenditure must be unbearable to you, and must throw you into disarray and how particularly unsettling it must be for a good housekeeper like you, as I know from living with you—but I'm in an exceptional state of mind. I wanted to see once more if my mother's money could help me—and I believe that it's indisputably certain to do so. I'm suffering too much not to want to end it *once and for all*. That expression has, I think, already appeared several times. Indeed, despite the terrible pain I'd feel at leaving Paris and bidding farewell to so many fine dreams, I've taken the sincere and violent decision to do so if I can't force myself to live and to work for some time on the money I'm asking you to spend. It would mean going far away. People I met on the *Ile de France*[15] have been kind enough to remember me; I'd find with them a post whose duties I could easily fill, with a generous salary in a country where the living is easy once one is established there, and *the boredom, the horrible boredom and the intellectual decay of warm and sunny countries*. But I'll do it as a form of punishment and atonement for my pride, if I don't carry out my resolutions. Don't look among the official posts for this job—it's almost a domestic situation. I'd have to teach *everything* apart from chemistry, physics, and mathematics to a friend's children. But let's not speak of that, for the possibility of having to make such a decision sends shivers down my spine. I'll add only that should I judge it necessary *to punish myself for failing to live up to all my dreams* I'd insist (because over there my life would be easy and secure) that *all my debts be paid*. The mere thought of debasing and renouncing my gifts in such a way makes me shudder. So I beg you not to show this letter to *M. Ancelle*, even in confidence, so shameful do I find it for a man to doubt that he'll succeed. I have until February to accept or refuse, and I hope to give you proof on New Year's day that your money has been well spent.

This is my plan. It's simple in the extreme. About 8 months ago I was asked to write two full-length articles, which I still haven't completed, one on the *history of caricature*, the other one on the *history of sculpture*. That would bring in 600 francs, and would cover only urgent needs. Articles like these are a mere game for me.

Starting on New Year's day, I'm embarking on a new career—the creation of works of pure imagination, novels. I don't need to prove to you here the seriousness, the beauty, and the infinite nature of that art. While we're dealing with material concerns, I'll just tell you that *any novel can be sold, good or bad*—you just need determination.

15. The ship that took Baudelaire to Mauritius and Reunion.

Well, I've *calculated* that the excessive weariness of most of my creditors who look on their loans as deplorable and have into the bargain the secret knowledge that they've *shamefully robbed* me, would enable me to reduce the total amount of money I owe to 6,000 or 8,000 at the most. With a bit of care and persistence, I could easily raise that sum, as I well know from all the experience I've gained in all the hustle and bustle of journals and booksellers. To whom will I give the unpleasant task of conferring with them—myself, M. Ancelle, or another? I don't yet know. But I insist that you promise me that once this first task has been carried out, and moreover, once a few months have gone by, as proof that I can not only pay my debts, but also refrain from contracting any more debts, you'll help me by bearing witness to this fact, and that you'll be the first to act in helping me get back full control of my affairs. You'll also give me back those cruel letters you spoke of—the ones that made you so severe. If you only knew what a complicated blend of large and small torments makes up my habitual suffering. At least I've forced myself this time to write you a letter that is entirely suitable and can prove the complete lucidity of mind I enjoy in good moments. The sad thing is that I need you and that there's nothing I can do concerning you without appearing selfish.

I'm very tired. It's as though a wheel keeps spinning around in my head. One last time, dear Mother, I beg you in the name of my salvation. I believe it's the first time I've confided in you at such length about so many plans that I cherish and consider so important. I hope this convinces you that from time to time I think of setting aside all my pride and dealing with my mother! Don't speak to me any more of my age. As you know, not all educations follow the same course and the question can be summarized in the following terms: the more time that has gone by between the day of one's birth and the instant that has been marked as the start of success, the more one has to hurry and profit from what time remains.

But once more I feel now in such a perfect state of mind that it really would be unfortunate if I couldn't make myself understood. Time passes, and a few more days of idleness could destroy me. I've told you, I've misused my strength so much that I've reached the outer limits of my own patience and will be incapable of a final great effort unless I gain some assistance.

If by any chance it occurs to you to ask M. Ancelle for money, don't tell him what it's for, since it's you I'm asking and since you might at least *let me have the pleasure of receiving this help from you alone.* Please answer straight away. *I've been urging myself to write to you for three days without finding the courage to do so.* You can trust the messenger. —One more thing. For a long time you've been trying to cut me completely out of your life. You probably hope that this isolation will bring my problems to an end. Whatever I've done wrong, it isn't my fault. Do you think I'm strong enough to put up with perpetual isolation? *I undertake not to visit you until I can bring good news.* But in exchange I ask to be allowed to see you, to be received by you warmly and in such a way that your expression, your looks, and your word protect me against everyone when I'm with you.

Farewell, I'm glad I've written to you.

3 · *The Republic: 1848–1851*

28 TO PIERRE-JOSEPH PROUDHON[1]

21 August 1848

Citizen,

A passionate and unknown friend *expressly wishes to see you*, not merely for his own instruction and to take up a few minutes of your time, as perhaps he'd be quite justified in doing, but also to tell you of matters concerning your safety of which you may be unaware. Even if the writer of this letter only tells you something you already know, I don't believe he'll appear ridiculous, for his admiration and sympathy are a sufficient justification.

I have for some time been struggling to overcome my laziness and write you a very long letter, but I've preferred to address you directly. Today policemen prevented me from entering whatever approach I tried, for I hoped to be able to have this note delivered by other representatives I know slightly. If you don't consider it odd for a lowly stranger to beg an immediate answer from a man as busy and worried as you—well in that case I'll wait as long as necessary in the cafe-restaurant on the corner of the rue de Bourgogne. Have the goodness to send me as soon as possible a note in reply—telling me your address and a time when I can see you. The confusion that dominates all minds at present demands the swiftest explanations among feeling men. Please accept my eternal and sincerest devotion and admiration.

29 TO PIERRE-JOSEPH PROUDHON

[21 or 22 August 1848]

This is what I had to tell you. I think it useful information. For either you already know, in which case, since I don't know whether you're aware or not, it's my duty to tell you; or you don't know and it's something you really ought to be aware of.

Disturbances have been predicted. Who'll cause them? We don't

---

1. Proudhon had been elected to the National Assembly on 4 June 1848. His demands in support of farmers and the press had made him a prime target for the forces of reaction.

know. But at the next demonstration, even if it's against the people—that is, at the very next pretext—you may be *assassinated*. This conspiracy really does exist. At first it was merely an intention, vague and latent, choosing you as a target in the same way that a few years ago people began to desire the death of Henri V along these lines: of course, it's evil to want anyone to die, but it would be a happy chance if an accident were to befall him. The other form this longing takes is more explicit: at the next opportunity, we know where he lives and we can find someone to track him down. We'll handle it. You are to be a scapegoat. Please believe that there's no exaggeration in this claim, although I'm not in a position to give you any proof. If I had any, I'd have sent it to the police without consulting you. But my conscience and my intelligence make me an excellent spy where my convictions are concerned. By that I mean that I'm sure of my facts: and they are that the man *we* value so highly is in danger. It's so serious that by recalling certain conversations I've overheard, I could, if there were an attempt, *give you names*, so imprudent is ferocity.

I thought you'd honor me with a reply today. What's more, I was only going to tell you of certain improvements I think you should make in your journal, for example concerning the weekly edition and the re-publication of the whole series. Second, I wanted to talk to you about making a gigantic poster signed by you, by other representatives, and by the editors of your journal. This poster would have an immense print run, and would ORDER the people not to move. Your name is at present better known and more influential than you believe. An insurrection can start out by being legitimist but end by being socialist. It's true that the opposite can also take place.

The author of these lines has complete trust in you, as have many of his friends, who'd walk blindfolded behind you if you guaranteed their safety. So, the next time the mob gets excited, however insignificant it seems, *don't stay at home*. If you can, have a secret bodyguard or demand police protection. Moreover, the government would eagerly welcome such a gift from the ravening beasts who uphold private property, so it's best perhaps to arrange your own protection.

30   TO M. R^ARD [2]

[1848?]

Dear Sir,

You think that by calling me an "ultra-liberal" you're insulting me. My only reply should be to thank you. But let's have a closer look at this

---

2. This man's identity remains unknown. The letter was never sent.

shaming adjective. I open the dictionary and find that the primary meaning of the word is "one who loves giving." In that sense I'd wager that you'd call yourself as well as me "ultra-liberal." Or perhaps you'd not give me that title anymore. But I'm sure you yourself would accept it and would consider yourself more liberal than I. Now, as I can't believe you sought to insult yourself I can take as flattering the major part of the word's meaning.

Figuratively speaking, it means "one who has lofty, open, noble and generous ideas." Once again, I think I can assert that you believe your thoughts noble, your acts generous, and your ideas as open as they are lofty. So this is another piece of praise that I've managed to wrest from you, or at least that I'm sharing with you.

There's a third sense associated with the word, one that is as yet not sharply defined and is better understood than defined, but which the mind nevertheless measures exactly in the statement "liberal opinions," *such as those professed by the pious Lanjuinas, the stern Beauséjour, the virtuous La Fayette, the severe Argenson.* If, by attaching to my name, as if it were a term of abuse, the word *liberal* taken in this meaning, you associated me with those renowned men, then I've no longer anything to be ashamed of. If there exist people who are more honest—and I do not doubt that there are, since I have your word for it—they've reached a pitch of perfection from which heights they shed such light that one cannot gaze upon them. The light I love is that which guides me, and not that which, by blinding me, leads my feet toward the precipices.

Perhaps by *ultra-liberal* you were thinking of those who live only in unrest and subversion. Let them step forward and I'll be the first to heap curses on their heads. But I find such men all about me. I see them near you, today, reddening in blood the color they describe as spotless, and which they have assumed only in order to use it as a barrier between themselves and their accusers.

So, upon close examination, I cannot believe that you would have wanted so to disfigure merely in my favor a word that is terrible only to fools of the upper classes and—generally speaking—to the enemies of governments based on virtue and justice because they guarantee freedom and equality. Now, as I do not consider you to be either stupid or the enemy of civilized freedom and equality, I thank you in all sincerity for the kindness you've shown in giving me the noblest title a citizen can bear.

My gaze will not be fascinated by the baleful results of evil passions! I feel it in the depths of my heart: there are truly liberal men, because there are men who still love true glory and virtue.

Sir, I salute you.

31   TO NARCISSE ANCELLE

[December? 1849]

Madier de Montjau,[3] on his way back from some legal triumph or other, a triumph concerning a trial, came through here and paid us a visit. You know that this young man is supposed to have a marvelous talent. He's an eagle of democracy. He filled me with pity! He was playing at being the enthusiast, the revolutionary. So I spoke to him about the peasants' view of socialism—the inescapable socialism, ferocious, stupid, as bestial as the socialism of the brand and sickle. He was frightened, his ardor cooled down. He backtracked in the face of such logic. He's a fool, or rather an extremely vulgar and ambitious man.

32   TO CAROLINE AUPICK

Sunday 22 June [1851]

My dear Mother,

The weather is so awful that I can't allow you to get wet and go to our absurd meeting in a cafe. I hope that this will reach you in time to stop you going out on my account. I'm returning to Neuilly *tomorrow morning*. So bring me my present there or send it to me, but do try to come.

33   TO CAROLINE AUPICK

Wednesday 9 July [1851]

The need to finish my article[4] and see the editor has prevented me from carrying out your request. But I *give you my word* that you'll have it this evening. You're not leaving until tomorrow morning. Your caretaker will bring you the little parcel this evening.

I thought it appropriate to write you a note this morning since I presumed you'd believe me neglectful enough to forget you.

34   TO CHAMPFLEURY

6 October 1850

Can you meet me tomorrow morning and have lunch with me at Neuilly, 95 avenue de la République? I'll translate your ballad straight through aloud. I'd have to write a whole article to make you understand the type of humor you get in an artist's studio.[5] A conversation would be better. So, let's make it Friday morning, 8 October. You know that buses

3. A socialist, canvassing votes for his election to the Legislative Assembly.
4. Baudelaire's study of the songwriter Pierre Dupont.
5. Champfleury shared Baudelaire's interest in caricature and the comic and published various studies on these topics.

from the Boulevard will drop you just opposite my place. Give your name to the concierge.

35   To Caroline Aupick

30 August 1851

Dear Mother,

I'm no doubt going to make you rather unhappy. I promised to write to you twice a month and now 6 weeks have gone past since I moved in and I've not written to you. That's connected with my vanity in wanting to have some good news for you in my first letter. Well, there's nothing of the sort—nothing or close enough to it. As I like to bring you up to date about what I'm doing, I'm sending you this little brochure for which I was well paid and that you'll read because it's by me—I attach no greater importance to it than that.[6]

When you left you thanked me in a charming letter for the promises I'd made you. And here I am about to break them. Now that I've sorted things out with M. Ancelle and the deficit has been recorded, I'd *almost forbidden* you to send me money. Well, today it's I myself who am calling on your boundless generosity. But it's for very little, and moreover I owe you some explanations. For the first two months—July and August—I lived on money I drew regularly from M. Ancelle, then I *paid* the inescapable deficit, that's to say, promises made to essential creditors— (50 francs to the tailor, 50 francs for furniture, etc.) with what I'd earned. Moreover, I paid off some long-standing debts. Up to now, I'd kept myself well under control. But the day before yesterday I drew my money for the month that's just beginning and feeling sure that my work on *Caricature* would be published immediately, I bravely spent the 200 francs at a stroke on purchases, which were, it's true, necessary but which I could have put off until my next payment (the explanation for this is that I'm going to move to another apartment at the back of the building I'm living in now, and because it has one more room than this one I needed a desk, a little iron bed, and some chairs). As a result of the sort of accident that is always befalling me and that I ought to know how to foresee, but which I didn't foresee, the work won't be published, and I won't be paid, for another two weeks, perhaps not until the end of the month. At the moment of writing to you I have 20 francs. I'm going to watch in terror as they fly slowly away. In a month, perhaps two weeks, I'll be rich, but what shall I do until then? Until then there'll be disorder and as a result—*no work*. The story of my life for the last 9 years is starting all over again. Moreover, as well as the full payment for my

6. The article on Pierre Dupont.

brochure I received some money from the bookshop as a loan which I promised to repay the day after tomorrow. *Please* don't scold me. For two days I've been wondering what to do and I thought that the best thing was to confess my foolishness to you. But *how many days* will pass between my letter and your reply? And your disappointment! And *you'll probably be hard up* as a result. If 200 francs is beyond the bounds of possibility, let it be 150; if 150 is too much, let it be 100—ANYWAY SEND SOMETHING—and if I can't reach the end of the month or even the first two weeks calmly with your help let me at least have a few days' respite to let me get things under control. Now my confession's over, I've only a few pieces of relevant information to add. I absolutely do not want M. Ancelle to be involved. I don't want to feel his suspicions of me. *I could have gone to him and turned his forgetfulness to my advantage but I preferred to turn to you. I don't think that one can use postal checks abroad* as in France. Besides, I don't think you know how to go about it. The only two people among our common acquaintanceship whom I can see without flying into a rage and even with some pleasure are M. Olivier and M. Lenglet (I don't know their addresses).

I've probably hurt you enough for today. I'll put off until my next letter, probably on September 16, the tale of an abominable trick Dr. Naquart played on me in regard to Mme de Balzac, whom I need. What the devil's got into that awful man, whom I've not seen for 20 years and whom I'd known only through the predictions he made about my death and the threat of the tortures he wanted to inflict on me! Moreover to recount the story I'd need to go into it in some depth.

I'm very anxious and unhappy. I have to confess that man is a very weak animal indeed, since habit plays such a great role in virtue. *I'm finding it extremely difficult to settle down to work again.* If I were being honest, I'd need to remove the "again," for I fear I've never really settled down to it. How extraordinary it is! A few days ago, I held in my hands Balzac's *juvenilia*.[7] No one will ever imagine how clumsy, simple and STUPID that great man was in his youth. And yet he succeeded in having, one could almost say, *procuring* not only grandiose conceptions but also an immense intelligence. But he ALWAYS worked. It's probably very reassuring to think that by work one acquires not only money but an unquestionable talent. But at the age of 30, Balzac had already formed the habit of permanent work over several years, and up to now the only things I have in common with him are debts and plans.

I am really very unhappy. You'll no doubt read with pleasure, or rather with the proud eyes of a mother, the weighty work that I'll send you next

7. At this stage Baudelaire seems to have been planning a study of Balzac as dramatist.

month—but when all's said and done I've made a bad job of it.[8] You'll see a few outstanding pages, no doubt, but the rest is only a farrago of contradictions and digressions. As for erudition, there's only a thin veneer of that. And what next? What will I show you after that? My book of poetry? I know that a few years ago it could have made my name. It would have provoked an enormous uproar. But today the conditions, the circumstances, *everything* in fact has changed. And if my book hangs fire? What next? A drama, a novel, even history perhaps. But you can't imagine what days of doubt are like. Sometimes I think I've become too much of a reasoner, too much of a reader, to think of something sincere and naïve. I know too much and I work too little. After all—in a few weeks' time I may be full of confidence and imagination. —In writing this it occurs to me that I wouldn't admit it to one of my friends for anything in the world. But there's no question of retreating. In the course of 1852 I must tear myself out of this state of mnd, this incapacity, and *before the new year I must pay off some debts and publish some poems.* I'll end by knowing that sentence by heart.

On the subject of Balzac, I was at the first performance of *Mercadet le Faiseur.*[9] Those who caused the poor man such torment in his lifetime insult him now he's dead. If you read the French newspapers, you'd have thought the play was appalling. But it's quite simply admirable. I'll send you a copy.

Answer this IMMEDIATELY. *Take all the necessary steps to prevent the letter going astray.* Tell me how to get in touch with you. Give me some details about your journey and ESPECIALLY *about your health.* Don't forget, as you always do, to date your letters. And now let me tell you how deeply happy I am again, and how calming it is for my mind, now that I've formed once more with my mother natural bonds that ought never to have been severed. With warm kisses.

36   TO THÉOPHILE GAUTIER

[late 1851?]

The *incorrigible* Gérard[10] claims that, on the contrary, it's because the good cult was abandoned that Cythera has been reduced to such straits.

Here then, my dear friend, this *second* little parcel. I hope you'll find something you can choose from it. I'm very eager that your taste and mine should be in agreement. For my part I prefer the following:

8. Probably the essay on laughter and the caricaturists.
9. *Mercadet*: a play by Balzac. Baudelaire had been to a performance of this play at the Gymnase theater.
10. The poet Gérard de Nerval.

The Two Twilights: ["Les Deux Crépuscules"]
The Caravan;   ["La Caravane"]
The Denial of Saint Peter;   ["Le Reniement de saint Pierre"]
The Unknown Artist;   ["L'Artiste inconnu"]
The Pleasure Gourd;   ["L'Outre de la volupté"]
The Fountain of Blood;   ["La Fontaine de sang"]
The Voyage to Cythera.   ["Le Voyage à Cythère"]

Protect me as well as you can. If there's not too much growling at this kind of poetry, I'll give some examples that are even more striking.

4 · *The Flowers of Evil: 1852–1857*

[early 1852?]

Madame,

Can it be possible that I am never to see you again? Therein lies the important question for me, since I've reached the stage where my heart suffers profoundly merely by being deprived of your presence. When I heard that you were abandoning your work as a model and that I was the unwitting cause of this decision, I felt a strange sorrow. I wanted to write to you although I am but little disposed to put things in writing. One almost always regrets doing so. I risk nothing, however, for I've taken the decision to give myself to you for ever.

Do you realize just how strange our conversation was last Thursday? It's that very conversation that has left me in a state I've never before experienced and that has provoked this letter.

A man who says "I love you" and who pleads—and a woman who answers, "Love you? Me? Never! Only one man has my love. Whoever comes after that man is doomed to unhappiness: he'll receive only my indifference and scorn!" And that same man, to have the pleasure of gazing at greater length into your eyes lets you speak to him about the other, lets you speak of him alone, lets you burn for him and think only of him! The result of all these confessions was very strange: for me, you are no longer simply a woman I desire, but one I love for her sincerity, her passion, her freshness, her youth, and her folly. I have lost much over these explanations, for you were so resolute that I was forced to yield immediately. But you, Madame, have gained much thereby. You have inspired in me respect and deep esteem. Be like that always and guard carefully that passion which makes you so beautiful and so happy.

Come back, I beg you, and I shall be gentle and modest in my desires. I deserved your scorn when I told you I'd be satisfied with crumbs. I lied. Oh, if you only knew how beautiful you were that evening! I hardly dare compliment you—that's so banal! But your eyes, your mouth, your whole person with all its animation and vitality now passes before my

---

1. The identity of this Marie is not certain, although it has been argued that she is Mlle Marie Daubrun.

closed eyes and I know only too well that it will always do so. Come back, I beg you on bended knee. I won't say you'll find me no longer in love, but you cannot prevent my mind wandering around your arms, those beautiful hands of yours, your eyes which are the mainspring of life, and all your adorable earthly being. No, I know you cannot prevent it: but fear not, you are for me an object of worship, and I am incapable of defiling you. I will always see you as radiant as before. Your entire being is so good, so beautiful, and so wonderful to breathe in! For me you are life and movement, not precisely because of the speed of your gestures and the violence of your nature so much as your eyes, which can inspire a poet with nothing less than eternal love.

How can I tell you how deeply I love your eyes and how fully I appreciate your beauty? That beauty consists of two contradictory graces which, however, in you do not contradict each other: the grace of the child and that of a woman. Oh, believe me when I tell you from the depths of my being that you are adorable and I love you deeply. The feeling that binds me to you for all eternity is a virtuous one. Despite what you yourself may say, you'll henceforth be my talisman, my source of strength. I love you, Marie, there's no denying it, but the love you inspire in me is the love a Christian feels for his God. So never give an earthly name—a name so often shameful—to this incorporeal, mysterious cult, this sweet and chaste attraction, which unites my soul to yours, regardless of your desires. That would be sacrilege indeed.

I was dead and you restored me to life. Oh, you don't know all I owe you. In your angel eyes I have captured unknown joys; your eyes have initiated me into the happiness of the soul in all that is most perfect, most delicate. Henceforth, you will be my sole queen, my passion, my beauty, you are that part of my being formed by a spiritual caress.

Through you, Marie, I shall be strong and great. Like Petrarch I'll immortalize my Laura. Be my guardian angel, my Muse and my Madonna, and guide my steps in the path of beauty.

Have the goodness to send me a word in reply, I beg you, a single word. There are, in every individual's life, days of doubt, decisive days when a proof of friendship, a glance, a scribbled message drives one to stupidity or madness. I swear to you that I've reached such a point. A word from you would be the blessed object one gazes on and learns by heart. If you but knew how deeply I love you! Let me throw myself at your feet; a word, say just a word . . . No, you will not say it!

How happy he must be, a thousand times happy, the man whom you have chosen among all men, you who are so rich in wisdom and beauty, you who are so desirable in your talent, your intellect, your heart! What woman could ever supplant you? I dare not beg for a visit; you'd refuse. I

44

prefer to wait; I'll wait for years and when you find yourself loved obstinately and respectfully, loved in a completely disinterested way, you'll remember that you began by mistrusting me and admit you acted badly.

In a word, I'm not free to refuse the blows it pleases you to send me, my idol. It pleased you to throw me out; it pleases me to adore you. There's no more to be said.

38   TO NARCISSE ANCELLE

Friday 5 March 1852

My head is quite literally becoming a diseased volcano. Great storms and mighty dawns. Have you read my article?[2] I'm forced to take from you tomorrow (*either very early or at lunch or dinner time*) the money I'm not supposed to have until the 15th, in nine days time, that is, 200 francs. I'll survive until the 15th of next month on the money I get from publishing this piece. I have your *Saint Priest* but I've only had it for four days, and the printer who works for the *Revue des deux mondes* lent it to me *only for eight days*. There was no way of buying it as *all the copies had been sold*. You didn't see me at the polling station but that's a decision I've taken. What happened on the 2nd of December[3] *physically depoliticized me. You can no longer talk of generally held ideas.* That *the whole of Paris* is *Orleanist* is beyond dispute, but that doesn't concern me. If I had voted, I could only have voted for myself. Perhaps the future belongs to the *declassés*.

Don't be surprised that my letter is such a hodgepodge. My head is full of worrying thoughts. The affair concerning the Tailor torments me horribly. Moreover you know that for me this is the *great* month, the separation.[4] I need a lot of money. I've only my pen and my mother. For I don't count you.—The strangest adventures have been befalling me. A man has just offered to lend me *22,000 francs* under *very strange conditions*. In another respect he's suggested to me that in a month's time I can be in charge of an honorable enterprise, one that has been my life's ambition. All the notes I've taken so far will be of use. And this time we'll proceed supported by *immense* amounts of money.

All this looks like a dream, but it does have a basis in fact. On rereading my letter I can see that it will appear *mad to you*. That will always be the case.

2. The first part of the study on Poe published in the *Revue de Paris*.

3. Louis-Napoleon's coup d'état, after which he declared himself emperor.

4. Baudelaire wanted to leave Jeanne at this stage. See his letter to his mother of 27 March.

20 March [1852]

My dear Malassis,

Several days have already passed by since I was given your letter at the Cafe Tabourey. But a string of unavoidable tasks and a thousand stupid errands have prevented me from replying.

Champfleury, Christophe, and Montégut are all in good health. Champfleury is now writing for the *Revue de Paris*. All the people I know are governed by mere stupidity and individual passions. No one is willing to take a *providential* point of view. You know what I mean by that. The president has given a kind of caress to the literary world by abolishing tax duty on novels. Napoleonic socialism has revealed its true colors through the conversion of government stocks. And there are daily fears of a decree imposing a 25% tax on collateral inheritences. Finally, the president has realized that in allowing open discussion about the seizure of the possessions of the princes of Orleans he has put himself in the right. So every play is being published and brochure is replying to brochure. There is also talk of restoring to the minister of the *interior* the department of literary affairs, which has recently been combined with Public Education. Some members of the Society of Men of Letters complained about this promiscuous partnership with the teachers, who, moreover, are merely Jesuits in disguise, and who seize all the funds, that is when there are any funds.

Moreover, I'm convinced that all suggestions and ideas repugnant to the university will flatter the president. As a result I'd really prefer to see only two sides together and I hate this pedantic, hypocritical *milieu* which has condemned me to dry bread and the cell. —I find all this greatly entertaining. But I'm determined henceforth to stay well away from all human polemics and I'm more determined than ever to pursue the loftier dream of applying metaphysics to the novel. —The *Semaine théâtrale* has died on us. The last number contained a *very good* article by Champfleury, a piece of literary criticism, and two poems by me, which aren't bad.[5] I published in the *Revue de Paris* a lengthy article about a great American writer.[6] But I'm very much afraid that this first effort will be my last. My article clashes with the rest. The first part appeared on 29 February and the second will come out in 10 days' time. There'll also be a short story by Champfleury.

In the meantime I dreamed *a beautiful dream. Amic* had told me he was

5. Baudelaire's two poems "Twilight: Evening" ("Le Crépuscule du soir") and "Twilight: Dawn" ("Le Crépuscule du matin"). Champfleury's article was a review of Nerval's *Travels in the East* (*Voyage en Orient*).
6. The study on Poe.

definitely going to found a review and that I'd be its director. I gave him my ideas on the subject but it seemed that *our* plans (I wanted Champfleury to help me) were *too* beautiful. He has cooled down greatly and I think we've missed out chance.

You must have lost my address: 25 rue des Marais-du-Temple. But I'll be here only until the end of the month and will then send you my new address. Farewell—and be convinced, as I am increasingly convinced, that Philosophy is All.

40   To Caroline Aupick

27 March 1852

It's 2 P.M. If my letter is to leave today I've only got 2½ hours in which to write to you and I have a lot to tell you. I'm writing this in a cafe opposite the long-distance post office, in the midst of noise, card games, and billiards, so as to be calmer and be able to think more clearly. You'll understand that in a moment. —How can it happen that in 9 months not a single day can be found in which to write to one's mother? Not even to thank her! It's really phenomenal. And every day I think of it and every day I tell myself: "I'll write to her today." And every day flies past in a mass of useless errands or in dashing off puny articles to earn some money. You'll find in this letter things that will certainly please you and that will prove to you that if I still suffer greatly through certain failings, my mind, instead of stultifying, is expanding: you'll find things that will distress you, too. But haven't you urged me to tell you everything and indeed to whom else could I pour out my sorrows? There are days when my solitude torments me.

My letter will be very disordered. That's the inevitable result of the state of mind I'm in and the little time I have at my disposal. I'll divide it into subject groups, in a manner of speaking, as I remember some of the most important things I have to tell you, things that have been in my mind for a long time.

I'm enclosing with this letter a few of my articles—I've cut them out of the newspapers in which they appeared to avoid making the letter too bulky. I'd be pleased if you'd read them when you have time. I'm very doubtful that you'll understand them fully; there's no impertinence in such a statement. The fact is that they're especially Parisian, and I doubt that they can be understood outside the *milieux* for which and about which they were written. *The Honest Plays and Novels* [*Les Drames et les Romans honnêtes*] numbered in pencil 0, 2, 3, 4, 5, 6, and *The Pagan School* [*L'Ecole païenne*]: 6. The two Twilights, 7, 8.

I've done other things that will please you more and with which I'm pretty satisfied. As I can't send you whole volumes in a letter, you'll have to be kind enough to borrow or buy, I don't know which, from M. Monier (is that a library or a bookstore?) who is Madrid's correspondent for the *Revue de Paris*, the issue that came out in Paris on 1 March and the one due here on 31 March and that will probably reach Madrid on 5 or 6 April. I've found an American author who has aroused in me a sense of immense sympathy and I've written two articles on his life and works. They're written with ardor, but you'll no doubt find in them a few lines that are quite extraordinarily *overexcited*. That's the result of the mad, painful life I lead; moreover, I wrote them at night, sometimes working from 10 P.M. to 10 A.M. I'm forced to work at night to have peace and to avoid being unbearably pestered by the woman I live with. Sometimes I escape from my rooms in order to write and go to the library or to a lending library, or to a wine shop or a cafe, as I'm doing today. The result of all this is that I live in a state of constant rage. Obviously that's no way to create works of any length—I'd forgotten a lot of my English, which made the task even harder. But now I know it very well. In short, I think I've brought that ship safely into harbor.

Don't yield to the maternal pleasure of reading all my articles before answering my letter. Please send my a reply first, even if it's only 3 lines—and put off for tomorrow or the day after the advice and reflections my letter inspires in your mind. This letter will leave this evening—27, 28. On the 29th it'll be at Bayonne. Supposing it arrives in Madrid on the 1st, which is unbelievable, and that you reply on the 2nd, I'll have your answer on the 7th. I didn't understand what you told me about the mail in one of your letters. Those 4 poor letters and 3 incomplete volumes of Racine are the only treasures I have from you, you who so often sacrificed yourself, without allowing anything your son does to disgust you. —Briefly, I went to the post office and was told that the diplomatic mail wouldn't come until the 10th. So it's impossible for me to use it and for you, too. You must therefore address your reply care of Mme Olivier—I'll pay for the postage—and not to M. Ancelle. It'd be just like him not to let me know for 2 days or even longer. I'd not ask you to reply to my home address. Not only does Jeanne know your handwriting but I do not have a single drawer I can lock!! How can I ever know what wind will blow over my mind and where I'll sleep next? There have been times when I've fled from my home for two weeks in order to refresh my mind a little. At the long-distance post office no one could give me precise information on the speed or slowness of the Bayonne-Madrid service and I was told that I couldn't stamp my letter and I was also informed that the embassy had the right to refuse it because it wasn't stamped. None of that makes any sense to me. So to be really sure it reaches you I'm writing on the envelope Private and Personal, with my initials C. B. Even if M. Aupick guesses, I can't see that that can be impertinent. To return to my affairs. I'm going to explain things very hastily—but in doing so I'll make the few words I use rich in thoughts for someone who knows me as well as you do.

Jeanne has become an impediment not merely to my happiness, which wouldn't be very important, for I, too, know how to sacrifice my pleasures, and I've proved it—but also to the improvement of my mental faculties. The past nine months have been a decisive experience. The great tasks I have to carry out, the payment of debts, the *conquest* of my claims to fortune, the achievement of my fame, the alleviation of the pain I've caused you—all this can never take place in such conditions. In the past she had some qualities but these she has lost and I for my part have gained clear-sightedness. To live with a person who shows no gratitude for your efforts, who impedes them through clumsiness or permanent meanness, who considers you as a mere servant, as her property, someone with whom it is impossible to exchange a word about politics or literature, a creature who is unwilling to learn a single thing, although you've offered to teach her yourself, a creature who *has no admiration for one* and who is not even interested in one's studies, who would throw one's manuscripts on the fire if that brought in more money than publishing them, who drives away one's cat, the sole source of amusement in one's lodgings, and who brings in dogs, *because* the sight of dogs sickens me, who does not know or *cannot understand that by being tightfisted, just for ONE month* I could, thanks to that brief respite, conclude a big book—is all this possible? Is it possible? My eyes are full of tears of fury and shame as I write this and to tell the truth I'm glad I have no weapons at home. I'm thinking of the cases when I cannot obey the voice of reason and of that terrible night when I cut her head against the side table. That's what I've found in the very place where 10 months ago I thought I'd find consolation and repose. To sum up all my thoughts in a single reflection, and to give you an idea of all my musing, I think, and I always shall think that the woman who has suffered and brought a child into the world is the only one who is the equal of a man. Giving birth is the sole act that gives a woman moral intelligence. As for young women, with no status and no children, they offer only flirtation, implacability, and elegant debauchery. Something had to be done. But what? My terrible vanity was even greater than my grief. I didn't want to leave that woman without giving her a fairly large sum of money. But where could I get it from, since the money I earned disappeared day by day, since I'd have to save up, and since my mother, to whom I dared not write, having no good news to tell her, couldn't offer such a large sum as she didn't possess it herself? You can see how carefully I've worked it out. And yet I must leave her. But it'll have to be forever.

So this is what I've resolved. I'll begin at the beginning—that is, by going away. Since I can't offer her a large lump sum, I'll still give her money from time to time, which is an easy matter for me since I can earn it without difficulty, and by working assiduously I can earn more. *But I'll never see her again.* She can do what she likes. She can go to hell if that's where she wants to go. I've used up 10 years of my life in this struggle. All my youthful illusions have gone. All that remains is a bitterness that may well be permanent.

And what's to become of me? I don't want to set up a little appartment for myself because even now, although I've changed a great deal, that would always be dangerous. Residential hotels sicken me. While I'm waiting for better things, I've decided to take refuge with a doctor who is a friend of mine and who has offered me, for 150 francs instead of the 240 francs he usually charges, a beautiful room, a fine garden, an excellent table, a cold bath, and 2 showers a day. It's a German cure which is highly suitable for my inflamed state.

So I want to take advantage of rent day, and move out on 7 April, for our apartment has already been allotted to our successors. That way I could escape. But I don't have a cent. I've written several things that will be published next month but not until after the 8th. Can you understand the scenario now? What can I do? I said to myself: M. Ancelle may have received nothing from my mother. Perhaps, too, she has absolutely nothing because when she left Paris she warned me she'd have heavier expenses than before. But at least she can *send me* a letter authorizing M. Ancelle to give me a sum sufficiently high for me to carry all this out on a single day. Subsequently she can let me have it in small doses, if that's at all possible. Apart from the deficit which you knew about before you left, I have stuck exactly to our agreement in dealing with Ancelle. Now, my dear mother, this is what I dare demand of you, in such decisive circumstances. There are two months' rent due, and all the bills one is obliged to pay on leaving an area—butcher, wine merchant, grocer, etc.—shall we say 400 francs. It would be best if I arrived at the doctor's establishment with 150 francs to pay the first month in advance. Finally, I'd like to buy a few *books* for I cannot bear being deprived of books, and a few toiletries. In spite of my sufferings I can't help laughing as I think of the lecture you gave me in your last letter on the link between a man's dignity and the clothes he wears, for the very clothes you bought for me nine months ago are still the only ones covering the animal who writes to you. Finally, I'd like to calm down a creditor of many years' standing who could get me into very serious trouble. All this certainly needs a lot, but please note, my dear mother, that any sum at all would be very welcome. At a pinch I'd do what I've often done, I'd deprive myself of everything that wasn't absolutely essential.

It's now 4:20. I must rush. I'll call at Mme Olivier's on the 7th of April. I beg and beseech you, don't confide in M. Ancelle about the use this money is to be put to. I'll entrust to him the secrets I choose to let him know. But you treat him as though he were my brother or my father and that doesn't suit me at all. I presume this letter is serious enough to provide a good guarantee that this money will be well spent. At a pinch 1,000 francs would suffice. But even with a mere 400 I could do something. But that would leave me only 5 francs for my personal needs and I'd be forced to wait for all the little sums due to me in April, using them as they fell due on my purchases and at the sanatorium.

I'll write to you again tomorrow; for I've still got another 20 pages worth of thoughts to share. But don't wait for my second letter before answering me, and even put off, if there's no other course for you, the thoughts and advice that occur to you. Think first of the letter I'll need for Ancelle. Tomorrow or the next day I'll try to write a more comforting letter, and a more cheerful one. One final point: M. Ancelle spoke to me about your *butterflies*.[7] The good old chap didn't understand what you meant by that. But *I* understood. So do something about your eyes and take lots of advice about them. Remember that one day I may be living with you and to have a blind mother constantly before my eyes would not only increase my obligations, which is unimportant, but would be a daily source of grief for me.

I'll tell you another time about the political events and the overwhelming influence they exerted on me. Farewell, pity me, and think of the unbearable punishments I've laid up for myself. I strongly recommend you to ask the bookseller for my two pieces on Edgar Allan Poe.

41   TO THÉOPHILE GAUTIER

{July 1852?}

[. . .] This year Paris has sizzled: every day Phoebus Apollo pours bucket on bucket of molten lead on the unfortunate citizens strolling along the boulevards. Were I in heaven, I'd call on the locals to set up barricades against this unceremonious god. He has already been exiled

7. An allusion to Mme Aupick's myopia.

once to the earth where Admetus made him guard sheep. If it were I I'd take into account his relapse into crime and set him to guard second-string poets in the French Academy.

42   To Apollonie Sabatier

9 December 1852

She for whom these lines were written,[8] whether they please her or not, and even if they strike her as utterly ridiculous, is requested in deepest humility not to show them to a soul. Deep feelings have a modesty that seeks to avoid all violation. Isn't the absence of any signature proof of that unconquerable modesty? He who wrote these lines, in one of those states of revery that is frequently provoked by the image of the woman who is their theme, loved her very deeply, without ever telling her, and will *always* feel for her the most tender sympathy.

43   To Maxime Du Camp

3 January 1853

I'd feel I was failing in my duty to obey the voice of conscience if I didn't immediately tell you of the *joy* I felt on reading the second part of your book.[9] If you write more books in that vein, you'll be what I call in my own private language one of the saved. I'd very much like to be able to claim that of myself. —As for pantheism, I always hope that those whose talents arouse my sympathy and who describe themselves as pantheists are using the word in a *new sense*. For it would be too unpleasant for me, given the many similarities I detect between myself and them, to discover that I'd long been a pantheist unawares.

By the way, the other evening I met the mad Philoxène who, embittered by all his adventures, despite the publication in a newspaper of his witnesses' statements, has provoked his adversary with excessive violence.[10] I repeated to him WORD FOR WORD, and I really put into this everything I had, what you told me this morning. I merely added that I felt that a visit to you would in no way violate his honor. I did that believing I was doing the right thing and hoping you could give him some good advice.

---

8. The poem "To the Woman Who Is Too Joyous" ("A celle qui est trop gaie").

9. *The Posthumous Book* (*Le Livre posthume*)—a work in the mold of *Werther* and *René*.

10. The dramatist Edouard Plouvier had accused Baudelaire's friend Philoxène Boyer of basing a character of a servant in a play Boyer had written on a character Plouvier himself had invented.

15 March 1853

My dear friend,

On Sunday, the day before yesterday, immediately after leaving you, I handed over—not to Barbara himself but to a man in uniform who acts as the hospital's porter—the money I'd undertaken to deliver. As for what I'm sending you today, you may decide not to use it, or perhaps you'll find it helpful to alter it, but I felt the best thing to do was to write a fairly long note—since English readers won't know the little group in question.[11]

One of those who has lived in close association with the people described by M. Champfleury in his story of *Mademoiselle Mariette* and by M. Henri Murger in the *Scenes of Bohemian Life* [*Scènes de la vie bohème*] has been kind enough to supply a *key* to the work we are offering today to our readers. We assume that readers will judge, as we did, that the extreme freedom and impartiality of this *key* are sufficient proof of its veracity.

Gérard — Champfleury
Author of the present volume and of [nine other works], several pantomimes and various articles of art criticism.—One of the main exponents of the so-called *Realist* school, which claims to put the study of nature and of the individual in place of the *Classical* and *Romantic* madness.

Streich — Henri Murger
Author of *Scenes of Bohemian Life*, *Scenes of Youth* [*Scènes de jeunesse*], *The Latin Quarter* [*Le Quartier latin*], and other short stories. One of the novelists working for the *Revue des deux mondes*.

De Villers — Théodore de Banville
The only writer to be truly maltreated in Champfleury's work, and, whatever the author may say about him, the most skillful poet of the recently established new school—so skillful is he that he's reduced the art of poetry to a set of purely conventional mechanical processes, and that he can teach anyone to become a poet in 25 lessons. Inventor of the Marmoreal Style. —Author of *The Caryatids* [*Les Cariatides*], *The Stalactites* [*Les Stalactites*].

Giraud — Pierre Dupont
The complete opposite of the foregoing, a poet of the people, a tireless songster, had the good fortune to predict the February Revolution and to

11. Baudelaire's commentary refers to Champfleury's novel *The Adventures of Mlle Mariette* (*Les Aventures de Mlle Mariette*), which recreates bohemian life in the Paris of the 1840s.

link his reputation as a rustic poet with the rising sun of a revolutionary poet. His works are by now numerous. Composes the music of his own songs.

Thomas — François Bonvin

First-class painter, a national and positive intelligence, member of the *Realist* school, loves above all to represent family life and household utensils.

The Poet of the Cats — Charles Baudelaire

Like Pierre Dupont and François, one of the author's closest friends.

45   TO CAROLINE AUPICK

Saturday 26 March 1853

I know I'll cause you a great deal of pain, for it's just not possible to prevent the mental distress I'm suffering from showing in my letter, let alone all the confessions I have to make. But I really can't do anything else. Despite the large number of letters I've written you, *in imagination*, since for a whole year I've imagined every month that I was going to write to you, my letter now will be brief. I'm in such dire straits and my life is so complicated, that I've scarcely an hour to devote to this letter, which ought to bring me pleasure but which is the exact opposite. For a long time now, I've been so wrapped up in my life that I'm no longer able to find time even for work.

—I'll begin with the hardest and the most painful of the things I have to say. I'm writing to you as my last two logs burn, and my fingers are frozen. I'm going to be prosecuted for a payment I should have made yesterday. I'll be prosecuted for another at the end of the month. This year, I mean from April of last year until now, has been a real disaster for me, although I've had at my disposal the means of making something entirely different of it. I have the most immense confidence in you. The admirable indulgence you showed by coming through Paris allows me to tell you everything, and I hope you won't think me completely mad, since I know my own madness. Moreover, what's the good of disguising the facts, of fabricating a letter full of feigned joy and confidence, at the very moment when my mind is so laden with anxiety that I hardly sleep anymore and when I do I have unbearable dreams, and fever?

Why didn't I write to you earlier? That's what you're thinking, isn't it? But *you* don't know what it's like to feel ashamed. —And moreover what prevented me from writing was the pact I'd made with myself never to write to you unless I had good news to give you. And the pact never to ask you for a cent. Today that pact is no longer possible.

After receiving your money *a year ago*—and, as a result of a perfectly innocent misapprehension on my part, I even received more than you had wished—I immediately used it just as I had told you I would. I paid my year's debts and I lived alone. —It's here that the misfortune begins yet again. I was living in a house where the landlady caused me such suffering, through her ruses, her grousing, her deceit, and I was so uncomfortable, that I went away, in my usual fashion, without saying a word. *I didn't owe her anything.* But I was stupid enough to keep up the rent even though I was no longer living there, the result being that the sum I owe her represents rent for an apartment I wasn't livingin. I discovered that this ignoble woman had the nerve to write to you. Well, I'd left with her, on the assumption that I'd be able to fetch them in the near future, *all my books, all my manuscripts, some complete, the others just started, boxes full of papers, LETTERS, DRAWINGS,* in a word, *EVERYTHING. Everything I hold most dear; papers.* During that time an editor, a rich and amiable man,[12] had conceived a passion for me and had asked me for a book. A portion of my useful manuscripts were *over there.* I tried to begin again from scratch, I bought books that I already owned, and I clung doggedly to my determination not to write to you. On 10 January when my contract insisted I produce the book, I had drawn my money and had delivered to the printer such a hodgepodge of a book that after he had composed the first sheets, I realized that the *corrections* and *reworkings* to be done were so considerable that it was better to break the forms, and recompose from scratch. You won't understand these expressions: I mean that the section that had been composed by the workmen was worthless, through my fault, and that my honor obliges me to pay for the costs. The printer, receiving no corrected proofs, grew angry; the editor thought me mad and he was wild! To think it was the very man who said to me: "Don't let anything worry you. You've been looking for an editor for several years, I'm just the chap you want and I'll print everything you write." The poor devil, I've made him miss the winter sales, and it's three months since I've dared either to write to him or to see him. The book is still on my desk, *interrupted.* I've paid half of the printing costs. A booksellers' treaty is certain to be established between France and the United States and that will make it impossible to publish our book unless we pay more costs. It really is driving me mad. That book marked the beginning of a new life. It was to have been followed by the publication of my poems, the reprint of my *Salons,* combined with my work on the caricaturists, which had stayed with that abominable woman I was writing about and for which I've been paid more than 200 francs by the *Revue de Paris*—a fact that now prevents me getting a cent from it.

12. Victor Lecou.

The man who thought me *mad*, who is totally unable to understand my *delays* and whose good will represented in my mind the beginning of my literary reputation, that man must now consider me a *thief*. Will I ever be reconciled with him?

That's not all. There is the Opera. The Opera's director has asked me for a new kind of libretto, to be set to music by a new musician who is making a name for himself. I even believe it could have been set to music by *Meyerbeer*. That was a real stroke of luck, perhaps even providing a perpetual income. There are people of 50, whose reputation is already established, who've never been able to obtain a favor like that. —But poverty and disorder create such listlessness, such melancholy, that I failed to turn up at all the appointments. *Luckily* I hadn't been paid a cent!

That's not all. The associate of one of the directors of the Théâtre du Boulevard has asked me for a play. It was to have been read this very month. *I haven't written it.* On the basis of my association with that gentleman, the leader of a claque lent me 300 francs, destined to avert another disaster last month. If the play had been written, this wouldn't matter. I'd get the associate to pay off the debt, or I'd have it subtracted from the income of the play or the cost of the tickets. But the play is not written. Bits of it are with *the woman of the house in question* and the money is due in six days' time, at the end of the month. What is to become of me? What will happen to me?

There are moments when I'm filled with the longing to sleep for all eternity, but I can no longer sleep because my brain is constantly thinking.

I don't need to tell you I've spent the winter without a fire. But that's stupid.

So, to sum up, it was *proved* to me this year that I really could earn money, and with a bit of hard work and consistency, I could earn lots of money. But dissolute actions in the past and an unceasing poverty, a fresh deficit to make up, the decrease in my energy as a result of small irritations, in a word, my tendency toward revery, has nullified it all.

I've still got something to tell you. I know you're so good and so clever that I consider it my duty to tell you everything. I haven't listed all my torments yet.

A year ago I left Jeanne, as I told you, —although you doubted the truth of this, a fact that caused me pain. Why do you suppose that I need or want to hide anything from you? For several months, I went to see her two or three times a month, to take her a little money. Well, now she is gravely ill, and in the direst poverty. I never speak of it to *Ancelle*. The wretch would be only too delighted at such news. It's obvious that a small

56

portion of the money you send me will go to her. Now I'm annoyed I've said that since you're capable, in your heavy-handed maternal way, of sending her money, without telling me, through M. Ancelle. That would be extremely improper. You don't want to wound me again, do you? That idea is now going to swell and root itself in my brain, and persecute me. Anyway, I'll tell you what I suffer in this regard. She caused me a lot of pain, didn't she? How many times—and to you quite recently, just a year ago—have I complained about it? But faced with a collapse of such proportions, with a melancholy as deep as hers, my eyes fill with tears, and to tell the truth my heart is full of reproaches. Twice I've devoured her jewels and her furniture, I've made her incur debts on my behalf, sign IOUs, I've beaten her, and finally, instead of showing her how a man of stamp behaves, I've constantly given her the example of debauchery and instability. She suffers—and is silent. Isn't there cause for remorse in that? Am I not as guilty in this regard as in all the other matters? [. . .]

Now do you understand why in the midst of the terrible solitude that surrounds me, I was able to understand so well the genius of Edgar Poe, and why I wrote such an excellent biography of his abominable life. [. . .]

46 TO APOLLONIE SABATIER

9 May 1853

Dear Madam,

Truly I offer my deepest apologies for this idiotic and anonymous bit of verse[13] which smacks horribly of childishness—but what's to be done with it? I'm as self-centered as children and invalids. When I'm suffering my thoughts turn to those I love. Generally, when I think of you I do so in verse, and when the verse has been written down, I can't resist the urge to show it to you who inspired it. —But at the same time I hide myself away, like someone who has an extreme fear of appearing ridiculous. — Isn't there something essentially comic in love? Particularly for those who are not affected by it.

But I swear to you that this really is the last time I'll expose myself to ridicule; and if my ardent friendship for you lasts as long again as it lasted before I said a word to you about it, we'll both be old.

However absurd this might appear to you, remember that there is a heart which it would be cruel for you to mock, a heart in which your image lives on.

13. "Confession" ("Confessional du cœur").

57

My dear Malassis,

I beg you—I'll not say "earnestly," which would be an insult—I beg you simply—if that's possible—to send me by post as soon as you receive this letter—a sum of money, any amount. You see I'm putting you at your ease—for it's clear that there can't be any question of a large sum. It's only a question of my finding a few days of rest, and of taking advantage of that respite to finish some important things that will bring a positive result next month.

In resolving to ask you for a little money I had to ferret about in my accounts to see what I already owed you. I find the sum of 36 francs. If I'm wrong do let me know. I presume that you'll tell me in person, for Champfleury informed me yesterday that you were coming to see us in January.

I can't describe to you all the very real misfortunes that have thrust themselves into my life this year, some through my own fault and some through no fault of mine. A sterile year. This whole grotesque poem doesn't concern you and wouldn't interest you. You're life is so calm now! *My* life, as you can guess, will always consist of outbursts of wrath, death, insults, and, above all, discontent with myself. These expressions, believe me, are in no way exaggerated: in writing to you I feel no sense of nervous overexcitement. All I know, all I feel, is that I've just lost a whole year through a series of misadventures in which my folly has its share of blame, and that I must write four volumes and three plays— these works are not yet done, at least not entirely. —I've been paid for several of them—and I don't have a cent to let me work, not even for a single day, let alone two weeks. You won't be surprised that my thoughts turn to you, for you've been so kind to me—always.

POSTSCRIPT: Whether you can let me have the money or not, answer this letter straight away—but, above all, dear friend, don't serve up to me the sort of excuse made for fools. I'll undersand that you *can't* help me through the simple fact of your not doing so. And so—my dear friend—not too much wit—it would be out of place, given my present state. Since you're coming here in January, I'll assume you'll come to see me—that goes without saying. I'll try to have enough foresight to put to one side the money I owe you. I'm going to publish a series of pieces in *Le Moniteur*—as soon as I have the short breathing space I'm begging for, and that will bring in a large sum.

ADDITIONAL P.S.: A few months ago Christophe gave me a number of the *Journal d'Alençon* where you implied that the translator and the enthusiast would soon become *the model to follow*. Now that's wit for you. I still have the article among my papers.[14]

You also say that my categories and psychological explanations are unintelligible and even, if I remember rightly, that I have no philosophical bent. It may be that I'm a bit obscure in works done at speed, when need drove me on and romantic brutes hounded me. But my new work,[15] which has doubled in size and is to appear in January, will prove to you that there's no question of any misunderstanding. I'm convinced, for my part, that you have not understood the GENIUS in question. You were discussing with that boisterous joy of the mind, a man you've never met. And what's more, the translation you included is not a good sample of the sense and poetic style of *The Raven*. Don't let my little outburst prevent you from doing what you can for me. If your mistress is still with you, and doesn't hate me too much, and if you think it appropriate, remember me to her.

Thanks for the money, if you send it, and for your diligence in answering if you only send a letter.

48   To Fernand Desnoyers

[late 1853?]

My dear Desnoyers,

You ask me for some poetry for your little collection, poems on Nature, I believe? On woods, great oaks, greenery, insects—the sun, too, if I'm not mistaken? But you know very well that the vegetable kingdom fails to move me and that my soul rebels at that strange new religion that will always be, so it seems to me, rather *shocking* to any *spiritual* being. I'll never believe that the soul of the gods inhabits plants, and even if it did, I really couldn't work up much enthusiasm for the fact and would consider my own soul as of much more importance than that of the sanctified vegetables. What's more, I've always thought that *Nature*, flourishing, rejuvenated Nature, possessed something impudent and painful.

As I'm in no position to give you complete satisfaction, according to the exact terms of your program, I'm sending you two pieces of poetry[16] that more or less sum up the reveries that assail me in the twilight hours. In the depths of the woods, shut in by those vaults that recall sacristies

14. Poulet-Malassis was the publisher of the *Journal d'Alençon*, for which he wrote an article on Baudelaire's translations of Poe's short stories.

15. The preface to the collection *Histoires extraordinaires*.

16. The two "Twilight" poems.

and cathedrals, I think of our amazing cities, and that prodigious music which rolls over the summits seems to me a translation of the lamentations of mankind.

49   To Champfleury

My dear friend,

After finding your prospectus[17] at my lodgings last night, I immediately wrote you a brief note which I burnt this morning, through some sense of decency, and in the fear that my letter, written under the influence of intense overexcitement, would give you some cause for laughter, partly through the highly enthusiastic friendship for you that I revealed, and partly through the maniacal or nit-picking observations—you can choose which adjective to use—that I inflicted on you. To make a long story short, you can see I'm beginning afresh.

Your title I consider to be very fine. In general the prospectus is well set out. It's obviously very important for you to break free from the lower ranks and you can't believe how happy I am about your publication from that point of view. But—and this is where the nit-picking begins: [there follows a series of criticisms of French expressions in Champfleury's usage].

You say, the author has only one belief: the Novel. That's as if Dupont were to say, I've only one belief: the Song. The Novel is a more useful, more beautiful art than the others, it's not a belief, any more than Art itself is. That's a piece of Romantic nonsense. Do you remember the days when people wrote such things as this: "As for me, I have *faith* in art—or—I have *faith* in beauty, that's my sole belief"? A belief is Buddhism, Christianity, Redemption, etc.

Do you really consider that at your age and with your present strength it's of much use to you to exhume compliments from Victor Hugo, who poured praise on the most vulgar of creatures? Is there not also throughout your prospectus a kind of jealous and involuntary preoccupation with Dickens and the vast machines of Eugène Sue? [. . .] "The first publications, apart from those of 1853, which are not of the short-story type." How can you imply that, from the point of view of normal and accepted usage, *Mademoiselle Mariette*, *Delteil*, etc., are anything but short stories? Or—have I totally misunderstood? In that case the sentence would be at fault.

One more thing. In thinking of your affair it seemed to me, and it

17. Probably the prospectus for Champfleury's novel *The Mirror of the Faubourg Saint-Marceau* (*Le Miroir du Faubourg Saint-Marceau*).

appears you feel this too, that six volumes sold over 10 years at 25,000 francs would hardly bring you 420 per volume per year. What's more, you're sacrificing all the different types of editions. Well, I've finished at last—don't give a damn about my comments, if you don't want to. In 2 or 3 days I'll write to you about the matter we discussed. [. . .]

50   To Hippolyte Tisserant

28 January 1854

I've received a letter from you, my dear M. Tisserant, which contains a fat bouquet of compliments. You should wait until I've earned them! We'll see later on if there are grounds for praising me; moreover, I'm well aware that I'm going to set myself—and it must be said, at your instigation—a great test. —In a short time, I'll know if I'm capable of conceiving a good play. What's more, it's on that score, and to bring you up to date on the present state of that play, that I'm writing you a rather lengthy letter that I've been planning for several days and that I've postponed each day.

First, let me tell you of something I'd be delighted to be freed from, for it borders on indiscretion and, however angelic we may be, our acquaintanceship is, after all, of recent date. My articles, my ill-starred articles, my damnable articles seem to be growing longer and longer; I still have several hours more work; I can't leave my desk for fear of putting off the blessed moment when I'll be generously paid. Well, I literally do not have a penny; 20, 25 francs would last me a whole week, when I'm locked away like this. I needn't add that if it weren't too much of a burden on your purse—I'd repay you soon, *perhaps* in the first days of February— and—if you were willing enough to be really kind—you'd bring them yourself instead of giving them to the man I'm sending with this letter— and you'd pay me a visit, *especially* if you have no money. When one lives shut away like this, a good visit is the best of distractions.

To return to our business, which greatly concerns me: I'm anxious that we should understand each other very well—I feel I may have need of you and I think that in certain matters you'll be more able than I to distinguish between the possible and the impossible.

Although it's a matter of some importance, I haven't yet thought of a title. THE WELL? DRUNKENNESS? THE SLOPES OF EVIL? My central preoccupation when I began to ponder my theme was: to what class, to what profession should the main character belong? I've chosen a heavy, rough, coarse profession: the sawyer. The thing that almost forced me into such a decision was that I have a song, written to a melancholy tune, which I believe would make a magnificent impact in the theater, if

61

we put on stage the man's normal place of work, or above all if, as I would very much like, I work into the third act a scene about a cabaret or a singing competition. This song is singularly raw. It begins with the following lines:

> There ain't nothing so lovable
> Fanfru—Cancru—Lon—La—Lahira
> There ain't nothing so lovable
> As the sawyer.

And what's even better is that it's almost prophetic; it could become the *Willow Song* of popular drama. This lovable sawyer ends by throwing his wife in the water and he says in speaking to the siren (It's very odd! I presume it's connected with the waves and the musical sounds, for to my mind there's a gap here):

> Sing, Siren, Sing
> Fanfru—Cancru—Lon—La—Lahira
> Sing, Siren, Sing
> You're right to sing
> For you have the sea to drink
> Fanfru—Cancru—Lon—La—Lahira
> And my sweetheart to eat.

I'll have to write to someone from the region to fill in that gap and set down the tune. My hero is a dreamer, a ne'er-do-well, he has, or believes he has, higher aspirations than his boring trade and like all dreamers and ne'er-do-wells, he gets drunk. The woman must be pretty. A model of gentleness, patience, and *good sense*.

The function of the cabaret is therefore to reveal the lyrical instincts of the people, instincts that are often comic and clumsy. I used to frequent cabarets in the past—I'll have to go back to them. —Or rather we'll go together. It could even perhaps be possible to copy down examples of the poems sung there. Moreover, this scene provides a short-lived oasis in the middle of a lamentable *nightmare*.

I don't want to give you a detailed scenario here, because in a few days' time, I'll do a proper one, and you'll analyze that with an eye to cutting out any blunders. Today I'm just providing notes.

The first two acts are full of scenes of poverty, unemployment, household quarrels—drunkenness and *jealousy*. You'll se in a moment the usefulness of this new element. The third act is *The Tavern*—where his wife, from whom he has separated, comes back to look for him, since she's worried about him. It's there that he gets her to agree to meet him the following evening—a Sunday.

Act 4. The crime—fully premeditated, fully foreseen. As for how it's carried out, I'll tell you that with the utmost care.

Act 5.—(In another town.) The conclusion, that's to say the guilty man's denunciation of himself, driven to confess by an obsession. What do you think of that? How many times have I been struck by just such cases in reading the *Gazette des Tribunaux*. You see how simple the plot is. No complications, no surprises. Just the unfolding of a vice, and the successive effects resulting from a particular situation.

I'm introducing two additional characters. A sister of the sawyer, a creature who loves ribbons, cheap jewels, taverns, and low dives—incapable of understanding the Christian virtue of her sister-in-law. She's the typical example of precocious Parisian perversity. A young man—fairly rich—from a loftier profession—deeply in love with the wife of our worker—but honest and full of admiration for her virtue. He manages to slip a little money into the household budget from time to time. As for her, in spite of her deep religious convictions, the pressure of suffering inflicted on her by her husband leads her sometimes to think of the rich young man and she can't help herself dreaming of the gentler, richer, more decent life she could have led with him. But she reproaches herself as if the very thought were a crime and she struggles against that tendency. I'm presuming that that will provide a dramatic element. You'll already have guessed that our worker will seize joyfully on the pretext of exacerbated jealousy to hide from himself the fact that what particularly irritates him in his wife is her resignation, her gentleness, her patience, her virtue. —And yet he loves her. —But drink and poverty have already affected his reason. Note moreover that theater audiences are not familiar with the very subtle psychology of crime and that it would have been very difficult to make them understand an atrocity that seemed to have no motive.

Apart from these characters we've only some minor figures—perhaps a worker fond of practical jokes, a ne'er-do-well who is the sister's lover. Some prostitutes, a few characters who hang about toll gates, taverns, and inns—sailors, police spies, and the like.

Now for the scene of the crime. Remember that it's already been premeditated. The man is the first to arrive at the meeting place, which he has selected. Sunday evening. A dark street, or a plain. In the distance, sounds from a tavern band. A sinister, melancholy lanscape typical of the outer edges of Paris. Love scenes, as sad as can be, between the man and his wife—he wants her to forgive him, he wants her to let him come back and live with her. He's never seen her looking so beautiful. He's filled with genuine tenderness. They walk past, go into the distance, walk back again. The stage can thus remain empty a couple of times—

it's against the rules, I'm told, but I don't care a fig for rules. I feel that the empty stage and the lonely night landscape can heighten the ominous effect. He almost falls in love again, he longs for her, and begs her to take him. Her pallor, her thinness, make her more appealing and act almost as stimulants. The audience must guess what's at issue. Although the poor woman also feels her former affection aroused, she refuses such wild passions in such a place. This refusal irritates the husband who attributes such chastity to the existence of an adulterous passion, or to the veto of her lover. "It must come to an end, but I'll never have the courage to end it, I can't do it *myself*." An ingenious idea, full of cowardice and superstition, comes to him. He pretends to feel very ill, which isn't hard, as the emotion he really feels comes to his aid. "Look, down there, at the end of this little path, on the left, you'll find a pear tree (or an apple tree), go and pick me a piece of fruit." (He could easily find another pretext—I'm just dashing this down on paper as I go.)

The night is very dark, the moon hidden. As his wife disappears into the darkness he gets up from the stone he's sitting on and puts his ear to the ground: "God can decide—if she escapes, all the better, if she falls in, it's God who has condemned her." He's sent her along a path where she must come across a well, almost flush with the ground. The noise of a heavy body can be heard falling into water, but preceded by a scream and the screams continue. "What's to be done? Someone might come, they might think—indeed they would think—that I'm the assassin. Moreover, she's done for. Oh, the stones! There are stones around the edge of the well." He runs off!

The stage remains empty.

As the noise of the falling stones increases, the screams decrease. They stop. The man reappears: "I'm FREE. Poor darling, she must have suffered greatly!" All this must be interspersed with the far-off noise of the band. At the end of the act, groups of drinkers and tarts—among them the sister—come back along the road, singing.

Here's a brief explanation of the conclusion. Our man has fled. Now we're in some sea port. He thinks of signing on as a sailor. He drinks terribly: sailors' inns, taverns where there is alcohol and music. That idea: *I'm free, free, free* has become an obsession. I'm *free*, I'm *calm, no one will ever know*. And as he drinks incessantly, and has been drinking terribly for several months, his willpower diminishes daily and the obsession finally surfaces through a few words spoken aloud. As soon as he realizes that, he tries to numb his brain by drinking, by walking, by running. But the strangeness of his behavior draws attention to him. A man who's always running has obviously done something. He's arrested and then—with extraordinary volubility, fire, and exaggeration, and with extreme preciseness—he quickly, very quickly as if he's afraid he won't have the time to complete it, recounts his whole crime. Then he falls senseless. Policemen seize him and carry him off in a cab.

That's very perceptive, isn't it, and very subtle? But it's very important that it be understood. Admit that it's truly terrifying. We could have the little sister reappear in one of those houses of ill repute where sailors go on a spree.

—Two more words in closing—are you influential with producers? Is it true that Royer insists on a secret collaboration? [18] I wouldn't accept that. I'm entirely at your disposal. My terrible financial needs guarantee my activity.

Let me know what you think of this. I'd be prepared to divide the work into several short scenes instead of adopting the awkward division into five long acts. Don't destroy this letter. In certain cases it could be used as a note, or rough draft.

51   TO APOLLONIE SABATIER
7 February 1854

I do not believe, Madame, that women generally know the full extent of their power, either for good or evil. It would probably be unwise to inform all of them of that power, equally. But with you one runs no risks. Your soul is too generously kind to yield to fatuousness or cruelty. Moreover, you've no doubt been so steeped in and saturated with flatteries that henceforth one thing alone can flatter you, that is, to discover that you're doing good, even unwittingly, even while you sleep, simply by existing.

As for this cowardly anonymity, what can I say, what excuse can I offer, except that my first fault determines the others, and that the habit has now been formed. Imagine, if you like, that sometimes, under the pressure of an intractable sorrow, I can find consolation only in the pleasure of writing poems for you, and that I'm then forced to reconcile the innocent longing to show them to you with the horrible fear of displeasing you. That's the cause of my *cowardice*. [19]

It's true, isn't it, that you think as I do—that the most deliciously beautiful woman, the best and most adorable creature—yourself, for example, can desire no better compliment than the expression of gratitude for the good she's done?

18. At this stage Royer was director of the Odeon theater.
19. Letter continues with "They Walk before Me" ("Ils marchent devant moi").

16 February 1854

I do not know what women think of the adoration they sometimes arouse. Some people claim that they must find such adoration perfectly natural, while others assert that they find it funny. For such people, therefore, women are nothing but either vain or cynical. For my part, I believe that well-constituted souls can feel nothing but pride and joy at their own benevolence. I do not know if I'll be granted the supreme sweetness of discussing with you face to face the power you've acquired over me, and of the constant radiance your image casts in my mind. I'm simply happy, for the moment, to swear to you again that love was never more disinterested, more ideal, more steeped in respect than that which I secretly nourish for you, and that I'll always hide with the care that such tender respect demands.[20]

53   TO CAROLINE AUPICK

8 March 1854

My dear Mother,

The little book[21] you'll find with this note is, I admit, hardly more than a piece of gross wheedling. I'm sure you'll find some wonderful things in it. Apart from the *Poems of Youth* and *Scenes from Politian*, which are at the end and contain some mediocre bits, you'll find nothing that isn't beautiful and strange. Although I don't need this book at present, because I've got some copies, don't lose it and above all *don't lend it*. It's a very attractive edition, as you see, and you know the trouble I have in collecting the various editions. Something strikes me as rather strange, something that I could hardly fail to notice, and that is how close a resemblance there is, although it's not actually highly pronounced, between my own poems and those of this man, once you make allowances for temperament and climate. [. . .]

54   TO EUGÈNE PELLETAN

17 March 1854

Dear Sir,

I've never seen you or had the honor of conversing with you. I'm told you were kind enough to mention my name in a recent article of yours (*Revue de Paris*) and that's the only thing that encourages me to write to

20. Letter continues with "What Will You Say Tonight" ("Que diras-tu ce soir").
21. *The Poetical Works of Edgar Allan Poe.*

you. This is what it's about. For a long time, indeed since 1847, I've been concerned with the fame of man who was at one and the same time a poet, a scholar, and a metaphysician—and he was a novelist, to boot. It's due to my efforts that Edgar Poe's name is beginning to be known in Paris. The funny thing is that others, aroused by my biographical and critical articles and by my translations, have turned their attention to him, but that none of them—apart from you—has deigned to mention my name. The world is paved with folly. What's more, these ill-starred fragments have been presented as resulting merely from obsessions. Sometimes they're described as too *bizarre*, too *eccentric*, too *terrible*, too *subtle* (why not too *beautiful?*). The fine book trade that exists in this wonderful age having forced me to draw a double profit from this, I thought of turning to the *Musée littéraire* that *Le Siècle* publishes, in its second review—M. de Tramont,[22] who specifically promised me he'd help me, has eight copies in his possession. I needn't add that to facilitate the sale I'll suppress the purely philosophical or scientific pieces. You would be the kindest exception in journalism if you were willing to say a good word for me to M. de Tramont or to M. Tillot.[23] Your position and your fame doubtless add great weight to your words. Only—it seems to me that one can be perfectly frank with a colleague—I'd be very happy in this matter if I didn't have to see the face and hear the voice of M. Desnoyers. I swear I bear him no ill will; his hatred of the beautiful is innocent because it's unconscious. With him, it's an animal instinct. And were he to be the best man on earth, he'd always do wrong where literature is concerned. It's because of the esteem I feel for your character and your work that I've written this letter, however odd the letter itself may be. —Pray accept, my dear sir, my sincere gratitude and do believe that this formula, when addressed to you, has none of the banality that a similar formula would have when addressed to a less sensitive man.

55   To Apollonie Sabatier

8 May 1854

It is a long time, Madame, a very long time since I wrote these lines.[24] The same deplorable habit continues: reverie and anonymity. Is it through a sense of shame at this ridiculous anonymity or through the fear that my poetry may be bad and my skills unequal to my lofty sentiments, is it for such reasons that I have been so timid and so hesitant this time? I

22. Administrator of *Le Siècle*.
23. Managing director of *Le Siècle*.
24. "Hymn" ("A la très chère").

really cannot tell. I am so afraid of you that I've always hidden my name, thinking that anonymous adoration—which would obviously appear ridiculous to all the brutish, materialistic women of the world we could consult on this score—was, after all, fairly innocent, as there is nothing it could disturb or trouble, and as it was infinitely better from the moral point of view than a stupid, conceited pursuit, a direct attack on a woman whose affections and perhaps also whose duty belong to another. Are you not—and I say it with a little pride—not only one of the best-loved but also most deeply respected of all creatures? I want to give you proof of this. Laugh at it, laugh at it a great deal if such is your pleasure, but do not speak of it. You'd find it natural, simple, and human, wouldn't you, that a man who is deeply in love should hate the happy lover, the one who is in possession? That he should consider him inferior, shocking? Well, some time ago fate decreed that I should meet *him*. How can I explain to you, without appearing comical, without bringing a laugh to your wicked face, always alive with gaiety, how happy I was to find him an amiable man, a man capable of pleasing you? Great God, doesn't such subtle reasoning suggest madness? To make an end of it, to explain my silences, and my ardor, an ardor almost religious in its intensity, I'll tell you that when my being has rolled in the black depths of its natural evil and stupidity, it dreams intensely of you. The stimulating and purifying dream generally produces some happy event.

For me, you are simply the most attractive of women, of all women, but you are also the dearest and most precious of superstitions. I'm an egoist and I use you. Here's my ill-starred scribbling. How happy I'd be if I could be sure that these high visions of love had some chance of finding a warm welcome in some secret part of your beloved thoughts. I shall never know. Forgive me, that's all I ask of you.

56   To Caroline Aupick

[28 July 1854]

Arondel has just left. How that man haunts me! Luckily I'd hidden myself in my dressing room. He waited for a while and then M. Lepage, entirely on his own initiative, had the inspiration to tell him that someone had come to take me to the press. I can only reply very succinctly to your long letter. Yes, yes, it will all work out, yes, this reconcilation will take place, and it will be an honorable one, provided your husband keeps his wits about him; yes, I know all I've made you suffer.

At present I'm realy hard-pressed. There's a mass of layabouts and wretches whose visits eat up my days. I'm going to seal myself hermetically away. In the evenings I'm at the press. I can't lose any more time, for the press would catch me up, it goes so quickly. You no doubt guessed about the ridiculous accident that befell me.[25] Those scoundrels took it into their heads to begin the publication at 4 o'clock on the 24th without letting me know. As a result, the edition sent to the provinces was really botched, an absolute scandal. Even in the Paris edition, where the errors were reduced during the night, for by chance I'd gone to the press, serious faults remained, particularly in the dedication to Maria Clemm,[26] a dedication to which I attached great importance. For example: *he* will embalm your name with *his* glory.[27]

Within the next two days I'll try to write you a note with a copy, one for yourself and one for Ancelle—do what you can to prevent him from losing his, as it could help you both in providing subjects for discussion and will show you at the same time that something must be done while we wait for the lucky breaks in my life. I am determined to find, in the midst of the unbearable weariness of translation, the time to write the scenarios of my play.

Oh, by the way, my 40 francs? Is there any chance of getting them today? They'll go to the steward as a small installment. Would it be possible for the 1st or 5th of August? Within 3 days at the latest I'll send you the note I mentioned.

57   To Paul de Saint-Victor

14 October 1854

You'll certainly take me for a recommender of the most indiscreet type and to tell you the truth I don't know how to go about the business. When it concerned Rouvière there was no problem, given his immense talent, but today the person in question is a woman, and to get it all off my chest at once, I'll say that it is my most heartfelt wish that you find a good word to say for Mlle Daubrun. This evening you were to have seen at the Gaîté theater a coarse melodrama entitled *The Bird of Prey*,[28] but I believe it's been postponed for 2 or 3 days. Yesterday I sent Théophile Gautier a letter, written at top speed, and making the same plea and I don't know how I have the audacity today to seek to use your pen to further my interests.[29]

25. A reference to the fact that the Poe translations were published before Baudelaire had checked the proofs.

26. Poe's adoptive mother, much venerated by Baudelaire.

27. The words "he" and "his" were omitted in the paper.

28. Marie Daubrun was to take the role of the duchesse de Guérande in this five-act play by Adolphe Dennery.

29. Saint-Victor did write favorably about Marie Daubrun in his review published in *Le Pays* on 23 October 1854.

Mlle Daubrun is one of those people who are sometimes good, sometimes bad, depending on weather, nerves, encouragement, or discouragement. While I'm waiting for the paper *Le Pays* to be good enough to embark on the publication of the remaining 32 numbers, I'm going to make up at my own expense an attractive little luxury edition of 50 copies including the poems of Edgar Poe.[30] It'll be absolutely outstanding. Need I say that your name is among the first 10 to be sent to the printer.

A thousand pardons and a thousand thanks.

58   To Hippolyte Hostein

8 November 1854

What timidity and suspicion I would feel were I taking the unusual step I'm attempting today, did I not know I'm speaking to a man of intelligence! The work[31] I'm sending you, and which I've been at infinite pains to discover, for the library was not willing to lend it and the *Revue retrospective* had disappeared, is more or less unknown. Perhaps you're familiar with it? In any case, it is not included either in the *Complete Works* or even in the *Posthumous Works*, and hardly anyone has read it except for those who love ferreting around in bookshops. For many years I've felt this work would be a great success in our day and age. Anyone but me would have considered the *Comédie française* or the *Gymnase*, but my choice is, I think, better, first because of the qualities of the director, but also precisely because of what you'll permit me to call the paradoxical nature of such a choice.

This is how my thinking went: Balzac counted M. Hostein as one of his friends. You were the one who so skillfully staged *The Stepmother* [*La Marâtre*],[32] if I'm not mistaken. M. Hostein, I thought, is sure to judge correctly the value of a work that seems to be one of the rare precursors of the sort of theater Balzac dreamed of.

In the subsidized theater, nothing happens, no decisions are reached, nothing works properly, everyone is timid and prudish. And I thought, too, that it would be interesting to check once and for all if this working-class audience, which is generally held in such scorn, would not be capable of understanding and applauding a work that has such a marvelous message—I don't want to pronounce the word *literary*, which belongs to the horrible jargon of our age. It occurred to me that the

30. Yet another of the projects Baudelaire never carried out.
31. Diderot's play *Is He Good? Is He Evil? (Est-il bon? Est-il méchant?)*. Hostein declined Baudelaire's suggestion.
32. Balzac's play, first performed on 25 May 1848.

indefatigable success of your theater authorized you to make a dazzling attempt without running any risks and that *The Cossacks* [*Les Cosaques*] and *The Boar* [*Le Sanglier*] could easily—if the worst came to the worst—pay for Diderot's welcome.

IF I wanted to arouse your pride, I could say that it would be worthy of a great man like you to lose money with this great author, but unfortunately I'm obliged to confess to you that I'm convinced of the possibility of making it a financial success. Finally—shall I continue my argument to the bitter end? For at this point, given that I'm unknown to you, I look as if I'm indiscreetly impinging on your rights and functions—it seems to me that an actor who is remarkable for his vehemence, his finesse, his poetic nature, an actor whose performance dazzled me in *The Musketeers* [*Les Mousquetaires*][33] (I've no idea if you share my judgment here), it seems to me, then, that M. Rouvière could find in the character of Diderot written by Diderot (Hardouin)—a blend of sensibility, irony, and the strangest cynicism—an entirely new development for his talent.

All the characters—and this is a curious fact—are *true*. M. Poultier, the navy clerk, died very old: I knew someone who knew him. There are numerous female characters, all of them amusing and charming. Strictly speaking this is Diderot's only dramatic work. *The Natural Son* [*Le Fils naturel*] and *The Paterfamilias* [*Le Père de Famille*] aren't in the same league.

As for alterations—I want our judgments to coincide on this point—I think that we can limit them to dealing with old-fashioned expressions, outmoded legal practices, etc. etc. In other terms, I think it would perhaps be good to commit a few innocent anachronisms to help a modern public.

And now let me take this opportunity to confess to you that I've long mused on a play as terrible and extraordinary as anyone could want, and that in the rare moments when I've been able to work on it, I've constantly had in my mind's eye the image of your strange actor. It concerns a play on *drunkenness*. Need I tell you that my drunkard isn't like other drunkards?

59   TO VICTOR DE MARS

[7 April 1855]

I'm at present at work on a very fine epilogue for *The Flowers of Evil*[34]—I hope it'll be finished in time. I wanted to tell you that whatever the pieces you choose I'm extremely eager to arrange them in

33. The play by Alexandre Dumas père.

34. This epilogue was never completed. Victor de Mars published in the *Revue des deux mondes* of 1 June a group of eighteen of Baudelaire's poems.

consultation with you, so that they form what we might call a sequence—just as we did for the first section.

I'll bring my *Epilogue* to you at 9 P.M. or 10 at the latest. The *Epilogue*, which is addressed to a lady, says more or less this: Let me find repose in love. But no, love will provide no repose. Candor and goodness are repulsive. If you wish to please me and rejuvenate my desires, be cruel, lying, libertine, debauched, thieving. And if you're not willing to do that, I'll beat you, but not in anger. For I am irony's true voice, and my illness is beyond all hope of cure. As you see, it creates a pretty firework of horrors, *a true epilogue*, worthy of the prologue to the reader, a real conclusion.

60 To George Sand

14 August 1855

Dear Madam,

I have a very great service to request of you and you do not even know my name. If any position can be called embarrassing, it's surely that of an unknown writer forced to call on the good offices of a famous writer. I could use the names of several famous friends to recommend myself to you, but what good would that do? I believe that the recital of my story will be of more use than anything else. And, too, I believe that asking for help from a woman is always less embarrassing than asking it of a man, and when one is pleading to a woman on behalf of another woman, it's no longer a source of humiliation, it's almost a joy. So I hope you won't be too displeased when I confess to you that despite your high literary position, I feel in addressing you neither too much embarrassment nor too much timidity.

Rehearsals for your play [35] are to start at the Odéon. Rouvière, one of my best friends, a brilliant actor, will play the main role. There is a part (Rouvière's wife) that was originally to go to Mlle *Daubrun*. Do you remember her? She played a remarkable role in *Claudia*. The matter had almost been decided. *Narrey* wanted her to have the role, the stage manager insisted on having her, M. *Vaëz* seemed to want her. As for Rouvière, who's a good judge in such matters, he likes her *almost* as much as I do. Mlle Daubrun is in Nice, returning from Italy, where her producer went bankrupt. She left the Gaîté for reasons that are not only highly pardonable but indeed very much to her credit. *Hostein* has said that he'll prosecute any *boulevard* theater that takes her but that he won't prosecute the Odéon. M. Narrey had undertaken to overcome that diffi-

35. *Maître Favilla*, first performed 15 September 1855.

72

culty and briefly it could be considered as having been overcome. Besides, it would take only a matter of hours to resolve that. Yesterday morning at 10, I met M. Vaëz who asked me eagerly if all were over: I told him Mlle Daubrun accepted with delight but that she wanted a slight, a very slight, increase in pay. It's such a trifling sum that I dare not tell you what it was. M. Vaëz asked me to meet him again at 2. At 2, Narrey had accepted the unpleasant task of telling me that the whole idea had been abandoned, that any negotiation was useless, that whole days would be wasted, etc. It's a 3-day journey between Paris and Nice and the Odéon doesn't reopen until September 15.

Need I tell you, Madame, what joy it would give me to see Mlle Daubrun return to Paris in honor, appear in one of your works, and repair rapidly in a theater appropriate to her talents the sorrows and misfortunes of last year? So I said that I would accept on her behalf and without consulting her the conditions that had been offered. But even that door was closed against me.

In all this discussion there was no question of asking what you wanted or seeking your opinion. It was when this simple realization struck me that I saw a chance of salvation, and it's for that reason that I'm writing to you. Not only am I asking for your opinion, a favorable opinion, but I'm also pleading with you as author and master to exert pressure that will annihilate that unknown pressure whose source I've been unable to guess. I beg you, unless you have already made your own plans, to write a brief note to these gentlemen, particularly M. *Royer*. You can see that I'm like those wretches who, displeased with the qadi, search for the sultan high and low. They count on his goodness and his justice. Whether you grant or refuse my request please be good enough not to reveal the eccentric means I've dared to use. It would really be too ridiculous now if I were to talk to you of my admiration for you and my gratitude. I await your answer in some trepidation.[36]

POSTSCRIPT: If I could at least make you laugh by telling you of a little misfortune that made me hesitate for *three hours* before sending you this note, perhaps I'd win a little ground. I didn't know your address—I had the absurd idea that Buloz ought to know it. He was correcting proofs, and when I mentioned your name he really gave me the rough edge of his tongue.[37] Moreover, I didn't know how to write your name: Mme Sand, Mme Dudevant or Mme the Baroness Dudevant? My greatest fear was that I might displease you. Finally, the last name appeared to

36. George Sand did her best to support Marie Daubrun but failed.
37. George Sand and Buloz had been on bad terms since 1841. Baudelaire's opinion of her as a writer was far lower than this letter would suggest.

me a mark of impertinence toward a genius and I thought you'd prefer
the name by which you reign in the hearts and minds of our age.

61   To Caroline Aupick

20 December 1855

Dear Mother,

I have lots of things to tell you, and M. Ancelle, who'll be taking this
letter to you, has up-to-date information about everything. Thank God
he and I have often discussed and debated these matters, not only for as
long as we've known each other, but above all over the last two months.

First and foremost, I want to see you. It's almost a year now that you've
been refusing to see me and I truly think that your—perfectly legitimate—wrath must be assuaged by now. Where our relationship is concerned there is something completely abnormal, completely humiliating
for me, that you really can't wish to maintain. If this prayer isn't enough to
satisfy you, at least be generous in your behavior toward me. I'm not yet
positively old, but may soon become so. It seems to me impossible that
you should wish to maintain this situation—all kinds of humiliations are
heaped on me; the least I can request is that I don't suffer any more
through *you*. And as I was saying to you, if you feel no pleasure and
confidence in allowing me to bring about this reconciliation at least do it
as a form of charitable act. Yesterday, as I knew I was soon to leave (it's for
tomorrow) I began to put a great bundle of papers in order. I found a pile
of letters from you, dating from different times and written under different circumstances. I tried to reread several of them: they were all imbued
with deep interest—a purely material interest, it's true, as if my debts
alone counted, as if spiritual joys and pleasures were nothing. But as they
were above all maternal, they eventually forced me into the most painful
train of thought. All these letters represented years I had spent, years I
had misspent. Soon I found it impossible to go on reading. There are
certain situations in which nothing is more hateful than the past. And as
one thought led to another, I said to myself that this situation was not
merely monstrous and shocking: it was even dangerous. Just because my
mind is framed in a particular way, which clearly you consider eccentric,
you shouldn't draw the conclusion that I take a morbid pleasure in
complete solitude, in separation from my mother. I think I mentioned a
moment ago that I may become old—but there's worse than that. One of
us could die, and it's truly painful to think that we're exposing ourselves
to the risk of dying without seeing each other again. You know how much
I hate any exaggeration. I know the wrongs I've done you and every time
I feel something deeply, the fear of expressing it in some exaggerated way

74

forces me to say it as coolly as I can. You won't be wrong then if you imagine that my words hide a warmth and an intense longing that I perhaps don't completely convey, as a result of habitual reserve. But above all, as I was saying to you a moment ago, grant me this: even if you granted me all the rest (that is, in material matters) I wouldn't be fully content. For a long time now I've been fairly ill, physically and spiritually, and I want everything, everything at once: a complete rejuvenation, an immediate physical and spiritual satisfaction. The years pass by with neither sort of satisfaction and that is truly hard to bear.

Ancelle will tell you of my desire—I'll go so far as to say my firm decision—to establish myself on a permanent basis in lodgings I chose 2 months ago. That means that almost as soon as I move in I'll have rent to pay, because the rooms have been held for 2½ months and I couldn't move in before because I didn't have enough cash.

I'm completely weary of my life in cheap cafes and furnished rooms: it's that that's killing me and poisoning me. I don't know how I've survived it. I'm sick of colds and migraines, fevers and above all the need to go out twice a day in snow, mud, and rain. I tell him that again and again but he wants you to authorize it before he agrees to my request. I lack everything so it'll need a bigger sacrifice or a bigger loan than normal. BUT it's also true that I'll draw from it almost immediately immense benefits. Above all, I won't waste any more time. That's my wound, my great wound, for there is a more serious state than physical suffering and that's the fear of watching as there wastes away, falls into jeopardy, and disappears in this horrible existence with all its upheavals, the admirable poetic gift, the clarity of ideas and the power of hope which alone make up my true wealth.

My dear mother, you are so utterly unaware of what a poet's life is like that you probably won't make much sense of this argument. Yet that's where my main fear lies. I don't want to croak unknown. I don't want to see old age come upon me without leading a regular life; I'll NEVER resign myself to that. And I believe that my personality is highly valuable, I won't say more valuable than others, but valuable enough for me.

To return to my house-moving—I lack everything—furniture, linen, clothes, even saucepans and a mattress and my books are scattered about in various binders' shops—I need everything and I need everything at once. Ancelle can't undertake such a complicated business, I made him see the truth of that. Moreover, all these costs are interdependent. My moving in depends on the possibility of getting away from the place I'm in now. My peace of mind depends on the move's being complete. Several of the objects I've mentioned have been ordered. It'll all be over in three days. As I have to leave the rue de la Seine tomorrow, or lose everything I own there, (and the book I'm working on?—and the printer?—and the bookseller?) if we suppose I can have the money today, I'll spend the next 2 or 3 days sleeping rough and I'll work wherever I can—for I must not stop. I chose the rooms in the quarter around the Boulevard du Temple— rue d'Angoulême, number 18. It's a fine house and above all it's quiet. At last I'll be lodged like an honest man—as I was saying, that'll be a true rejuvenation, I need to lead a completely secret life in absolute chastity and sobriety.

My two volumes are at last going to appear, in the course of the new year. They'll be published by the *Revue des deux mondes*[38] and thanks to Ancelle I'll be able to live in a suitable manner. I'm not worried on that score. And at last I'll have a place of my own. Henceforth you won't have to put up with my importuning you like this. There'll no longer be any reasons why I should! I've taken all the precautions necessary to safeguard these new lodgings from any threat of misfortune.

Oh heavens! I was forgetting to tell you the precise sum. With 1,500 francs everything would be over in three days. Truly, a poet's life is worth that. The sum is neither higher nor lower. I've done and checked all the calculations 50 times. It's not much, but it's exactly what's needed. I strongly insisted to Ancelle that he should not create any difficulties for me through his timidity, his fears. I insisted that he should not dream up ways of giving me this money in several stages that would remove all its worth and usefulness. I'm forced to move so quickly, so very quickly! Then, as I was telling you, all these expenses are closely connected with each other, like a block of shares. As for the very simple matter of self-respect and decency, it's too obvious to need stating.

When I think of all I'm forced to spend uselessly and fatally, without either pleasure or profit, I'm filled with exasperation. I've just added up all I've received *from you*, *from Ancelle*, from *Le Pays*, from *Lévy's booksellers*, this year. It's a vast sum, and still I live like a wild beast, like a drenched dog. And that'll be the case for ever, until my imagination fades away with my good health—unless I immediately take this big step.

This very morning I was saying to Ancelle something I find pretty reasonable. I said to him: "Would you prefer me to do what many literary people do, when they have less pride than I have, something I've never done under any minister, under any government? Asking a minister for money fills me with horror and yet that's almost accepted practice. There are funds for that purpose. As for me, my pride and my prudence have always kept me well away from such means. My name will never appear

38. The two collections entitled *Histoires extraordinaires* and *Nouvelles Histoires extraordinaires*.

in a government's despicable archives. I prefer to owe money to all and sundry. I prefer to argue with you, to torment my mother, however painful that may be."

You won't take offense if you receive my volume after everyone else has received their copy. I want to offer you a beautiful book. And I'm going to have a special edition made for three copies.

As for my literary plans—but you have so little interest in them! I'll tell you of them another time. Moreover, I've the same plans for the coming year as I had for the one just gone, plans that my horrible way of life prevented me from carrying out. One volume of criticism (completed), poetry (completed)—those are all but sold—a novel and an important play.[39] My love to you. I won't say: "I beg you." I'll just say: "Have a little boldness and trust."

It's tomorrow that I have to leave. I should have left my rooms today. Having thought everything out, I've come to the conclusion that I've so rarely hidden from M. Ancelle any detail of my existence that I decided it was better to show him this letter, before handing it to him to give to you. I presume you won't find anything offensive in this conduct. He pointed out to me that in telling you how deeply I longed to see you again, I didn't include sufficient apologies. But these regrets, these apologies, are obvious, they leap out from the page. I've twice expressed them to you in two letters you didn't read. When one thinks of certain things, those thoughts can be seen in the thinker's face, so to speak. Could you suppose that I took pleasure in giving you offense and in worsening the really false opinion you have of me? Once again, I beg you with all my strength to be generous and you'll be satisfied. What prevents us, once I've been able to establish a regular way of life, from seeing each other and from meeting at least once a week? That would let me keep you up to date with what's happening in my life and thanks to the new kindness I've asked of Ancelle, there would be no question of further upheavals.

62   To Caroline Aupick

9 January 1856

My dear Mother,

I'm sure you were thinking I'd forgotten to write you a few lines of thanks. Not a bit of it. The truth is that I was snowed under with problems and worries. The truth is that these problems, and all the

---

39. All these, except the poems from *The Flowers of Evil*, were merely projects in Baudelaire's mind.

errands involved, made me waste a lot of time and that, naturally, as soon as I was a bit calmer I had to make up the work I hadn't been able to do. At last, for the first time in ages, I've been able to work for long stretches in peace—but I was forgetting to tell you that the real reason for my delay is that I wanted to send you the first volume of my book[40] with this letter. But there are delays, there are always delays. My publisher screams like a madman at the expense I'm causing the printers, and at my slowness. But I'm determined always to do what I want—at least where literature is concerned. And yet in three days' time I'll at last be able to set to work on the the second volume.[41] I had to see Ancelle this morning and I made up my mind to write to you. As soon as my dustjackets are finished I'll send you a copy, and later, if it's possible, and I hope it will be, I'll get hold of some copies on good-quality paper and you can return the first copy to me. As soon as the second volume is completed, and that won't take *four* months but simply *one* month, I'll begin to work for the *Revue des deux mondes* on a regular basis.[42]

You wanted me to read the long letter you wrote to Ancelle. I read it and to tell the truth I think that Ancelle, who's beginning to know what I'm like, was afraid I'd be offended. But I've a little more common sense than he thinks and your letter could have contained twenty time as many maternal details and I'd still have felt deeply touched by it. The characteristic of true poets—forgive me for this little outburst of pride, for it's the only one I'm allowed—is the ability to step outside their own personality and understand a personality that is completely different from theirs.

One section alone—and I'm convinced you're expecting an answer on that score—surprised me excessively, as much for the belatedness of the feelings it expresses as for its peculiarity. I'm referring to the lines about my brother. My brother hurt me deeply in two circumstances, one that you know about and another of which you're unaware. My brother's crime is no more than stupidity—but that's a great deal. I would never have believed that you'd conceive of giving me advice on this subject. I prefer *evil* people who know what they are doing to those who are good but stupid. My repulsion for my brother is so intense that I don't even like to be asked if I *have* a brother. The world contains nothing more precious than the poetic spirit and chivalrous emotions. His incapacity as regards politics and science, his cynicism concerning women, toward whom one should at least make a show of gallantry, if not passion, everything,

40. The translation of Poe's tales entitled *Histoires extraordinaires*.
41. The second volume, *Nouvelles Histoires extraordinaires*, was not to appear until 1857.
42. Another unfulfilled dream.

everything in a word, alienates me from him. Now do I need to tell you that if ever an unexpected occasion arose, not only am I incapable of harming my brother but even of causing him the slightest hurt? It's not a question of friendship but purely the awareness of what is fitting.

Let me hug you and offer you once more my thanks which are as real and as deeply felt as you could ever imagine.

My address is 18 rue d'Angoulême-du-Temple. I'll certainly write to you when I send the work mentioned. I sent you a biography of a friend of mine and an abominable article about me, but Ancelle tells me you hadn't received anything.[43] It's very odd.

63   TO ALPHONSE TOUSSENEL

21 January 1856

My dear Toussenel,

I really want to thank you for your gift to me. I didn't know the value of your book[44]—I admit it crassly and ingenuously. The day before yesterday I suffered a disappointment, a rather serious upset, serious enough to prevent me from thinking—so much so that I interrupted an important piece of work. Not knowing how to take my mind off it, I picked up your book this morning—very early in the morning. It riveted my attention and put me back on an even keel, restoring my peace of mind—as all good books always will.

For a long time I've been rejecting almost all books, with a feeling of disgust. It's been a long time, too, since I've read anything as absolutely *instructive and amusing*. The chapter on the falcon and the birds that hunt on man's behalf is a masterpiece—all on its own.

There are expressions in your book that recall those of the great masters and which are cries of truth—expressions whose tone is irresistible and philosophical, such as: "Every animal is a sphinx," and in regard to analogy: "What repose the mind finds in a gentle quietude, sheltered by so fertile and so simple a doctrine, for which none of God's works is a mystery!"

And there are many other things that are philosophically moving— the love of the outdoor life, the value placed on chivalry and women, etc. What is beyond doubt is that you are a poet. I've been saying for a very long time that the poet is supremely intelligent, that he is intelligence *par excellence*—and that imagination is the most scientific of faculties, for

43. The study of the actor Rouvière, and Louis Goudall's review of the eighteen poems published in the *Revue des deux mondes*.
44. *L'Esprit des bêtes* (*The Mind of the Animals*).

it alone can understand the *universal analogy*, or what a mystic religion calls *correspondence*. But when I try to publish such statements I'm told I'm mad—and above all that I'm mad about myself—and that the only reason why I hate pedants is that my education is flawed. But what is absolutely certain is that I have a philosophical cast of mind that allows me to see clearly what is true, even in zoology, although I'm neither a huntsman nor a naturalist. That at least is what I claim—don't behave as my bad friends do, and laugh at me.

Now, since I've moved into greater subjects and closer familiarity with you than I would have allowed myself had your book not aroused such sympathy in me—let me be completely open with you.

What is *indefinite progress*? What is a society that is not aristocratic? It seems to me that it wouldn't be a society at all. What is a *naturally* good man? Where has such a being been encountered? A *naturally* good man would be a *monster*, by which I mean a God. Anyway, you can see what kinds of ideas scandalized me, by which I mean scandalized rational thought as it has been expressed from the beginning of time on this earth of ours. —Pure quixotry of a fine soul.

And for a man like you to insult in passing, as if you were merely a reporter working for *Le Siècle*, that great genius of our time, de Maistre—a prophet! And you've included colloquialisms and slang, which always undermines a fine book.

One idea has been uppermost in my thoughts since I started reading your book—and that is, that you're a true intelligence that has wandered into a sect. All things considered—what do you owe to *Fourier*? Nothing, or very little. Without Fourier you'd still be what you are. Rational men didn't await Fourier's arrival on earth to realize that Nature is a language, an allegory, a mold, an *embossing*, if you like. We know all that, and it's not through Fourier that we know it. We know it through our own minds and through the poets.

All the heresies I mentioned a moment ago are, after all, only the result of the great heresy of our times, the doctrine of artifice, which has taken the place of the doctrine of nature—I mean the suppression of the concept of *original sin*.

Your book arouses in me a great many dormant thoughts—and where *original sin* is concerned, as well as the concept of a form molded on an idea, I've often thought that noxious, disgusting animals were, perhaps, merely the coming to life in a bodily form of man's evil thoughts, the transformation of those thoughts into material shape. Thus the whole of nature participates in original sin.

Don't hold my boldness and my straightforwardness against me, but believe that I am your devoted servant.

13 March 1856

My dear friend,

As you take a delight in dreams, here's one that I'm sure won't fail to please you.[45] It's now 5 A.M. so my dream is still perfectly warm. Note that it's only one of the thousands of samples that assail me, and I've no need to tell you that their strangeness and their general tenor, which is absolutely alien to the occupations and events of my life, always encourage me in the belief that they are an almost hieroglyphic language to which I do not hold the key.

In my dream it was 2 or 3 A.M. and I was walking alone through the streets. I met Castille who, I believe, had several errands to perform, and I told him I'd go with him and take advantage of the carriage to do an errand of my own. So we took the carriage. I believed it to be my *duty* to offer the madam of a great brothel a book of mine that had just been published. When I looked at the work I held in my hand, I discovered it was an obscene book, which explained why it was *essential* that I present the work to that woman. Moreover, in my imagination, this need was basically a pretext, providing the chance to make love to one of the prostitutes, which implies that had it not been essential to present the book I wouldn't have dared go into such an establishment. I didn't say a word of this to Castille, but had the carriage stop at the door and left Castille in the carriage, promising not to keep him waiting long. Immediately after I'd rung the bell and gone in, I realized that my prick was hanging out of my unbuttoned trouser fly and I thought it indecent to present myself in such a state even in a place like that. Moreover, as I felt my feet were wet, I suddenly realized that they were bare, and that I'd stepped into a great puddle at the bottom of the staircase. "Oh well," I thought to myself, "I'll wash them before making love, and before going out." I go up the stairs. From that moment on, I don't give the book another thought. I find myself in a series of vast, interconnecting galleries which are poorly lit and seem gloomy and faded, like old cafes or old-fashioned reading rooms, or low-grade gambling saloons. The prostitutes, scattered throughout these vast galleries, chat with men, among whom I see various schoolboys. I feel very sad and greatly intimidated. I'm afraid people will see my feet. I look at them and realize that *one* has a shoe. A bit later I see that both have shoes.

What arouses my attention is that the walls of these vast galleries are decorated with all kinds of paintings, in frames. Not all are obscene.

45. For an interpretation of this dream, see M. Butor, *Histoire extraordinaire: Essay on a Dream of Baudelaire's*, trans. R. Howard (London: Jonathan Cape, 1969).

There are even some drawings of architecture or of Egyptian figurines. As I feel increasingly intimidated and I don't even dare to approach a prostitute, I amuse myself by a close examination of all the sketches.

In an out-of-the-way corner of one of those galleries, I find a very unusual series. In a mass of little frames I see drawings, miniatures, photographs. They represent colored birds with very bright plumage, whose eyes are *alive*. Sometimes there are only halves of birds. Sometimes they represent pictures of strange, monstrous, almost amorphous creatures, like meteorites. In one corner of every drawing there is a note. Prostitute so-and-so, aged . . ., gave birth to this fetus in such-and-such a year. And other annotations along those lines.

It occurs to me that such drawings are hardly calculated to arouse thoughts of love. Another thing that comes to mind is that there's really only one daily paper in the world—and that's *Le Siècle*—that would be stupid enough to open a house of prostitution and to put into it at the same time a kind of medical museum. Indeed, I suddenly say to myself, it's *Le Siècle* that has provided the funds for this speculation and the medical museum can be explained through the paper's mania for *progress*, *science*, and the *spread of light*. Then it occurred to me that modern stupidity and folly have a mysterious usefulness, and that often something made for the cause of evil turns, by a form of spiritual mechanics, toward goodness. I am filled with admiration in my dream for the correctness of my philosophical thinking.

But among all these creatures is one that has survived. He is a monster born in the brothel who stands permanently on a pedestal. Although alive, he is therefore part of the museum. He is not ugly. His face is even attractive, very swarthy and Oriental in color. There are many shades of pink and green in him. He is squatting, but in a bizarre, twisted pose. Moreover, there is something blackish that is wound several times round him and his limbs, like a great snake. I ask him what this is, and he tells me it's a monstrous appendix that comes out of his head, something elastic like rubber, and so very, very long that if he rolled it on top of his head like a plait of hair, it would be much too heavy and absolutely impossible to wear. As a result, he is forced to wind it around his limbs, which, moreover, creates a more attractive impression. I chat with this monster for some time. He tells me of his problems and sorrows. For several years now he's been forced to stand in this room on this pedestal to satisfy public curiosity. But his principal problem comes at dinner time. Because he is a living creature, he's forced to eat with the prostitutes of the establishment, stumbling along with his rubber appendage to the dining room, where he has to keep it wrapped around him or to put it like a pile of rope on a chair, for if he lets it drag along on the ground it pulls him over backwards. Moreover, he's forced, he who is small and squat, to eat beside a prostitute who is tall and well built. He tells me all these details, what's more, without any bitterness. I dare not touch him—but I take an interest in him.

At this moment (this is no longer a dream)—my woman makes a noise in the room with a piece of furniture, and that wakes me up. I awaken weary, aching, my back, legs and hips stiff. I presume that I was sleeping in the twisted position of the monster. I don't know if all that will seem as funny to you as it does to me. Dear *Minot* would, I guess, find it very difficult to draw a moral conclusion from that.

65   TO CHARLES-AUGUSTIN SAINTE-BEUVE

19 March 1856

Here, my dear protector, is a form of literature that may well not inspire as much enthusiasm in you as it does in me, but which will certainly interest you. Edgar Poe, who is not highly regarded in America, *must*, by which I mean I wish he could, become a great man in *France*. I know how good you are and how much you love new things, so I've boldly promised Michel Lévy your aid.

Could you send a note telling me if you'll write something for *L'Athenaeum* or another paper? In that case, I'd write to M. Lalanne asking him not to give that task to anyone else—your pen has a *special* authority which I need.

You'll see at the end of my *Notice* (which turns topsy turvy all the fashionable opinions of the United States) that I'm announcing some new studies. At a later date I'll discuss this extraordinary man's opinions in regard to the sciences, philosophy, and literature.

I place in your hands my still-troubled soul.

If the newspaper's editor needs another copy he can collect it at the printer's.

66   TO CHARLES-AUGUSTIN SAINTE-BEUVE

26 March 1856

You were well aware that your good little piece of news would delight me.[46] Lalanne was informed of it by Asselineau and the arrangement was that the book would be given to someone else only if you weren't able to write your article. As regards the rest of your letter, I can provide some

---

46. Sainte-Beuve replied that he would write an article, not on Poe but on the translation.

details that may be of interest. There will be a second volume and a second preface. The first volume was designed as bait for the public: tricks, divination, leg-pulls, etc. *Ligeia* is the only important piece connected, from the moral point of view, to the second volume. The second volume is of a loftier kind of fantastic: hallucinations, mental illness, pure grotesque, supernaturalism, etc.

The second preface will contain an analysis of the works I won't be translating and above all a study of the author's *scientific* and *literary* opinions. I'll even have to write to M. de Humboldt on this matter to ask him what he thinks of the little book Poe dedicated to him, *Eureka*.[47]

The first preface—the one you've seen—in which I tried to include a sharp protest against Americanism, is more or less complete as far as the biography is concerned. People will pretend to consider Poe a trickster, but I return, to the point of exaggeration, to the supernatural character of his poetry and his short stories. He is American only insofar as he is a *charlatan*. As for the rest, he reveals almost anti-American thinking. Moreover, he mocked his compatriots to the best of his ability.

Therefore the piece you refer to is in the second volume.[48] It's a dialogue between two souls that takes place after the destruction of the world. There are three dialogues of this kind that I'd be happy to lend you at the end of the month before I give my second volume to the printer.

Now let me thank you with all my heart—but you're so kind that you'll run great risks with me. After the *Poe* there will be two volumes of my own, one of critical articles and one of poems. So I give you my excuses in advance and moreover I fear that when I no longer speak through the mouth of a great poet, I'll appear to you as a noisy, highly disagreeable creature.

POSTSCRIPT: At the end of the second volume of Poe I'll include a few examples of his poems. I'm sure that a man as careful as you are won't be offended if I ask you to observe the spelling of Edgar Poe's name. No *d*, no diaeresis, no accent.[49]

47. No letter from Baudelaire to Humboldt had been found.

48. See *Lettres à Charles Baudelaire*, p. 330. Sainte-Beuve asked Baudelaire about a short story in which a man, living in the last moments of earth's existence, recounts his emotions as the world approaches its final destruction: this is the *Conversation of Eiros and Charmion*. The other tales alluded to are *The Colloquy of Monos and Una* and *The Power of Words*.

49. Poe's name was frequently spelt *Edgard Poë* in contemporary French newspapers.

12 April 1856

My dear Mother,

However carefully you seem to avoid giving me the slightest thought, I'm convinced that you'll be pleased if I do you a favor. I'm sending you copies of two newspapers; one, *Le Figaro*, which a few months ago devoted 7 columns to libeling me, thought it appropriate to insert a portion of my book together with an article that is such a eulogy as to be almost dangerous. The section from my book is in the *feuilleton*,[50] the critical article is on p. 6. The other newspaper, *L'Assemblée nationale*, is worthy of a virtuous, polite old fool.[51] I almost died laughing when I read it. All in all it's a good article from the point of view of sales, which moreover are going very well. Please don't lose this cutting. As the old ass has a fairly high reputation, I may want to start my preface to the second volume by correcting his errors and in that case I'll need the article to hand. And it's the very devil to buy old numbers of newspapers.

I recall that at one stage I sent you an issue of *Le Figaro*—the one in which your son was treated more badly than even a thief or convict would have been. I hoped that you'd be brave enough to laugh at it, and I sent with it a pamphlet I'd written. Those papers never reached you. To prevent that happening again, I'm writing *Madame* on the envelope in enormous letters.

Two more reviews have been published, favorable on the whole, but stupid; one, in the *Revue de Paris*, the issue for 1 April in the bibliography article at the end—the other, in the *Revue des deux mondes* for 1 April, the bibliography article on the last page but one. Some reviews or articles by Gautier, Barbey d'Aurevilly, Sainte-Beuve, and Philarète Chasles are to appear, and they are serious critics.[52]

I'm not sure that anger gives one any talent, but if it did, I'd be stupendously talented, for I only ever work in the intervals between quarrels and legal seizures. I've noticed about all these monstrous scribblers, above all the democrats and supporters of Napoleon III, that not one of them is willing to tackle sincerely the question of poverty and suicide. I was hoping they would do so. Not one so far has fallen into the trap I sprung for them, but it's bound to happen.

50. The *feuilleton* was that part of a newspaper devoted to reviews or serialized novels.

51. The conservative critic Armand de Pontmartin, whose reviews are not quite as ridiculous as Baudelaire claims.

52. Neither Gautier nor Sainte-Beuve reviewed *Histoires extraordinaires*. Barbey d'Aurevilly's article appeared in *Le Pays* in June 1856. P. Chasles reviewed the work briefly in the *Journal des débats* on 20 April. For a full list of reviews, see my *Baudelaire's Literary Criticism* (Cambridge: University Press, 1981).

A great piece of news! As a result of various circumstances, I'm forced to begin putting my *ideas on theater* in order, starting next month—that is, if God and my creditors permit.

My second preface is giving me utter hell. I have to speak of religion and science. Sometimes I don't have enough knowledge, sometimes it's money that's lacking, and calm—which amounts almost to the same thing.

68   TO CAROLINE AUPICK

11 September 1856

My dear Mother,

Please don't answer this with a letter like the last one you sent me. Recently I've been suffering too many torments, humiliations, and even physical agonies for there to be anything to be gained by your adding your share. A few days ago, perhaps ten, I wanted to write to you to beg you, as Ancelle was off traipsing around the South, to send me a little money, the amount didn't matter, to let me get away from Paris, enjoy myself, and kill a little time; but I would have had to give you an explanation and in a moment I'll tell you why I didn't. But the days have gone by and the misfortune that has befallen me has so sapped my strength that I cannot bring myself to do any work, so it's no longer a question of pleasure or of amusement but of need, absolute need. I've gone back to work just to stupefy myself. But you know how exhausting it is to nag and argue with idiots. Ancelle will not be back for another 8 to 10 days perhaps, and this man, the one whose house I'm living in, is hounding me beyond belief for a paltry 200 francs or so. Michel Lévy is making me wait day after day to sign our third contract;[53] my desk is piled with uncorrected proofs, so it's a bad moment to ask him for a loan. This man wants his money tomorrow. Mind you, I could calm him down with less, say 100 or 150 francs, but I've taken it into my head that I must use the rest to visit you, not for a long time, just a day or so, and not at your place, rest assured of that! I'd just go to a hotel, you'd come and give me a hug there, and then I'd go back. Besides, I've got a lot of work to do, and I don't intend to stay away for long. Of course I was due to receive some money from Ancelle on his return. If you sent me some, I wouldn't take the money from Ancelle, to make amends, and I'd let him know what I'd done.

I said a moment ago that I haven't written, although I very much wanted to, and although at that stage I thought you were in Paris,

53. The contract for Baudelaire's translation of *Arthur Gordon Pym*.

86

because the necessary explanations would of course have delighted you, filled you with a kind of maternal joy I couldn't have borne. My state of mind must have been pretty obvious, since Michel Lévy, seeing me in such a state, sometimes depressed, sometimes in a rage, didn't ask any questions, left me alone, and didn't even press me for work. My relationship, my 14-year-old relationship with Jeanne has broken up. I did all that it was possible to do to avoid the break. This breaking up, this battle, went on for two weeks. Jeanne just told me calmly over and over again that I had an inflexible nature and moreover that one day I'd thank her for her decision. There's womankind's great middle-class wisdom for you. I myself know that whatever happens to me, whatever happy relationship, pleasure, money, or flattery I may find, I'll always miss that woman. So that my grief, which perhaps doesn't make much sense to you, won't seem too childish, I'll admit that I'd placed all my hopes in her, like a gambler; that woman was my only distraction, my only pleasure, my only companion, and despite all the internal upheavals of a tempestuous relationship, the idea of an irreparable separation had never before entered my head with any clarity. Even now—and yet I'm perfectly calm—whenever I see a beautiful object, a lovely painting of a country scene, anything pleasant at all, I find myself thinking: why isn't she at my side to admire this with me, to buy that with me? You see I make no attempt to disguise my wounds. It took a long time, believe me, so intense was the shock, for me to realize that perhaps work would give me pleasure and that after all I had obligations to fulfill. In my mind there ran a constant echo of: "What's the use?"—not to mention a kind of dark veil over my eyes and an eternal racket in my ears. That went on for a pretty long time, but at last that's all over. When it was perfectly plain that the situation really was *irreparable* I was seized with a nameless fury: for ten days I couldn't sleep, I vomited constantly, and I had to hide myself away because I wept all the time. My obsession moreover was purely selfish: I saw myself living out an unending sequence of years, bereft of family, friends, mistress, endless years of loneliness and hazards. And nothing for the heart. I couldn't even draw consolation from pride. For it's all my fault. I used and abused her; I took pleasure in making a martyr of her, and now it's my turn to be martyred. Then I was seized with superstitious dread, I imagined you were ill. I sent word to your house; I learned of your absence and that you were well; at least, that's what I was told, but please tell me so yourself in a letter. What's the use of continuing with this story which will probably seem only bizarre to you? I could never have believed that emotional suffering could cause such physical torture, and that two weeks later one could go about one's business like a different man. I'm alone, very much alone, forever, that's more than likely to be

87

the case. For, morally speaking, I can no longer place my trust in people, any more than in myself, having henceforth only matters of money and vanity to interest me, and no pleasure save literature. [. . .]

69   To Caroline Aupick

4 November 1856

Dear Mother,

I didn't want to let this day[54] go by without showing you by a brief letter that you are never out of my thoughts. Just a few lines—for you know my laziness, which ends by forcing me later on to rush through essential work. That's my current position. Moreover, you can, so it seems to me, have absolute faith in my future. Your fears are empty. If the financial problems are difficult to sort out, my moral health—which is all-important—is excellent. The accident that at first plunged me in such despair—a despair that seemed childish to those who lack imagination but which was so frightful for me—has ended by giving me an intense taste for life. I'm in the middle of my second preface, that is, the introduction to *Nouvelles Histoires extraordinaires*, which you'll receive in a few days' time. As for the third volume, you'll read it day by day, as you get *Le Moniteur*.

Will you let me laugh a little, just a little, at the desire you ceaselessly express to see me like everyone else, and to consider me worthy of your old friends whom you name with such pleasure? Alas, you know only too well that I haven't reached that stage yet, and that my destiny will be very different. Why don't you talk about marriage, like all other mothers?

To speak in all sincerity, the thought of that girl has never left me, but I'm so perfectly versed in the task of living, which is nothing but lies and empty promises, that I feel I'm incapable of falling a second time into the same inextricable traps of the heart. The poor dear is ill now and I've refused to visit her. For a long time she avoided me like the plague, for she knows my terrible nature which is nothing but ruse and violence. I know she is to leave Paris and that pleases me, although, I admit, I'm seized with sorrow at the thought that she may die far from me.

To sum up, I've the devil of a thirst for pleasure, glory, and power. That, I should add, is crossed often, though not often enough, by the desire to please you. So please take good care in future not to send me such boring people as that Senate usher, the *Tony*, who has acquired rogue's credentials and who installed himself in my rooms for three

54. The feast of Saint Charles.

hours, talking away like a servant, and who I only got rid of by behaving brutally. All my love, Charles.
Send me a few words, I beg you, about the state of your health.

70   To Auguste Poulet-Malassis
9 December 1856

My dear friend,
Nothing could be more judicious, nothing could be wiser, than your letter. To tell the truth, those are almost the conditions that Michel laid down before he started on his system of volumes at 1 franc with a print run of 6,000. But, with you, I'd get the books made honestly and elegantly.

I can now admit to you how very much pleasure your letter gave me. Don't hold it over much against me, but I'd come to see your hesitations as reflecting a real lack of confidence in my work. Moreover, I'd got into one hell of a mess. One day, in a rage with Michel, I'd boasted to him that I could count on you.

Finally, the money itself (above all the 200-franc note) is like a gift from the gods. For after you left me my jinx made *Le Moniteur's* editorial board decide to begin by auditing the accounts of the year that's just past, and *Arthur Gordon Pym* won't be paid for until 15 January. The first issue will appear, come what may, on the 8th.[55] You can guess how anxious I was and you see I have the odd reason to be pleased.

I'm very glad that you don't want to start until February, and that we're beginning with the poetry. I'll have the whole of January to find various homes for the 3 or 4 unpublished pieces from the prose volume, to bring in some money, and, at the same time, the two of us can work out the order of the pieces in *The Flowers of Evil—together*, you understand, for the question is of importance. We must make a volume that contains nothing but good things: only a little material, but giving the impression that there's a lot, and it must be very remarkable. Your reference to *popularity* made me really laugh. No popularity for me, I know only too well, but a fine drubbing from all and sundry which will arouse curiosity. And we'll be able to get a few articles in foreign reviews.

I don't know if you're going to include both books in a single contract, but whether you only have one or whether you draw up two separate ones, if you don't leave the title of the prose work blank, put "The Mirror of

55. In fact there was a further delay. The first issue did not appear until 25 February 1857.

89

Art," "An Æsthetic Cabinet," or whatever occurs to you. You can alter that to suit yourself, when you're ready to deposit the title at the Ministry.

The type of contract that I asked of you and that you made for me is excellent insofar as it is hard to imagine that you could lose anything and if the book runs into a second edition the author's future benefits are safeguarded.

So, two volumes, 1,000 copies all at 100 sous. Put the case that Malassis does not reprint within a year (?) and in which Baudelaire would be free. Send your contract or contracts, already signed, together with the money. I'll return them to you with the copies. In your letter let me have your advice on discounting the first 200.

I don't know what role your brother-in-law plays in your decision or even if he plays a role at all. In any case, send him my regards—that is, if you think he's susceptible to the satanic ceremonies of etiquette. Another thing that's happened to me is that my definitive apartment can't be ready until 15 January. So you'll find me here and I remain until 15 January stuck in the lodging house named after that so-and-so whom M. Havin and Léon Plée consider a great poet.[56]

Please set aside for me anything by or about Laclos that you can lay hands on. You'll get this tomorrow morning, which is Wednesday. I'd be happy if I received your parcel on Thursday morning. If I were not afraid that you'd treat me as mad or insolent, I'd add a word about some money I owe you. But you'll have plenty of time to be angry when you come to Paris.

POSTSCRIPT: If you see Lord Donkeyherd,[57] cure him of his exaggerated superstitions about me.

71   TO AUGUSTE POULET-MALASSIS

10 February 1857

My dear friend,

The manuscript was returned to Mme Dupuy on Wednesday 4 February—it's no fault of mine, therefore, that you received it so late. So I'll receive, at the same time as the galleys for half of *Spleen and Ideal*, the packet of poems we've abandoned and that were not typeset. You're right on that score. But I thought it legitimate to ask, because of my inability to assess the value of a line or a word unless it's in type.

As for the proofs—why the little sermon? *I know you're right*. But you seem to believe that I want to misuse them. I requested a galley proof and

56. Voltaire.
57. Punning reference to Baudelaire's friend Asselineau.

a page proof. You erroneously inferred that I meant "always two proofs"—
that is, two copies of the same proof—because I wanted to provide
quotations (perhaps) to reviews and papers *before* the volume goes on sale,
which could only be to your advantage anyway.

As for the question of typography, I don't understand anything about
it, or at least, I understand only with my eye. The only recommendation
I make is that when you set up the pages, don't be miserly with the white
spaces and do set the *Dedication* in rather solemn style—your excellent
taste will enable you to find one. Still, it would perhaps be a good idea
not to give a modern text the archaism and prettiness of red print. No
coquetry.

I was utterly astonished when you talked of 350 or 400 pages. I'd
never have believed it, particularly with the octavo format. Please be
good enough to explain to me how one uses the post to send proofs. It
was Michel who sent all my proofs from Corbeil. I'm longing to see
you. [. . .]

72   To Charles-Augustin Sainte-Beuve

9 March 1857

Dear friend,

You are too indulgent to have taken offense at the impertinent question mark I put after the words "in memory" in the copy of *Nouvelles
Histoires extraordinaires* that I left yesterday at *Le Moniteur*. If you can help
me, I'll find it completely natural, for you've spoiled me so much; if you
can't, I'll see that as natural too.

This second volume is more lofty in character, more poetic, too, than
two-thirds of the first volume. The third volume (being published at
present in *Le Moniteur*) will be preceded by a third notice. The story
about the end of the world is called *The Conversation of Eiros and Charmion*. The first volume has just gone into a second edition, from which
the main errors have been removed. Malassis knows that he is to keep one
for you. If I don't have the time to bring it to you, I'll have it sent.

73   To Auguste Poulet-Malassis

[16 or 17 March 1857]

First, it seems to me that it would be better to lower the whole
dedication so that it's right in the center of the page—but I leave that to
your judgment. Second, I think it would be good to have *Flowers* in
italics—in sloping capitals, given that it's a punning title. Finally,
although each of these lines and letters is well proportioned in relation to

the others, I find them all too thick. I think the whole thing would gain in elegance if you took a slightly smaller thickness for each line, while keeping the same proportions. The C.B. alone seems to me a little small.

I note that your pagination doesn't take into account the title and the subtitle. That too I'll leave to you. Be kind enough to return the corrected proofs. I give you moreover permission to print.

74   TO AUGUST POULET-MALASSIS

18 March 1857

Dear friend,

In reply to your letter of this morning:

First, it's absurd that you should be angry. Look, my very dear friend, I never said to you that I wanted Egyptian characters or thick characters, English or slender characters, etc. I know all about unity and have always thought exactly as you do on that score, and I know how important it is for the characters to be in harmony. You talk to me of the *Title* and I reply by mentioning the dedication. You tell me: it's published. What you mean is that it's printed.

The dedication cannot go ahead as it stands and since our tastes differ on this subject (I maintain the need to reduce the length or the height, or if you prefer, to thin down all the letters, making then all one "eye" thinner)—I'm willing (and don't be angry) to reimburse you for the cost of the paper and the printing of this sheet. But henceforth, don't run anything off until I've given you the go-ahead. Let me know how much all this costs you and you'll receive it on the first of the month.

For the new run, correct all the errors I've indicated on the proof (the printed sheet) sent by me (apart from *poëte* and your inverted commas, if you really prefer them). *As for my punctuation, remember that its purpose is to indicate not only the meaning, but the WAY IN WHICH IT SHOULD BE READ ALOUD.* As for those letters that are badly formed, you're right, but it's not my fault if my eye is too keen.

So we're agreed on this. That sheet must be redone. I'll pay the costs, and you won't print it without my permission. I'll return the next two sheets to you this evening.

Your very devoted,

C.B.

A reply *soon, very soon.*

NO, NO CREBILLON—[58] I've enough as it is with the other, which is causing me a great deal of trouble.

58. Malassis wanted to publish an edition of Crébillon fils with a preface by Baudelaire: the latter, already struggling with his Laclos essay, which he never completed, refused.

18 March 1857

My dear friend,

Many thanks. I received this evening the second sheet and the large parcel. Now everything will go smoothly. I still haven't been able to write to you today about everything I have to say to you. I'll just dash off 3 or 4 remarks:

1. Your strangely hooked inverted commas—do you have to use them throughout?

2. I entrust my dedication to you with infinite love. Something slim, elegant, well proportioned, and revealing rather more clearly the three or four main parts.

3. Isn't your running head too close to this first line? There ought to be at least as much space between the first line and the running head as there is between the verses.

4. Your second volume! I plead with you to let me finish this one first. Otherwise you'll have me putting verses into the prose and prose into the poetry, or ornithology, or a ship's rigging—subjects that are currently filling my mind. What (apart from the fear of disorder) stopped me from letting you whisk away from Paris this second volume, which needs only three more articles: Caricaturists, Opium, and Reasoning Painters? But the gaps! and the revising needed! Devil take it! No doubt you're cursing me down there but in a few days' time you'll see how right I am.

As for the letter, you were probably right to suppress it. It seems you guessed that what would exasperate *me* was the thought that your brother-in-law was exasperating *you*, and that this might lead to a change in our excellent and long-standing relationship. My regards to your mother if she remembers me. Please show me the first sheet when you've corrected it. I gave you the go-ahead as a means of pouring balm on your wounds. As for the notes, we'll have to make a decision, and if you're determined to spoil the volume I'll dream up a combined means of doing it.[59]
Equality of line spacing!
Broken letters, etc. etc. . .
I presume there's still time for all the little things, which are moreover important.

---

59. Baudelaire had written two footnotes, one to the poem in Latin "Franciscae meae laudes," the other to the section entitled *Rebellion* (*Révolte*). He wanted these placed at the end of the volume; Malassis wanted them incorporated in the text, at the bottom of the relevant pages. In the 1857 edition the note on *Rebellion* appears on the part-title of that section, that on "Franciscae" between the title and the poem itself.

25 April 1857
My dear friend,

I've just received your very surprising letter which took me a long time to understand aright and which, despite all the fine protestations, for which I'm deeply grateful to you, has proved to me that the relationship between us has now altered. Of the two of us, it's obvious that I'll be the one to feel most distressed by this change, but my character adapts to all great emotions, even resignation. I was counting on asking you to perform yet another service for me: the *Nocturnal Poems* [*Poèmes nocturnes*],[60] which will be completed after the *Curiosities* [*Curiosités esthétiques*]—so another project bites the dust.

The sheet you ask me to return is already in your possession. On this score I'll beg you (it seems there's still time!) to substitute in one of the last *Spleen* poems a line just before a new section full of corrections. Instead of "boredom, *son* of dull incuriosity" put "boredom, *fruit* of. . . ." This correction, which may seem childish, has particular importance for me. I'll send off your galleys tomorrow. But you know the post doesn't operate on Sunday as it does on other days. So I think it's highly unlikely you'll receive them before Monday evening or Tuesday morning. I trust you'll be indulgent over this 12-hour delay.

The three missing pieces of the *Curiosities* volume are going to be published (*Le Moniteur*, *La Revue française*, *L'Artiste*). If you want me to start by reworking the beginning of the volume I'll do so.

Théophile Gautier thinks I'm at Alençon at this moment. Indeed, I wanted to go and see you, as soon as the last *feuilleton* had come out. I wanted to behave at Alençon as I do at *Le Moniteur*, installing myself either at a hotel or at your press and, determined to concentrate on one thing at a time, I wanted to work day by day until *everything* was done. A combination of different reasons prevented me from doing so.

A little while back Théophile asked me if you'd be willing to publish *The Novel of the Mummy* [*Le Roman de la momie*]. I didn't write to you about it because I thought I was going to set off for Alençon. He attaches great importance to this book and charged me to tell you that he'd take out all the little light-hearted love affairs and all the silly horseplay and that he'd lift the whole tone to accord with the archaic solemnity of the opening. At the last moment I asked him what sort of contract he had in mind. He told me that what had led him to approach you was the hope of finding typographic purity and the kind of zeal needed for a work he values highly, and that, as far as costs are concerned, he'd want you to do what

60. One of the titles Baudelaire considered for his volume of prose poetry.

Hachette does, 1,200 francs for 4,000 copies or even 4,500 or more. I replied that the only problem was the small size of your print runs. To that he answered that you could, if you approved, do the run four times, reset the type, recompose the forms, whatever you wanted, but that he wanted there to be at least 4,000 copies. The sum in question spread over 4,000 copies, is the same as your usual price for 1,000 or 1,200 copies. There's only one problem for you, then, and that's whether you can be sure of doing such a run.

I hope you'll understand that, given my friendship with Théophile and the services I owe him, it would be painful for *me* to present him with a refusal. You could write to him—he's got enough wit to take anything you say in good part. What encouraged me to undertake this negotiation is the fact that you praised his work.

77   To Auguste Poulet-Malassis

14 May 1857

No, dear friend, I shall still not be finished today—I won't be free until tomorrow and you, of course, won't be free for another 2 or 3 days after that. I'm fencing with 30-odd lines which I find weak, displeasing, made badly, and rhyming badly. Surely you don't believe I have the suppleness of a Banville! I received a proof that was clearly meant for him and that wasn't a good sheet. I drew the conclusion he'd received mine— that is, the eighth sheet—unless it hasn't yet been run off.

This morning I corrected my ninth sheet. It's perfectly plain to me that you shouldn't correct a sheet before sending it to me—that only serves to introduce errors. My note on *Rebellion* is despicable: I'm amazed that you didn't criticize me on that score. I sent you a little pamphlet by d'Aurevilly. I presume your packet (ninth sheet, now ready to print— and part of the tenth, plus a little fragment that you'll print on a quarter sheet with the table of contents) will leave tomorrow morning in the morning post.

And my cover!!!

A thousand pardons for not franking this—I've neither stamps nor money.

78   To Caroline Aupick

Wednesday 3 June 1857

[. . .] I want to let you know briefly the reasons motivating my conduct and my feelings since the death of my stepfather. You'll find in these few lines the explanation both of my attitude during this great misfortune and of my future behavior. —That event was for me something very solemn, a kind of call to order. I've sometimes been very harsh and dishonest in my treatment of you, my poor mother. But after all I had every right to consider that someone had taken charge of your happiness, and the first idea that struck me when this death occurred was that henceforth that burden would naturally fall on my shoulders. Everything I've allowed myself hitherto—my nonchalance, my selfishness, those violent outbursts of uncouthness, the sorts of things you always find in lives that are disorderly and isolated—all that is henceforth forbidden to me. Everything humanly possible to grant you a happiness both unique and new for the last part of your life *will be done*. After all, this isn't such a difficult matter, since you attach such importance to the success of all my projects. By working for myself I'll be working for you.

Don't worry too much about my miserable debts and my fame, so indolently sought up until now and henceforth so painful to capture. Provided that every day one does a little of what there is to do, all human difficulties can be solved quite naturally. I'm only asking you one thing (*on my own behalf*) and that's to devote yourself to being well and living for a long time, as long as you can. [. . .]

79   To Caroline Aupick

9 July 1857

I assure you that there's no need to worry about me: but *you* cause *me* very deep concern and the letter you sent me, utterly full of despair, is certainly not calculated to calm my fears. If you give in like that, you'll fall ill and that will then be the worst of misfortunes and the most unbearable of wounds for me. I want you not only to seek out amusements but also to find new pleasures. I certainly think Mme Offila is a sensible woman.

As for my silence, don't look for any other cause than one of those bouts of languor that to my great shame sometimes take hold of me and prevent me not only from doing any work but even from performing the simplest of duties. Moreover, I wanted not just to write to you but also to send you your prayer book and my book of poems.

The prayer book is not completely finished yet—the workers, even the most intelligent, are so stupid that there were a few small things that needed rectifying. That caused me a few problems, but you'll be happy. As for the Poems (published two weeks ago), as you know, I first intended not to show them to you. But on second thought it seemed to me that since you would after all hear the work mentioned, at least through the reviews I'll be sending you, modesty on my part would be as silly as prudishness on yours. I received for my own use 16 copies on ordinary paper and 4 on fine-quality Holland paper. I've kept one of the latter for you and if you haven't received it yet it's because I wanted to have it bound for you. You know I have never considered literature and the arts as pursuing a goal at odds with morality, and that beauty in their conception and their style is all I demand. But this book, whose title, *The Flowers of Evil*, says everything, possesses, as you'll see, a beauty that is sinister and cold: it was created with fury and patience. Moreover, the proof of its positive value lies in all the attacks made upon it. The book infuriates people. Moreover, alarmed myself by the horror I was going to inspire, I cut out a third of it at the proof stage. Critics are denying me everything—from the ability to invent to knowledge of my own language. I just laugh at all those idiots and I know that this volume, with all its qualities and faults, will make its way into the memory of the literate public, along with the best poetry of Victor Hugo, Théophile Gautier, and even Byron. I'd just make one recommendation. Since you're living with the Emon family, don't let the book fall into Mlle Emon's hands. As for the priest, whom you no doubt see, you can show it to him—he'll think I'm damned and won't dare to say so to you. There's been a rumor that I'm to be prosecuted, but nothing will come of it. A government concerned with the terrible elections in Paris hasn't time to prosecute a madman.

A thousand apologies for these childish acts of vanity. I had indeed thought about going to Honfleur but didn't dare mention it to you. I thought of cauterizing my laziness, cauterizing it once and for all, beside the sea, through a period of strenuous work far from all frivolous temptations. I'd either work on my third volume of Edgar Poe or on my first play, to which I really must give birth, willy-nilly.

But I have tasks to perform that can't be done in a place that has no libraries, no prints, no museum. Above all I must get rid of *Æsthetic Curiosities*, *Nocturnal Poems*, and *Confessions*. The *Nocturnal Poems* are for the *Revue des deux mondes*: the *Opium Eater* is a new translation of a magnificent author, unknown in Paris. It's for the *Moniteur*. But I had to give some thought to M. Emon (why shouldn't I come out with it all?). He is your friend and I'm anxious not to displease you. Yet can you really imagine that I could forget his inferiority, his brutality, and the churlish way he condescended to shake my hand on that awful day when to please you, and for that reason alone, I humiliated myself even more than you have humiliated me over so many years?

Ancelle is well. I've only seen him twice since you left. He's always absent-minded, always slow to see things, and he still loves his wife and daughter unashamedly. [. . .] When I went to visit my stepfather's tomb

I was very surprised to find myself in front of an empty ditch. I went to the guardian who told me of the transfer and who gave me the enclosed paper as a guide. Your wreaths, spoiled by the heavy rains, had been meticulously taken to the new grave. I added others.

80   To Achille Fould

[20 July 1857]

A copy of my letter to the minister of state, written after I learned of the seizure of *The Flowers of Evil*.

Dear Sir,

The letter I have the honor of addressing to your Excellency is written with the sole aim of expressing my thanks for all the good offices I've received from you and *Le Moniteur*. I'm merely carrying out a duty at a moment when, as a result of an incomprehensible misadventure, I have perhaps caused you some disagreement, a possibility that would deeply distress me.

Le Moniteur published an excellent article on the second volume of the works of Edgar Poe whose very proud translator I am. M. Turgan shed light on the third volume (*Arthur Gordon Pym*), an admirable novel. Finally, *Le Moniteur* printed a marvelous article by Edouard Thierry on a book of mine which is at present the subject of a court case: *The Flowers of Evil*. M. Thierry, with truly praiseworthy prudence, made it clear that this book addresses a very small readership. He praised it merely for the literary qualities he was kind enough to discern in it. And he concluded wonderfully well by saying that despair and grief provided the sole, but sufficient, moral of the book in question.

What do I owe you, Minister? I owe you even more than all those lowly satisfactions of literary vanity. I have long hesitated over thanking you because I didn't know how to go about it. Perhaps M. Pelletier has told you that Mme Aupick, whose husband left her penniless, had, before leaving Paris, spoken to me of the part your Excellency had taken at the Council of State's discussion.[61] I watched my mother write a certain letter of thanks to you, but a stupid shyness prevented me from joining her. Today I'm seizing the opportunity of expressing to you my gratitude for this great and truly personal service.

Yesterday, I had intended to write a form of secret speech in my defence to the Privy Seal but I thought that such an act almost implied guilt and I do not consider myself guilty in the slightest. On the contrary, I'm very proud of having produced a book that expresses only the terror and horror

61. To establish a pension for the widowed Mme Aupick.

aroused by evil. I therefore decided against taking such a step. If I'm forced to defend myself I'll be able to do so fittingly.

And so, Sir, why should I not tell you candidly that I'm requesting your protection as far as it's possible to obtain it. I'm addressing myself to you, whose intelligence even more than your position, makes you the natural protector of literature and the arts. And literature and art, alas, are never sufficiently protected. But do believe that if you cannot grant me your protection I'll still continue to consider myself indebted to you.

81   To Caroline Aupick

27 July 1857

Dear Mother,

You should never accuse me for my delays, particularly in the present case. Ask your library at Honfleur for the edition of *Le Moniteur* dated 14 July and you'll find in it a sumptuous piece in my praise. After which, when I tell you that *M. Abatucci* sought an argument with *M. Fould* about that article, saying to him: "Why do you praise a book I'm prosecuting?" you'll see that I'm the cause of a conflict between three ministers. *M. Fould* is forced to defend me. Will he sacrifice me? That's the nub of the whole question.

M. Billault is so enraged that he forbad *Le Pays* to speak of me. That is completely illegal for I'm not convicted, only accused. I'm to be shown the article M. Billault has illegally prevented from being published.[62] I'll have it printed on galleys in the press of a friend of mine and will send one to *M. Fould*, one to *M. Pietri*, one to the *presiding judge*, one to my *lawyer* (I don't yet have one), and one to *M. Billault* himself.

I have on my side *M. Fould*, *M. Sainte-Beuve* and *M. Mérimée* (who is not only famous as a writer but is the only person to represent literature in the Senate), and *M. Pietri*, who has a lot of power and, like *M. Mérimée*, is a close friend of the emperor. *I need the support of a woman*—I could perhaps find the means to enlist Princess Mathilde but I rack my brains in vain to think up a way. I've appeared before the Judge. I was interrogated by him for 3 hours. Moreover, I found him a very benevolent magistrate. Your copy has been bound. I'll find out how to send it to you without running any risks, for the seizure has gone into effect. The same goes for your prayer book, for I can't entrust the binding to the post office. Don't worry about anything: I've already given the binder some money.

I wanted to hide all this from you. But frankly, that would have been

62. An article by Barbey d'Aurevilly.

absurd. Don't get uselessly worried in your usual fashion. My back is solid enough. Don't confide in M. Emon. You'll understand that my trip to Honfleur has been delayed in a very strange way. Moreover, in spite of all the time this business devours, I must finish 4 volumes: 3rd volume of Edgar Poe, the nocturnal poems (by me), the æsthetic curiosities (by me), and the opium eater (translation of a work by De Quincey). What's more, before the year is out I must write my play and a novel at Honfleur.

Everyone urges me not to say a word at the hearing. They're afraid I'll yield to one of my outbursts of rage. I'm also advised to take a famous lawyer, one who has good relations with the *Minister of State*, someone like M. *Chaix d'Est-Ange*.

Warmest love, and please don't consider this scandal, which is causing a great fuss in Paris, as anything but the foundation of my fortune.

POSTSCRIPT: I needn't tell you that the book is still being sold, but secretly and at twice the normal price.

82   To Apollonie Sabatier

18 August 1857

Dear Madam,

You didn't for a single moment believe that I could forget you, did you? From the instant the book came out I reserved a special copy for you and if its garb is unworthy of you, the fault is not of my making, but of the binder's, whom I'd asked to provide something far finer.

Would you believe that the scoundrels (I mean the judge, the attorney, etc.) have dared condemn among other pieces two poems written for my dear idol ("Tout entière" and "A celle qui est trop gaie")?[63] The latter is the very poem that the venerable Sainte-Beuve declared the best in the volume.

This is the first time I've written to you with my true handwriting. Were I not overwhelmed by business matters and letters (the trial is the day after tomorrow) I'd take advantage of this occasion to beg your forgiveness for so many childish and silly deeds. But anyway, haven't you exacted sufficient revenge, above all through your little sister? Oh, what a little monster! My blood froze when, on meeting us one day, she burst out laughing at me and said: "Are you still in love with my sister, and do you still write her such superb letters?" I realized first that when I wanted to hide I did so very badly, and second that your charming face hid a not

---

63. "Altogether" ("Tout entière") and "To the Woman Who Is Too Joyous" ("A celle qui est trop gaie").

very charitable nature. Rascals are "in love" but poets are "idolaters" and your sister is ill-framed to understand the eternal truths, I feel.

So allow me, at the risk of amusing you, to renew those protestations that so amused that little madcap. Imagine a blend of reverie, sympathy, and respect, together with 1,000 childish deeds, full of seriousness, and you'd have a rough idea of something very sincere that I feel incapable of defining more sharply.

To forget you is beyond my capacities. It is said that there have been poets who have lived out their entire lives with their eyes fixed on a cherished image. I do indeed believe (but I'm too deeply involved) that *faithfulness is a sign of genius*. You're more than an image I dream about and cherish—you are my *superstition*. When I do something particularly stupid, I say to myself: "Oh God, what if she found out about it?" When I do something good, I say to myself: "That's something that brings me closer to her—in spirit!"

And the last time that I had the joy (greatly in spite of myself) of meeting you! For you've no idea how carefully I avoid you! I said to myself: "It'd be a strange thing if this carriage were waiting for her, perhaps I'd better take another route." And then: "Good evening" in that beloved voice whose quality enchants me and tears me asunder. I went away, repeating for the whole length of my journey: "Good evening"— trying to mimic your voice.

I saw my judges last Thursday. I won't say they're not beautiful. They're abominably ugly and their souls must resemble their faces. Flaubert had the empress on his side. I have no woman to support me. And the bizarre idea that perhaps you, through your connections and by using channels that might be complicated, could make a sensible thought penetrate their thick skulls, took hold of me a few days ago.

The hearing is for the morning after tomorrow, Thursday. The monsters' names are:

President	DUPATY
State Advocate	PINARD (dangerous)
Judges	DELESVAUX
	DE PONTON D'AMECOURT
	NACQUART

Sixth Court of Jurisdiction.

I want to put all those trivial matters to one side. Remember that someone thinks of you, that one person's thoughts are never trivial in any way, and that he bears you a little grudge for your malicious *gaiety*.

I beg you most ardently to keep to yourself henceforth everything I confide to you. You are my Companion-in-ordinary, and my secret. It is this intimacy, where I have for so long replied to my own questions, that has made me bold enough to use this very familiar tone with you.

Farewell, dear lady, I kiss your hands with all my devotion.

POSTSCRIPT: All the verses between pages 84 and 105 belong to you.[64]

83   To Gustave Flaubert

25 August 1857

My dear friend,

I'm dashing off this brief note to you before 5, just to show you how sorry I am not to have replied to your friendly greetings. But if you knew what an abyss of infantile occupations I've been plunged into! And my article on *Madame Bovary* postponed yet again for a few days. How deeply a ridiculous adventure can disrupt one's life!

The comedy was played out on Thursday. It lasted a long time. Conclusion: a fine of 300 francs, 200 for the editors, and poems numbers 20, 30, 39, 80, 81, and 87 have been suppressed. I'll write to you at greater length tonight.[65]

All yours, as you know.

84   To Apollonie Sabatier

31 August 1857

I destroyed that torrent of childish outpourings that had accumulated on my desk. I didn't consider it serious enough for you, my dear beloved. I'm taking up your two letters and replying to them anew.

That demands a great deal of courage, for my nerves are horribly on edge, to the point where I feel like screaming and I woke up this morning with the inexplicable sense of moral uneasiness that I brought back with me from your place last night.

[. . .] *absolute lack of modesty.*[66]

That's the reason why you are even dearer to me. It seems to me that I've been yours since the day I first set eyes on you. Do with me what you will,

64. A reference to the poems entitled "Altogether," "What Will You Say Tonight," "The Living Torch," "To the Woman Who Is Too Joyous," "Reversibility," "Confession," "The Dawn of the Spirit," "Evening Harmony," and "The Flask."

65. No such letter has been found.

66. Part of this letter is missing. Mme Sabatier's answer is in *Lettres à Charles Baudelaire*, p. 322.

but I am yours entirely—body, soul, and heart. I urge you to keep this letter well hidden, wretch that you are! Do you really understand what you say? There are people who would imprison those who don't pay their promissory notes—but the promises of friendship and love—no one ever punishes their violation!

So I said to you yesterday: "You'll forget me, you'll betray me; I may amuse you now but later I'll bore you." And today I add: "The only one who will suffer is he who is idiotic enough to take seriously matters of the soul." You see, my most dearly beloved, that I have *odious* prejudices where women are concerned. In a word I have no *faith*. You have a beautiful soul, but when all is said and done it's a woman's soul.

Look at how a few days have been enough to overturn our situation completely. First, we're both possessed by the fear of hurting a nice chap who has the good fortune to be still in love. Then we're afraid of our own storm, since we know (I, above all, know) that there are knots that are hard to untie. And finally, finally, a few days ago you were a goddess— and that was very handy, very beautiful, very inviolable. Now you are a woman. And what if, for my misfortune, I acquire the right to be jealous! It's horrible even to think of it! But with someone like you, whose eyes are full of warmth and grace for everyone, a lover must suffer martyrdom.

Your second letter has a seal whose solemnity would please me if I were really sure you understood it. *Never meet or never part.*[67] That means indisputably that it would be far better never to have met, but once two people have met, they must never part. On a farewell letter that seal would be very droll.

Well, what will be, will be. I'm a bit of a fatalist. But what I do know well is that passion fills me with horror—because I know it, and all the ignominy attached to it—it means that the beloved image that dominated every episode of one's life becomes too seductive.

I hardly dare reread this letter, for that would perhaps force me to change it, since I'm so afraid of causing you pain. I feel I must have revealed something of the vile side of my nature. I don't think I can make you enter that filthy rue Jean-Jacques Rousseau. But I've got a lot of things still to tell you. So you must write and let me know how to contact you.

As for our little project—should it become possible, let me know a few days beforehand. Farewell, dear beloved. I bear you a slight grudge for being too charming. Just think that when I carry off with me the scent of your arms and your hair, I also carry off with me the longing to return. And what an unbearable obsession that is!

67. This sentence is in English.

85   To Apollonie Sabatier

25 September 1857

Dearest friend,

I made a terrible blunder yesterday. Knowing your love of bygones and knickknacks, I'd long had my eye on an inkwell I thought you'd like. But I couldn't pluck up courage to send it to you. One of my friends showed the intention of buying it, and that made my mind up for me. But just think how disappointed I was when I found a worn, cracked, rough-edged object, which had looked so pretty from behind the window. The terrible blunder was this: I gave the salesman neither my card nor a line for you, so that the inkwell must have arrived at your place like a bolt from the blue. Well, the guilty party is me. So don't suspect anyone else. It was only this evening that I realized how silly I'd been.

86   To Empress Eugénie

6 November 1857

Madame,

It demands all the prodigious presumption of a poet to dare draw your Majesty's attention to a case as minor as mine. I had the misfortune to be condemned for a collection of poems entitled *The Flowers of Evil*, since the terrible frankness of my title was not sufficient protection. I thought I was creating a fine work, a great work, above all a work that was clear. It was judged obscure enough for me to be condemned to rework the book and cut out several pieces (6 out of 100). I have to admit that I was treated by my judges with admirable courtesy and that the very terms of the judgment imply a recognition of my lofty and pure intentions. But the fine, swollen by costs that are inexplicable to me, is beyond the faculties of a poet's proverbial poverty and, encouraged by so many proofs of esteem that I've received from friends in very high places, and also convinced that the Empress's heart is open to pity for all tribulations, spiritual as well as material, I have formed the project, after timidly hesitating for 10 days, of calling on the most gracious goodness of your Majesty and begging you to intervene for me with the Minister of Justice.

87   To Caroline Aupick

25 December 1857

My dear Mother,

This afternoon or tonight (alas, if I have the time!) I'll write you a long letter and send you a parcel that I've had ready for you for a long time. I say, if I have time, since for *several months* I've been in one of those terrible bouts of listlessness that disrupt everything. Since the beginning of the month my desk has been piled with proofs I can't find the heart to tackle and there always comes a moment when one must, in great pain, pull oneself out of these abysses of indolence.

These wretched feast days have the advantage of serving as cruel reminders of the swift passage of time and how ill we use it and how full of grief it is! This evening I'll explain how, after resolving to devote myself constantly to you, I've been led to break off abruptly all confidences and if you don't understand me fully, at least you'll admit that I was to some extent excusable.

Solitude, with neither a shred of affection or work, is certainly horrible, but I'm sure, since you have more courage than I, that you bear your solitude better than I bear mine. I'm in such an awful state, spiritually and physically, that I envy everyone else's position.

The parcel I've been keeping for you contains, first, some articles of mine published in the second half of the year (I was again summoned to appear before the public prosecutor for the review of *Madame Bovary*, a book that was taken to court but acquitted); then there is a *sample* of the reviews of *The Flowers of Evil*; this *sample* (for there were so many that finally, equally tired of flattery and of stupid attacks, I didn't even deign to read them) will let you judge the sinister luster shed by this book in which I sought to express some of my sources of anger and melancholy; —finally, the *book itself*, which you so strangely rejected when you thought it right to join your censure to the outrages that were piled on me from all sides.

I wanted to give you as a Christmas present the third volume of Edgar Poe but, as I've confessed, the proofs have been piled up on my desk for a month and I've been unable to shake off this awful weakness.

The copy of *The Flowers of Evil* is my own. I owe it to you because I'd given yours to M. Fould. These are the last two on Holland paper. I'll be able to get hold of an ordinary one. I shudder with indolence at the thought that if this book is to be sold legally I'll have to republish it all over again and write six new poems to replace the six that were censured.

So this evening or at the latest tomorrow morning I'll send you the parcel together with a more detailed letter. I hug you and beg you to be in future full of indulgence, for I swear I have great need of it. If ever a man were ill, with an illness that doesn't concern doctors, I am that man.

88   TO CAROLINE AUPICK

11 January 1858

My dear Mother,

You will have guessed that I'm snowed under by tasks and worries. I never talk to you about them because that would upset you needlessly. Moreover, as if to increase my problems, I now have the greatest difficulty walking, for my right leg is swollen, I can't bend it, and it gives me the most exceptional pain. Some say it's cramp, others that it's a form of neuralgia.

Many thanks for your pharmaceutical recipes. I've put them carefully away and will make use of them. For the rest, my stomach, at least for the moment, is better, thanks to ether, and the colic has been suppressed thanks to opium. But opium has terrible drawbacks.

You tell me to go to you immediately! But you're forgetting all the manuscripts that I have to finish first and all the debts I have to repay. Moreover, as I've told you, there are manuscripts that I can't finish over there. If I were to explain why, it would take me an excessively long time and there'd be no point in it anyway.

I repeat that I've formed the firm resolution of installing myself at Honfleur and hope to do so at the beginning of February. As soon as winter is over, I'll start sending you, one after the other, parcels and chests containing my possessions. I must earn a lot of money if I'm to free myself of Paris. You'd never believe how much I pay in interest, in bailiff's fees, etc. I have neither the heart nor the genius of Balzac and yet I have all the problems that made him unhappy. I'll only pay what is absolutely necessary and I hope that at the last moment the director of *La Gaîté* will arrange a loan of 1,000 or 1,500 francs on the play I've begun writing. That would solve the final questions.

I told some friends about my plan to settle in Honfleur. Every one tells me it's a stroke of genius. It will indeed put an end to all the agitation, all those sterile errands, and will bring the solitude I love so much. Moreover, I hope that if I can earn money in Paris—in the midst of innumerable, nameless torments—5,000 or even 6,000 francs, even though I work so little, I'll earn a lot more in good conditions of tranquillity.

There remain two problems that are difficult to solve. I'll need to make frequent trips to Paris to see theater directors, editors of reviews and newspapers, and to sort out lots of little jobs. This will be expensive, and I'll have to do it regularly, and I believe that the railway officials are unfortunately very mean with free tickets.

Second, I'll cause you at least one expense, that of food, and we'll have to sort out some compensation for that.

So you didn't realize that *The Flowers of Evil* contained two poems about you or at least alluding to intimate details of our former life, at that time of your widowhood that has left me with such strange, sad memories. The first of them is "Je n'ai pas oublié, voisine de la ville" (Neuilly) and the other, which follows it, "La servante au grand cœur" (Mariette).[1] I left these poems without titles and without clear indications because I detest prostituting intimate family matters.

This is horribly scribbled. I didn't notice I was doing it.

89   TO CAROLINE AUPICK
                                              19 February 1858

Dear Mother,

You wrote me a most charming letter (the first in such a tone for many years) some three weeks ago, and I've not yet answered you. You must have been hurt and surprised. For my part, when I read that letter I realized you still loved me, more than I had believed, and that many things could be repaired and that much happiness was still permitted.

In considering various reasons for my silence you may perhaps have lacked indulgence. To tell the truth this perfectly good, motherly letter almost caused me suffering. It hurt me to see how sincerely you wanted me near you and to think that I'd be forced to hurt you because I was not yet ready.

First, I don't have enough faith in Michel Lévy to go away from Paris leaving behind me a book which is currently at the printer's. You know what frightful care I give such matters. I'd be anxious, and with good reason. The book has eight sheets; I'm on the fifth and if I really work I can do the rest in 10 days.

Second, think about the horrible life I lead, which leaves me so little time for work. Think of all the problems I have to solve before leaving (for example, I was forced to lose 6 days at the start of the month, when I had to hide away because I was afraid I'd be arrested. And I'd left my books and manuscripts at home. That's only one of the multiple details of my life.) To have happiness only a step away, almost within my grasp and

1. "I have not forgotten" and "The Maid-Servant."

107

no to be able to seize it! And to know that not only am I to be happy but also that I'll be giving happiness to someone who deserves it!

Add to that cause of suffering this one, that you'll perhaps fail to understand: when a man's nerves are greatly weakened by a morass of worries and sufferings, the devil, despite all resolutions, slips into his brain every morning in the form of this thought: "Why shouldn't I take a day off and forget about everything? Tonight I'll do in a single burst of activity everything that's urgent." And then night falls, the mind is horrified at all the things that are overdue; a crushing sense of sorrow renders you powerless to do anything and the following day it's the same palaver—all in good faith—with the same trust and the same conscience.

I sincerely long to be rid of this accursed city where I've suffered so deeply and where I've lost so much time. Who knows but that my mind may be rejuvenated at Honfleur, in repose and happiness? I have in my head 20 novels and 2 plays. I don't want an honest, commonplace reputation. I want to crush people, astonish them, like Byron, Balzac, or Chateaubriand. Is there still time? Oh, if only I'd known when I was young the value of time, health and money. And those damned *Flowers of Evil* that I have to begin all over again. I need peace of mind for that! To become a poet again, artificially, by an act of will, to get back into harness when you thought your task finally done, to deal yet again with a subject you thought you'd milked dry, and all that just to obey the whim of three stupid magistrates, one of them a *Nacquart*!

I seriously believe, with no exaggeration and no illusions, that by assiduous work in Honfleur I can pay all my debts in two years, that is earn three times as much as here. What a pity you didn't offer me this wonderful arrangement almost a year ago when I wasn't deep in such horrendous problems!

(As far as *The Flowers of Evil* is concerned I want no more praise— you've given me four times as much as I asked for. —I've been asked to provide a complete new edition in Belgium. It's a serious question and I'm not sure what to decide and it's possible that there are drawbacks. The *Revue contemporaine* here has published a new article, a real horror. I'll send it to you. I really fear that I've committed a very wicked act. The *Revue contemporaine*, which is an official publication, committed a serious act with this contradiction of the *Moniteur's* praises. I went to complain to the minister of state and to complete my revenge, I borrowed a few hundred francs from the *Revue contemporaine*, as an advance on some work I'm doing. I feel that my conscience is not entirely clear. It's the first time I've asked for help from people I wanted to hurt. But my excuse lies in my terrible financial difficulties. —And then, finally, to get back to my plans of happiness, I'll be able to *read, read, and read again*! without harming my output. All my days will be spent forging my intelligence anew. For I must confess to you, dear mother, that my ill-starred education was cruelly interrupted by all my follies and all my tribulations. And youth flees and I sometimes think in terror at the flight of the years. Yet they're only made up of hours and minutes. But when we waste time we think only of fractions of time, not of the total.

These are certainly good plans and I don't think they're impracticable, since at Honfleur I'll have no excuse not to put them into practice. I don't want you to think as you read my letter that it's only egoism that drives me on. A great part of my thought is: my mother does not know me, she scarcely knows me at all, we haven't had the time to live together. Yet we must find a few years of happiness in each other's company.

You mentioned Valère again. The first time, a few months ago, I confess I was tempted to mock my mother for seeking nobility in servants, but truly I knew nothing of that disgusting detail—the theft of the jewels. We must avoid having the kind of excessive sensitivity that makes us susceptible to wounds inflicted by the lower classes. You have to be a dupe, to know how to shut your eyes and forget. Farewell, it's 4:30. I embrace you with all my heart. This letter is horribly scribbled. But at least I've scribbled it in large letters thinking that that would tire your eyes less.

90   To Caroline Aupick

26 February 1858

My dear Mother,

The letter I'd awaited in trepidation and which filled me with such sudden joy had the same result as a letter announcing a misfortune. You can gauge how agitated it made me when I tell you I spent two days with almost no sleep at all. Yesterday and the day before I was in such turmoil I couldn't sent you a reply. I was so doubtful of the success of my request that I'd attempted to raise money through a usurer. I was asked for 800 francs per year in interest and only on condition that I repaid the sum monthly or quarterly. I'm only telling you this to give you an idea of how desperately I want to leave. *I've just written to that rogue telling him I don't need his services any more.* I've just sent word to various people whom I want to pay before leaving, telling them that I'll pay them next week.

At last, at last, I've made myself understood! This time, if I fail to take real advantage of this final service, it means that my willpower and intelligence are destroyed and that I'm no longer good for anything. Oh, the time was more than ripe. I'm pinning all my hopes on this new setup. Rest, work, and health. For I believe I'm ill and someone who is ill, even if it's all in his mind, really is ill. What are all these perpetual fears, these moments of breathlessness, these palpitations, above all during my sleep?

Ten days after the money has been put in my hands I'll be in *Honfleur*. I assume you'll receive only three chests—the first to come will be the books. Two objects worry me as they are awkward to pack—my table and my lamp. But I don't want to sell them.

How could you think I'd run the risk of going to see Ancelle before you'd told him what I planned, what you wanted, and what goal I'm pursuing? I'd be willing to bet that even after your letter he'll do everything, not to avoid carrying it out, but to carry it out as slowly as possible. This visit frightens me. I'm convinced I'll have to go and see him several times, which will be a great waste of time—and I have so little time at my disposal! You can have no idea of how many times when, in the past, you were kind enough to send money, he reduced the benefit of it by paying me a little at a time. On each occasion I wasted time and there was a pretty large loss of money, too. You've no idea what a visit to Neuilly is like. It causes me painful worry and wearying uncertainty. And then I sometimes have to spend several hours with him chatting about politics and literature before coming to the point and that when my mind is on other matters. That fine Ancelle has no suspicion how many times I've cursed him.

He'll get the money from whatever source he pleases and I'll give him a receipt stating that I'll only take 50 francs per month until he's repaid me in full. I'm resolved to stick to this—it's more prudent, although at first I had the heroic intention of taking nothing at all.

I believe my accounts (from January 1857) will prove that I'm *in advance* by 400 francs. Truly it's not much over 14 months. [. . .]

I almost forgot the question of lodging. Truly dear mother, you are far too kind in worrying so much over whether I'll be happy. A hole, a veritable hole would do, provided it's clean! How could you imagine I'd have the idea of taking over the dead man's room? You must think me incapable of any delicate thoughts. I'd be most ungrateful if I were not completely satisfied with whatever you offer.

But to tell the truth I've had a question on the tip of my tongue for nearly two months without daring to express it: *Will I see the sea from my room?*[2] If it's not possible, I'll resign myself to the inevitable. Should I buy one or two shelves for my books? My dear, beloved mother, you were probably expecting a really great outburst of joy. But I'll tell you just how grateful I am when I see you, —that'll be much better—and moreover

2. The window overlooked the Seine estuary.

the best way of expressing my gratitude would be by putting these plans into action. One final word, which is not without importance. I absolutely insist that I must have all the money at once to avoid wasting time and so that I can act quickly and by myself. I don't want to have to account for my spending to Ancelle. With you it's a different matter. I'll tell *you*, if you want. That's only fair.

91   To Caroline Aupick
27 February 1858

I've had three days of wonderful joy—that at least is something to be grateful for, since joy comes so rarely. After all, I thank you for it most sincerely. But it was merely an attractive dream. I'm not giving up my plan of going to Honfleur. My desire to do so will increase daily. But I'll go with my own money, and when I've been able to get out of this mess under my own steam.

Please, dear Mother, don't be angry. I'll certainly go, but when? I don't know. I'll do everything I can to bring about this goal. I received your fatal letter this morning. So the letter I sent yesterday, with all its minute recommendations, is rendered null and void. I'm obliged to provide rapidly for the financial difficulties that are about to overcome me. They're even greater than before. For, as I told you, I've arranged to meet several people in the coming week and I've refused money offered by another source. It's enough to drive a man mad.

But however frightening all that may be, it's not yet the worst. Ancelle, to whom you've probably already written, is going to come and assassinate me with his services and when he sees me refuse his money he'll try to help me in spite of myself. He's going to weary me with his hateful conversations. I'm so in need of rest. He'll force his way in here, he'll try to force his way into my affairs, he'll try to force me to tell him my problems. The mere thought of his visit turns my suffering to rage. Seeing me so determined to refuse everything, he'll try to cause me the most suffering he can, always on the pretext of being useful to me. I can't leave Paris to escape him, for the remedy would be worse than the disease. He's going to force himself into my affairs as he did at the hearing during my trial. He forced his way into conversation with my friends, who were completely unknown to him, so wild is he to get to know people and to meddle with everything. And my friends would ask who was this great gentleman who seemed to know me so well. I constantly kept a worried eye on him, afraid that he would compromise or ridicule me. There, I hope, is a fine detail of manners.

So, I beg you, for pity's sake, if you haven't yet written to him, don't write anything at all. If you have written, write him another letter, telling him that your resolution and our agreement must be canceled. I want to live, and I don't want that plague of an Ancelle to steal my time and my peace of mind! —*my peace of mind!*

I'm going to try to numb myself through work. What will happen will happen! I'll keep you up to date about how my project is progressing, that is, if there is any progress. I beg you, dear Mother, don't be annoyed with me for preferring my own hell to an intervention that has always been ruinous to me. The usurer would have been preferable, but it's too late for that.

I hope I can count on you to stop Ancelle getting involved in anything. Rejecting his money gives me the right to reject his services. I've never had very serious quarrels with him and I've never insulted him. That could come to pass: I'd be ashamed and sorry about it, but the harm would have been done already.

Bear in mind that one of my greatest joys in the thought of going to Honfleur was that I'd be escaping him.

I hug you tenderly.

POSTSCRIPT: It didn't occur to you either that supposing I accepted his invitation he would make me lose an awful amount of time, and that coming to an agreement with him would necessitate 50 journeys. Just think of the cataract of problems you've loosed over my head, in thinking you'd give me pleasure. I've just reread your letter and I see the harm has already been done, that Ancelle must have received your letter this morning at the same time as I got mine. To parry the blow I'm going to write to him telling him that I'm staying in Paris and have no need of money. In that way he may perhaps be made to leave me alone. Now I'll renew my promise to do my level best to join you in Honfleur as soon as possible.

POST-POSTSCRIPT: I open my letter for the third time, for two reasons. I know you're going to be hurt when you read this—I beg you not to be annoyed with me. I know what I'm doing. I know that my reasoning is right. I know that I'm right to prefer the worst of torments to the fatigue of seeing Ancelle.

I swear to you that I'll do all I can to go to Honfleur and be free of him. This letter is very sincere, and very clear. All these mishaps upset me. Let's leave this question behind us and do believe that unhappiness and shock have not altered all my good resolutions one jot.

13 May 1858

I've never seen such a gift for imagining catastrophes. And what a bizarre idea to lecture me on the theme that it's in my best interests to go to Honfleur! *I know it is*; but I'm guided by a loftier sentiment. I've never had a change of mind, therefore, so you mustn't sign your letters "your poor mother," or reproach me for writing to you so frequently when I had worries and not writing any more now those worries are gone. All those accusations, dear Mother, are equally unfair. I'm still very worried and I've never changed my mind. I was wrong not to keep you up to date about what I was doing and I was above all wrong not to set off for Honfleur as soon as I got back from Corbeil. It's true that I would have been forced to return to Paris for three or four days when my book[3] came out, but on the other hand I would already have begun that calm life I long for with all my heart. Here's a brief explanation of my delay.

I was naturally held up for a few days when my volume went on sale. After that I was determined to finish my *Opium Eater* in Paris, above all because I wanted to receive the money for it before I left. 1,000 francs from the *Moniteur* (but the *Moniteur's* dragging its feet because the bizarreness of the work horrifies them) or perhaps 600, only 500 perhaps in a small review. There are still a few small sums I want to pay off, so I'm sticking to my plan. To make things worse, M. Mérimée, whose help I needed in this business (and for another more serious matter) was away from Paris—he didn't return from England until yesterday morning.

I have had no change of mind whatsoever. What a bizarre idea of yours that was! As for that other great matter which is even more serious, I beg leave to keep it secret for a few more days. In many cases I don't like you to give me your advice—I like to do things in my own way. I'll make it up to you by telling you of my defeat if I fail.

So as soon as I have fixed up about *Opium* I'll write to you and tell you the date when I'll finally settle in. I wanted to show you that I think of you, so a few days ago I sent you some English books that have been much discussed here, at least among people I know.

So you thought I was badly treated by the *Revue contemporaine*. Those people, dear Mother, are simple idiots, turkeys, brainless numskulls. Moreover, they can't guess what a mass of plans and projects I mull over in my mind. In parentheses I'll add that the *Revue contemporaine* is one of my current bugbears. They frequently send someone to my place to get an article in exchange for the 300 francs I took in advance. I'd have done

3. *Arthur Gordon Pym.*

better to take 1,000 francs in advance—they wouldn't have bothered me so much.

For the last three or four years I've become utterly familiar with such insults. I sometimes send them to you to amuse you—but you don't think as I do. To tell the truth I must admit that all these people who heap abuse on me are in no position to guess how hale and hearty my mind is. In a word, I've hardly shown any indication of what I could really do. How cruel this laziness is! How terrible this tendency to dream! The strength of my thought is for me a painful contrast when I think of how I dawdle to put those thoughts into action. And that's why I must go to Honfleur.

Gustave Flaubert, whose novel you asked me to send, and who has so strangely achieved glory at his first attempt, is a good friend of mine. In the papers we're generally insulted together, although there's no comparison between us. He knows you very well and has often spoken to me about the charming way you received him in Constantinople.[4]

93   TO JEAN-HIPPOLYTE VILLEMESSANT

[9] June 1858

The *Figaro* of 6 June contains an article ("Tomorrow's Men") in which I read: "M. Baudelaire, esquire, is reported to have said on hearing the name of the poet who wrote *Les Contemplations*: 'Hugo! Who's Hugo? That's not a name anyone knows—Hugo?.'"

M. Victor Hugo occupies so high a place that he has no need for anyone's admiration, but a remark that would be a proof of stupidity if it were expressed by your average reader becomes an impossible monstrosity when attributed to me.

Further on, the article's author completes his insinuation in the following terms: "M. Baudelaire, esquire, now spends his time speaking ill of Romanticism and abusing the *Jeunes-France*.[5] The reason behind such an evil action isn't hard to find: it's the pride of the former Jovard that drives Baudelaire today to deny his masters. But all he had to do was hide his flag in his pocket. Was there any need for him to spit on it?"

In simple French that means: "M. Charles Baudelaire is an ungrateful devil who sullies the fame of those whom he considered his masters when he was young." It seems to me that I'm toning the passage down in attempting to translate it. I believe, sir, that the author of this article is a

4. In November 1850 when Flaubert was traveling in the East and General Aupick was a plenipotentiary minister and an envoy for the Republic in Constantinople.
5. Allusion to Gautier's collection of short stories, *Les Jeunes-France*, itself a witty mockery of Romanticism.

young man who does not know yet how to distinguish properly between what is permissable and what is not. He claims that he spies out all my acts: doubtless he does so with the utmost discretion, as I've never set eyes on the man.

The energy the *Figaro* devotes to attacking me could well lead some ill-intentioned people, or people who are as ill-informed about your character as this journalist is about mine, to think that your newspaper hopes to find great indulgence in the law, the day that I ask the tribunal that condemned me to have the goodness to protect me.[6] Take note that where criticism is concerned (I speak of literary criticism) my ideas are so liberal that I even favor abuse of liberty. So if your paper finds ways of taking its criticism of me even further (provided it doesn't accuse me of dishonesty) I'll be able to rejoice as though it didn't concern me.

Sir, I take advantage of this opportunity to tell your readers that all the jokes about my resemblance to the writers of an age that none has succeeded in replacing have filled me with a most justifiable vanity and that my heart is full of gratitude and love for the famous men who have enveloped me in their friendship and advice—those to whom, in a word, I owe everything, as your collaborator so rightly remarks.

94   TO CHARLES-AUGUSTIN SAINTE-BEUVE

14 June 1858

My dear friend,

I've just read your study of *Fanny*.[7] Need I tell you how charming it is and how amazed I am to see a mind that is at once so abounding in health—possessing Herculean health, indeed—and yet has such sharpness, such subtlety, such femininity? (On the subject of femininity, I wanted to obey you and read the Stoic's[8] work. Despite the respect your authority commands, I really would not like to see the suppression of all that is gallant, chivalrous, mystic, and heroic, in a word, all that excess and overflow which is the greatest source of charm, even in honesty.)

In dealing with you, one has to be quite brazen, for you're too sharp for trickery to be other than dangerous. I'll admit then that your article made me dreadfully jealous. There has been so much talk of Loève-Veimars and the service he paid French literature.[9] Will I not find some good soul to say as much of me? How should I pay court to you, my

6. Baudelaire was convinced *Le Figaro* was acting under the instructions of the government in attacking him.
7. A novel by Ernest Feydeau.
8. Proudhon's antifeminist diatribe in *De la justice devant la Révolution*.
9. In translating the works of E. T. A. Hoffmann.

powerful friend, to obtain such a favor? Yet my request is not unjust. Didn't you make such an offer right from the start? Aren't the *Adventures of Pym* the perfect excuse for a *general* survey? You who love to show your prowess at all depths, won't you make a journey into the depths of Poe?

You'll have guessed that my request for this service is linked in my mind to the visit I was going to pay M. Pelletier. When you've money in your pocket and you're going to dine with an old flame you forget everything; but there are days when the insults of all the idiots fill your mind and then you beg help from your old friend Sainte-Beuve. Well, it so happens that these last few days I've been literally dragged through the mud, and (pity me, it's the first time I've lacked dignity) I was weak enough to reply. I know how busy you are and how hard you work for your classes, and all your tasks and duties. But if one didn't occasionally show a little exaggeration in kindliness and in benevolence, where would we find the heroes of benevolence? And if we didn't overdo the praise for the good chaps, how could we console them for the insults of those who want only to damn them too thoroughly?

I'll end by saying as usual that whatever your decision is, it'll be a good one. As ever. I like you even more than I like your books.

95   To Ernest Feydeau

14 June 1858

The very evening I received your book [10] I read it and before morning I'd read it a second time. It's certainly a good book, compact, solid, all its sections well assembled, and it will linger in people's minds. The impression it made on me was so intense that I wrote to you immediately and without caring whether the pleasure of having seen you once at the house of a mutual friend gave me the right to such familiarity, I began a letter full of the impressions of the moment, a real article, which would have swollen to 40 pages if I hadn't stopped at 10, considering it more fitting and discrete simply to thank you for this real gift and all the pleasure it gave me. And then the days went by, always full of worries, and I constantly put off my duty to the following day. I lent my copy and passed it round. I've heard some childish, stupid, bitter discussions and despite the prodigious decency of your book I've heard again the cry of veiled hypocrisy. (Among the enthusiasts there are some people who ask if there's been a special print run, some copies on high-quality paper.) To sum up, you've every right to be proud. You possess astonishing analytical powers. And you give your analysis an expression and a tone that

10. *Fanny.*

are *lyrical*, the natural tone of the man who is high-strung and has nothing to do, the only man who is truly adapted to the experiences of love. The only things of yours I'd read before were some charming prose poems on the *Seasons* and I was far from expecting this most energetic display of an entirely modern talent.

I've taken the book apart, analyzed its structure until I found—or thought I'd found—the method you used to create it. I'm sure nothing has escaped me, neither the art in the thought nor the the the art in the style (the modern forms of elegance, the Parisian scenes, the types of suffering and pleasure experienced by a man of our times).

Contrary to those who complain that your novel violates modesty, I admire the decency of expression which increases the depths of the horror and that excellent art of allowing so much to be guessed. It's truly impossible to give a clearer view of the terrible results of two little things that seem childish and lightweight—love and adultery. And the lover's immense credulity when he thinks he's the husband, and the way he naturally becomes comic just as animals do, without knowing it! But are you aware that the husband, this great Hercules who *wants* to be the strongest in life, and who is indeed the strongest, are you aware that this conqueror has the all-powerful grace of success and that many imaginative readers will love him, preferring him to the other? I'd be curious to know if George Sand has read this little book and what a blow it was to her![11] I feel I'm about to set out on an article again. I'll content myself with asking you to accept all my sympathy. You could not believe it as great as it is.

96   To Auguste Poulet-Malassis

3 November 1858

My dear friend,

I went to see Uncle Beuve last night. He looked in vain for the contract with Charpentier to see exactly what his rights were. So you'll have to have a chat with him when you next come to Paris. When I see you I'll tell you all about this very long conversation. Only three things for the moment: he was greatly struck by your idea of doing portraits. As Charpentier has neglected the sales of his work[12] and as he'll keep the right to continue his edition in his own format, Sainte-Beuve wants to

---

11. Feydeau replied by quoting, with his habitual complacency, the praise George Sand had sent him (*Lettres à Baudelaire*, p. 146).

12. The work in question is Sainte-Beuve's *Historical and Critical Tableau* (*Tableau historique et critique*) of French poetry and theater in the sixteenth century. Malassis wanted to reedit this work but the project fell through.

make up for the disadvantage you'll be at (you'll be selling in competition with him, at a higher price) by creating so to say a completely new edition: he'll make a lot of alterations and will add some new figures, such as Louise Labé. Finally he asked me if your press could allow him to work over the proofs carefully and copiously. You see I'm not the only one with that particular bee in his bonnet.

My dear, you can see therefore that an overture has seriously been made. Now as I'm your friend as much as Sainte-Beuve's friend, I'll say that I'm a little worried on your behalf. Were you aware that if the book were rejuvenated by the writer and perfectly produced you'd have to sell it at three times the cost of Charpentier's volume, and that the only people who'd buy it would be those who didn't already have a copy in their library? When I say three times the cost, I may be exaggerating, but it's inevitably going to be more expensive.

I thought you were angry because I'd slipped into the collection of signed pieces two letters from you in which you were threatening to prosecute me. The truth of the matter is that I thought it would be fun to get you to read them. But after I'd taken the parcel to the post, I reflected that you might think that what I said of certain letters was directed against you. So to make up for that involuntary impertinence, I'm sending you a handwritten letter from Gérard de Nerval. It's not beautiful, but such autographs are rare. It's very wrong to give letters away. I very much hope you won't compromise me and that you won't tell people, "M. Baudelaire has given me a ridiculous letter you sent him under such-and-such a circumstance."

Don't lose the plan for the drawing. We're not in any hurry. You know there's to be a third preface and it's not yet completed. Among the names you mentioned to me the one I prefer is M. Penguilly. I'd thought of Nantueil. I was forgetting something. I said to Sainte-Beuve: "But when Charpentier sees that your work has been improved for Malassis he'll order you to enable him to profit, too, from these improvements, won't he?" He answered that Charpentier, as the seller, has no right to ask for more than he has and that he, Sainte-Beuve, would answer: "The question of taste has changed residence. As far as I'm concerned, taste is treated at another press." Indeed, nothing could be clearer than that. I'm still preparing my new dual installation, for in that way I'll make up for the 16 years of laziness. At rue Beautreillis and at Honfleur. I've been to see the place. It's perched above the sea and the garden itself is like a theater backcloth. It's all designed to astonish the eyes. Just what the doctor ordered. Meanwhile, I'll be at quai Voltaire for another week.

10 November 1858

Dear Sir,

Although I've once again kept you waiting longer than I should, I'm not absolutely discontented with myself. I'll be with you tomorrow evening or the morning of the following day. *Opium* can come out on 30 November.[13]

I assure you it was no easy task to fit into such a small space the description of a very complex book without omitting any of its subtleties. You'll see that for yourself—the tone is different from that of *Hashish*; it appears to be more free-wheeling, more abrupt. The biographical details take up a fair space but they're not merely entertaining, but also essential in providing a key to the utterly individual phantasmagoria of *Opium*. Let's hope that M. de Quincey will send the paper a fine letter of thanks.

POSTSCRIPT: I've begun work on your painters. With your approval I'll call it *The Painters Who Think*. That'll provide the little hint of irony which will give the title its spice. As far as your friend M. Janmot[14] is concerned, I'll do it ad hoc, using my memory and his little book of verse, and if later we discover there are things in need of verification I'll go to Lyon.

I've begun work on the *Nocturnal Poems*. I've started on the new *Flowers of Evil*, but I won't give you any poems until there are enough to fill a sheet. The Tribunal demands only that six be replaced. I may well do 20. The Protestant professors will see to their grief that I'm an incorrigible Catholic. I'll pitch it so I'm properly understood—sometimes very low and sometimes very high. Thanks to this method I'll be able to sink to the most ignoble passion. Only people who are acting in utter bad faith will fail to understand the deliberate impersonality of my poems.

As far as the vagabondage that's made me undertake three things at once is concerned, don't worry about it. There is a method in it. I may ask your permission to include in *The Painters Who Think* an appreciation of *Humorous Sonnets* [*Sonnets humoristiques*].[15] All these Lyonnais are alike. I've known Lyon. Painters, poets, philosophers, they're all much of a muchness.

13. The adaptation of De Quincey's *Confessions* was not published until January 1860.

14. Janmot is mentioned in the unfinished *Philosophical Art* as marked from youth by Lyonnais bigotry.

15. Joséphin Soulary's collection of poems.

11 December 1858

My dear Mother,

I'm sending you another parcel, for all my delays don't mean that I've abandoned my goal. Don't write to me, or if you do, send it to 22 rue Beautreillis. The thing is, I may be at Alençon when your letter comes. Tomorrow I'll be taking the last of my bits and pieces from the hôtel Voltaire. I've still got four things to send off to you, and I'll have them packed in crates and wraps after my very brief stay at Alençon.

My *Opium* is causing me a lot of worry. I have the feeling that what I've done is awful. It's hardly worth getting to know the poisons if I can't draw more talent out of that knowledge. You've received Michelet's *Love* [*L'Amour*]—an *immense success*, among women: I haven't read it but I think I can guess that it's a disgusting book. *Fanny*, an *immense success*, is a disgusting book, an absolutely disgusting book. As for the *Humorous Sonnets*, now there's a charming work. If I have a little money left over, I'll bring you some New Year's gifts.

99   To Alphonse de Calonne

8 January 1859

Dear Sir,

I have a big, big favor to ask of you—please believe that I feel no embarrassment about this at all, for our relationship is by now sufficiently close for that.

The first advance you made me has been more than repaid by the *Hashish*. The second advance is all but repaid by what I sent you from the *Opium* manuscript, which is to act as a pair to the *Hashish*, —and more than repaid if you add the price of the poems I've given you. So I have every right to think you trust me enough to allow me to request a third advance, but this time a large one: a *monstrum ingens*: 1,000 francs, which may well suffice to help me flee Paris. Are you fully aware of the fact that I've been determinedly sticking to that project for a year now? I'm horribly bored, all my time is whittled away in a mass of empty errands, to the point where I really fear I can only give birth to the last pages of *Opium* at Honfleur, in the little spot I mentioned to you.

I'm aware that this is a pretty awkward habit of mine—that of taking money in advance and then paying it back through work, but it's what I've always done, with Malassis, with Lévy, and with all the journals. And, too, I'm truly very impatient to be off; Mme Aupick expects me, and as it would be wrong to upset an old and lonely woman I hide from her my problems and the reasons for my delay.

As you know, after *Opium* it'll be the *Idealist Painters* [*Les Peintres idéalistes*]. You already know the general thesis. The age is mad and talks nonsense in all areas, but above all where art is concerned, because of the *heretical* confusion between good and beauty. Everyone who seeks the pure ideal where art is concerned is regarded as a heretic in the eyes of the Muse and of Art. So I'll speak of the idealist painters as if they were ill; sometimes they reveal genius, but it is a genius that is ailing, etc., etc.

After the *painters*, no more general articles, never again, never, neither for gold nor for silver. Nothing but novels or poems. As regards novels, since I'm writing to you completely openly, allow me to make a few brief remarks. I could renew here my eternal thesis: the goal of moral teaching is goodness, that of learning is truth, but poetry and sometimes the novel have beauty as their unique goal. Any man who cannot devote his faculties to these corresponding goals is neither a philosopher nor an artist: now sometimes I see you rather tired and that freezes my very blood. If I saw that you were leaning more to boldness and innovation, if I felt more supported and protected by you, I'd be able to give you a series of really surprising short stories that would be neither in Balzac's manner, nor in that of Hoffmann, nor Gautier nor even Poe, who is the best of them all.

When we're at a certain stage—I warn you in advance—I'll demand of your benevolence that our contract be renewed. Two hundred fifty francs is not enough for a brain that gives birth only with the aid of forceps. A mind that depends on combinations and analysis is the slowest of all and it's always discontented with itself. I am one of those (and we're very rare) who believe that every literary composition, even a piece of criticism, must be created and composed with the conclusion constantly in mind. Everything, even a sonnet! Just imagine what a struggle that entails!

I think I've told you everything. I'll never become rich and I'll never possess my full talent until I have solitude. Before turning to you (I'm referring to the advance, which may throw your accounts out) I thought of turning to one of the government ministers who dispose of money for art. But although I've been highly cautious in that regard (I've only used it two or three times and then only in the last few years), I must point out to you first that there are writers even poorer than I am, second that there are *delays*, and finally to put it quite crudely, the ministers are poor.

When one asks a favor from a friend, one must thank him for earlier services. This provides me with a marvelous opportunity to thank you, not only for your helpfulness but also for all the good literary connections you've drawn on to assist me. When I had the idea of writing to the *Revue contemporaine* at the same time as you invited me to do so, several people predicted I'd run into problems and numerous worries. Well, it's not without its humorous side that the author of *The Flowers of Evil* himself was granted in a progovernment review a freedom of expression that was greater than he'd encountered anywhere else. You'll grant me greater liberty still, won't you? Oof, what a long letter! A wasted manuscript. All yours and my respects to Mme Calonne.

100   To Alphonse de Calonne

11 February 1859

Dear Director,

1. The envelope I'm sending back to you certifies that if you don't receive this packet until the 12th the reason is that your own packet didn't leave Paris until the 10th. Will there be time?

2. You'll cause me *very intense grief* if you cut out the dedication[16] again. The same postman who delivered your letter gave me one from M. Christophe announcing not only his skeleton, but an additional little statue much nearer completion. Truly the least I can do to thank him is to inscribe his name at the head of a little poem. You can rest assured that M. Christophe is a more than distinguished man whose name cannot compromise your review. He is the creator of the figure of *Grief* (at the World Fair) and of an excellent statue for the courtyard of the Louvre.

3. First stanza. I'll remove the masculine adjective (which referred to the absent word 'squelette') and substitute a feminine which will be instantly comprehensible.

Twelfth stanza. You've chosen a bad variant. First, the stanza above has the line: "Gulf of your eyes full of terrible thoughts." So "Eyes full of horror" is a repetition. I'll look as if I have no imagination. *Gouge* is an excellent word, a unique word, belonging to the language of the past and applicable to a Dance of Death as it dates from the time of the dances of death. UNITY OF STYLE. Originally "a beautiful *gouge*" meant simply "a beautiful woman." Then the *gouge* was a prostitute who followed the army in the days when neither the soldier nor the priest marched without a rear guard of prostitutes. There were even regulations controlling these mobile pleasure machines. Now, isn't Death the *Gouge* that follows the Great Army of Man, wherever it goes, and isn't she the prostitute whose embraces are literally irresistible? Tone, antithesis, metaphor—everything is exact. How could your critical sense, usually so clear, have failed to guess my intentions at this point?

16. The dedication to Baudelaire's sonnet "Dance of Death" is to Ernest Christophe, the sculptor whose statue inspired it.

I draw your attention to *Lovelaces*. If it's a noun, it needs a small "l" and a final "s." If it's a proper name that we occasionally use in a generic sense, a capital "L" and no "s," according to the rule. Generally speaking Lovelace is almost a conversational noun, so I plump for the lower case and the plural.

The dance of death is not a person but an allegory. It seems to me that it should have no capital letters. An extremely well-known allegory meaning: the way of the world leads to death.

You tell me all is going well. All the better, for I've met people who want it not to go at all. Greetings to M. Hervé and my friendly regards to Mme de Calonne.

I'm working for you.

POSTSCRIPT: No need to put *Christophe* in the list of contents. All that was badly punctuated.

101   To Charles-Augustin Sainte-Beuve

21 February 1859

Dear friend,

I don't know if you subscribe to the *Revue française*, but the fear that you do read it prompts me to protest against a certain comment (concerning *The Flowers of Evil*) on p. 181 where the author, who nevertheless has plenty of intelligence, commits a few injustices concerning you.[17] Once a newspaper accused me of ingratitude toward the leaders of the old Romanticism, the *movement to which I owe everything*, as this infamous rag added—though in that at least it was accurate. This time as I read that wretched comment I said to myself: "Damnation! Sainte-Beuve, who knows how faithful I am, but who is aware of my links with the author, will perhaps think me capable of ghosting this passage." It's the complete opposite that's true—I've many a time argued with Babou to convince him that you always did all that you could or should do.

Only a short while ago I was talking to Malassis of the great friendship between us. It's a friendship that brings me much honor and I owe that friendship much good advice. The monster wouldn't leave me alone until I gave him the long letter you sent me at the time of the trial and which may perhaps provide the basis for the preface.

I've created some more *flowers*, which are passing strange. Here, where all is tranquil, my inspiration has returned. One of these (*The Dance of Death*) was to appear on the 15th in the *Revue contemporaine*, for, partly

---

17. In the *Revue française* of 20 February the critic H. Babou attacked Sainte-Beuve for glorifying *Fanny* but ignoring *Flowers of Evil*.

123

because of my contract and partly through a kind of heroic dandyism, I've stayed loyal to the defeated.[18] If you have any news either on Calonne's position or on the progress of the new review, I'd be very grateful to hear it. I don't know if you've been consulted and what you think about it. I feel that Old Buloz must have been delighted and that where literature is concerned, monarchy is the best solution. Sooner someone off the street than a committee. I'm chattering on like a man who has no one to talk to. Forgive me. I haven't forgotten your Coleridge, but I've been a month without receiving my books and to skim through the 2,400 pages of Poe is a bit of a task.[19]

102   TO THÉOPHILE GAUTIER, JR.

27 February 1859

Dear friend,

Do me a favor. The article on your father has been completed for three weeks and I was still expecting the proofs this morning. I've discovered that they're awaiting your father's return to consult him: they are all mad. Théophile said to me before he left: "I have complete confidence in you. Everything you say will be *fine*. If you need any precise details, ask my son." Moreover, Mlle Grisi[20] tells me Théophile would have been delighted to receive the article at Saint Petersburg.

So it's precisely because I've dragged my heels over this that we must now profit from Théophile's long absence to send him the article in Russia. It seems to me that I've enough wit and friendship not to do anything unsuitable. It was all written in great heat and at top speed. That's another reason why I must revise it all (and all together) with great care. Go and see Ducessois and Arsène[21] then, since (and this I've heard this very morning) L'Artiste's star has entered into the zodiacal sign of Arsène. In truth there's only one thing missing and that would be for the new editorial staff to cause me problems now that I've taken such pains over it! I'll just add that it's *essential* that *everything* be published at once, however many columns it runs to. The article was conceived and written with that aim in mind.

If you see Mlle Grisi show her my letter.

POSTSCRIPT: This is all very tedious. First I put myself into a frame of mind that I'll probably have lost when the proofs arrive. Moreover, if I

18. The government had supported the *Revue européenne* against Calonne's paper, the *Revue contemporaine*.
19. Sainte-Beuve must have asked Baudelaire if Poe had written on Coleridge.
20. Ernesta Grisi, Gautier's companion.
21. Arsène Houssaye, editor of *L'Artiste*.

gave it my all, it wasn't just to be agreeable to Théo, but also to satisfy my own vanity. Finally, I'm not really sure why, but it seems to me that Arsène isn't particularly well disposed to me or to your father. Therefore, he's got no desire to be agreeable to me.

Another problem: please check personally that all the sheets are consecutive. Here's an extract from Asselineau's letter: "I've been told that you were eager for your proofs to be sent to Théophile, who, they say, won't be back until April." I wrote that to Ducessois at a time when I thought Théo had already returned. "The gentlemen have decided to set that motion aside but will send the proofs to Gautier's son." That's what I was planning to do. "Moreover, I've heard that Arsène has decided to make the publication of your article coincide with Théophile's return." Absurd!

103   TO AUGUSTE POULET-MALASSIS

[28 February 1859]

So, you sniffed out the Sainte-Beuve-Babou business! A few days ago I received a *frightful* letter from Sainte-Beuve. It seems the blow really knocked him sideways. I have to give him this, however, that he never believed I'd have ghosted such an article for Babou. I told him that the compliments and advice he'd given me at the time of my trial were in your hands, and that we'd thought of using them as a base (to be developed) for a preface to the second edition.

Either Babou wanted to help me (which implies a certain degree of stupidity); or he wanted to play a trick on me; or he wanted, without giving a thought to what was in my interest, to pursue some kind of strange revenge. I informed Asselineau of my discontent and he told me that I had no cause for complaint since it brought me a long letter from Uncle Beuve. [. . .]

You can see how this Babou affair could cause me problems, particularly if you look at it in relationship to the ignoble article in *Le Figaro* where it was stated that *I spent my life mocking the leaders of Romanticism, to whom, moreover, I owed everything.* [. . .]

104   TO AUGUSTE POULET-MALASSIS

1 May 1859

First of all, warmest thanks for your punctuality and your kindness. The *Gautier*. I don't want to abandon my plan of a portrait. Either de Broise can run off straightaway the frontispieces he'll need later, or the frontispiece of my brochure can be like that of *Enamels and Cameos*

125

[*Emaux et Camées*].[22] But how does one make proofs for prints of several colors? Can't one cover with some foreign matter (that can be removed later) those parts one doesn't wish to reproduce? There must be a way, but I've no skill in the matter. Afterwards, we'll do the title in bizarre letters. In a word there'll be two runs, as for the red and black ornaments.

The portrait will guarantee sales.

The two epigraphs are to be seen as antithetical[23] and it's clear to me that virtuous, pedantic Laprade has read *L'Artiste*. A very small size of letter could solve our problems here. The idea of the verso is not completely detestable. When will I receive the proofs? There are errors in *L'Artiste*'s version.

Opium and Hashish. An attractive little book. I'm counting on it to get me back into circulation a little. You'll be satisfied with the *Opium*. It'll be brilliant and dramatic. In total it will be 80 pages of the *Revue contemporaine*. I'm sure it will sell.

Calonne will come round. I know he will, but I can't tell you why. I can't forget your 3,000 francs.[24] This is my situation: I still owe him his 500 francs, less the money for *Dance of Death*, 45 francs. His *Opium* (which I'm currently rereading) has been delivered and will now provide you with a series of payments. It was for your sake that I made him promise that if I gave him two good short stories in June and July—published or not—he would pay me for them immediately either in silver or in notes. Do you take me for an ingrate or a fool? He won't have any more poetry. You tell me you've reread my poems. You'd have done better to have reread Edgar Poe's *Philosophy of Composition*. Your letter caused me much pain. I can see that your changeable mind experiences the whole range of temperatures. If I could dash off to Alençon, I'd go immediately, not merely for a little fun, but to shake you. You're wrapped up in your political brochures and you forget that it's part of human nature always to spend 5 francs to buy a novel or a theater ticket. So I'm not thanking you in the slightest for the honor you're kind enough to pay me in making an exception for my books. My *Flowers of Evil* will remain; my critical articles will sell, perhaps less swiftly than at a better time, but they will sell. Even if the war moves from Italy[25] to the Rhine men will want to read theories of literature, and novels. And it's above all when the nation goes mad that there's a benefit, a great benefit that must

22. Gautier's best-known collection of poems.

23. The first epigraph, the only one to be published, is from Gautier's *Caprices and Zigzags*. The second was an attack on Victor de Laprade, a minor poet much read at the time.

24. The amount Baudelaire owed Poulet-Malassis.

25. The war initiated by Napoleon III to liberate Lombardy from Austrian rule.

not be lost. In complete contrast to you, *I'm afraid, for you, because of your neglect of matters literary*. Of the 80 pages of the *Revue contemporaine* we should make if possible 250 pages. You're always telling me of your debts. I'm convinced that with a little ingenuity you could resolve your difficulties. But I don't know enough about your affairs to advise you. Write to me less sadly if you can, and always be friendly. My regards to your family. M. Mistral, the author of *Mirèio*, is a poet writing in *patois*, whose mahout is Adolphe Dumas.[26] The ne'er-do-well[27] regrets that Mistral is not completely wild. He was grieved to see that M. Mistral, through his commentaries, proved that he knew French. Moreover, this jargon-monger is our current star. I expect a note from you. Make sure the characters are as widely spaced as possible and that you use the widest possible margins.

105   TO NADAR

14 May 1859

My dear Nadar,

I'm like a soul in torment. I carelessly let my mother set off on a short journey without asking her for money and I'm here on my own, lacking neither butcher's meat nor bread, etc., but completely penniless and for that reason exposed to countless little problems. I thought that if it wasn't a complete nuisance to you you might be charitable enough to send me (immediately, alas!) a postal check for 20 francs. I'd return the money on the 1st of the month, if you consent not to laugh too much at that promise. Indeed, I'm obliged to return to Paris at that time. I can have your reply tomorrow morning if you're kind enough to think of me before 5 o'clock. Charles Baudelaire, Honfleur, Calvados: that's all the address you need.

To give you an idea of my difficulties, which alone can justify so ridiculous a request, let me tell you that I *need* to spend a few hours at Le Havre (don't go and imagine that it's for a debauch) and can't do so because I don't have the money.

2

There is a cafe here that, by some unlikely chance, gets *your* newspaper[28] so that I had the pleasure of seeing a whole procession of follies, injustices, caresses bestowed on fools, in a word, all the bizarre behavior

26. A pioneer of the revival of interest in Provençal language and literature.
27. Nickname for Barbey d'Aurevilly.
28. Nadar was at this time editor of the *Journal pour rire*.

that makes up the exceptional nature of Nadar. Recently, when you were mocking those who had or have a passionate love of cats, you confused Poe with Hoffmann. Note that there are no *cats* in Poe, apart from one whose eye is torn out and who is then hanged, and whose successor, which is also one-eyed, serves to reveal a crime.[29] More recently still, I don't know why, you took it into your head in connection with a Belgian or Polish poet to throw an unpleasant word at me. I dislike passing for the Prince of Corpses. You've probably been spared reading a mass of things about me which are nothing but musk and roses. After that, you're probably mad enough to say to yourself: "I'll give him a great deal of pleasure!"

3

If you were an angel, you'd go and pay homage to a certain Moreau, a picture seller, rue Laffitte, hôtel Laffitte. (I'm certainly determined to pay him homage myself concerning a general study I'm preparing on Spanish painting.) And you'd get from him permission to make a beautiful double photographic copy of the *Duchess of Alba*,[30] by Goya (vintage Goya, utterly authentic). The copies (life-size) are in Spain, where Gautier saw them. In one of the frames, the Duchess is wearing national costume, and in the counterpart she's naked, in the same position, lying flat on her back. The very vulgarity of the pose increases the charm of the paintings. If I were ever to consent to using your horrible jargon, I'd say that the Duchess is a bizarre lay; she looks angry, her hair is like Silvestre's, and her breasts, which hide her armpits, have a squint which is simultaneously crossed and divergent. If you were a very rich angel I'd advise you to buy them—it's a chance that won't arise again. Imagine a gallant or ferocious Bonington or Devéria. The owner is asking 2,400. It's certainly not much for an art-lover mad about Spanish painting, but it's also enormous compared with what he paid for them. For he confessed to me that he bought them from Goya's son, who was in great financial difficulties. If you tell this man that you want to make several copies he'll be afraid to give you permission, precisely because your name is so well known. Moreover, since the beauty of Goya's work is generally little appreciated, you'd be well advised to make only two copies, one for you, one for me. If you decide to do so, don't make them too small. That would destroy some of the flavor.

29. The tale in question is "The Black Cat." Hoffmann's novel *Kater Murr* intersperses the autobiography of a cat with the story of the musician Kreisler.
30. Baudelaire is thinking of the twin portraits of *La Maja vestida* and *La Maja desnuda*. The subject is not the duchess but a prostitute.

What I find particularly disagreeable in writing all this is that you're going to laugh like a maniac when you read all these recommendations. But I've not yet finished.

4

Who, then, is a certain German artist who did a certain miraculous or fantastic hunt scene on sale at Goupil's? Everyone advises me to approach him. I don't want Malassis's eternal friend Duveau for the frontispieces I need for my Poe articles (a portrait wreathed in emblems), my *Opium and Hashish*, my new *Flowers*, my *Curiosities*.

You'd make my happiness complete if, drawing on your numerous connections, you could unearth some biographical information on Alfred Rethel, author of *The Dance of Death in 1848* [*La Danse des morts en 1848*] or *The Good Death* [*La Bonne Mort*], which acts as a counterpart to *The First Invasion of Cholera at the Opera* [*La Première Invasion du choléra à l'Opéra*]. Do you know Knaus? He must know something about this.

I'm really in torment. Before publishing my *Curiosities* I'm still doing some articles on painting (the last!) and I'm currently writing a *Salon* without having seen it. But I have a catalog. Apart from the difficulty of guessing what the paintings are like, it's a first-class method and I recommend it to you. It means you're afraid to praise or blame too much so it makes you impartial. Do I need to tell you that of all these recommendations, the most urgent concerns the check?

5

I beg you, dear friend, don't scribble any farcical suggestions—as you used to in the past—on the envelope of your letter. All yours and forgive me for bothering you in your terrible routine.

106   To Nadar

16 May 1859

My dear friend,

Since you're not one of those who poke fun at long letters, you'll get your money's worth, for I've two hours of leisure before me. First of all, my thanks, not just for the 20 francs, but above all for an *excellent, charming sentence in your letter*. Now that's true friendship. I'm not much accustomed to displays of affection. As for your compliments, my vanity takes advantage of them to encourage you to read a few pieces that you've probably not yet read and which, with a few other unpublished articles, will, I hope, breathe new life into my wilting *Flowers*. They'll show you how little attention I pay to the critics and how much I sink pigheadedly into my state of *unpolishability*.

Now, back to my letter.

If the poems of M. Karski (have I got that right?) are really fine, you ought to get a copy for me, but if I've understood correctly they're not for sale in Paris. Yes, for my sake I hope you succeed in the Moreau affair, but I'm also convinced that it would be equally pleasant for you to have good proofs based on those extraordinary paintings.

So you don't know those wood engravings based on Rethel's drawings? The *Dance of Death in 1848* is now on sale for 1 franc (6 sheets). *The Good Death* and *The Invasion of Cholera* cost, I think, 7 francs. You can get them through a German bookseller who also sells German prints, rue de Rivoli, near Palais-Royal. Some people have told me that Rethel has decorated a church (perhaps at Cologne); others say he's dead; others that he's been put into a madhouse. I possess the works mentioned above and would like to know, in addition to the biographical information, if there are any other prints.

The German artist whose name is unknown to me was drawn to my attention by Ricard, who claims he has just the right sort of talent for illustrations and frontispieces. We'd need to see this *Hunt*.

Yes, I had indeed thought of Doré, and can't remember if it was I who on reflection rejected him because of the childishness that can so often be glimpsed through his genius, or whether we rejected him because Malassis feels antipathetic toward him. Again, I'm not sure if I'm right in making that final suggestion.

The various books and pamphlets I'll be ready to publish soon are: all the critical articles on Poe; (with these a portrait [I'll be responsible for providing what's needed for the portrait] framed in allegorical figures representing his main ideas—rather like Jesus Christ surrounded by the elements of the passion)—all in wildly Romantic style, if possible;

—*Opium and Hashish*: an allegorical frontispiece expressing the main pleasures and torments I've related;

—all my critical articles on literature and the fine arts. I believe Malassis doesn't want a frontispiece for these;

—The second edition of *Flowers of Evil*. For this I want a skeleton turning into a tree, with legs and ribs forming the trunk, the arms stretched out to make a cross and bursting into leaves and buds, protecting several rows of poisonous plants in little pots, lined up as if in a gardener's hothouse. This idea came to me when I was leafing through Hyacinthe Langlois's history of the *Dance of Death* theme.

To return to Doré. He has a remarkable talent for giving clouds, countrysides, and houses a positively supernatural aura. That side of his talent would be perfect for what I need: but the figures! There's always something childish even in his best drawings. As for the *Divine Comedy*, you really surprise me! How could he have chosen the saddest and most serious of poets? Moreover, you'll have noticed that I want to return to the ancient form of frontispiece, but treated in an ultraromantic way.

Finally, to confess all, among the names I've mulled over, I was above all attracted to those of Penguilly and Nanteuil. But I don't know if Penguilly would agree, and as for Nanteuil, I'm afraid he's watered his wine a great deal and won't be able to find anew the element of exaggeration that he used in days gone by for the benefit of Victor Hugo. Nevertheless, those two names had what I considered the great advantage of offering a Romantic meaning in perfect harmony with my tastes and corresponding in its brashness to the ingratitude and neglect of the age.

But most important of all, it doesn't suit me to visit a distinguished artist and engage him to perform a little piece of work for which I'll be particularly demanding, before I'm sure he'll be decently paid for it. With these reservations in mind, if you can give me information without committing me, I'd be most grateful.

As for the *Salon*, alas, I lied to you a little, but only a little! I have visited it, but only once, when I devoted my time to seeking out new things, but I found very little. And for all the old names, or the names that are just known, I'll trust my old memory, stimulated by the catalog. This method is not, I repeat, bad, provided one has a good knowledge of the cast.

Among other really remarkable things that no one will notice, don't miss two little paintings in a large, square room, right at the back at the left, among heaps of worthless religious things. One of them, no. 1,215, *The Sisters of Charity* [*Les Sœurs de charité*], by Armand Gautier. The other, no. 1,894, *The Angelus* [*L'Angélus*], by Alphonse Legros. This one isn't a particularly lofty style but it's particularly searching.

Among the sculptures, I also found (in one of the alleys in the Garden, not far from the exit) something that could be called "Romantic Vignette sculpture," and which is very attractive. A young girl and a skeleton rising up like an Assumption. The skeleton is embracing the girl. To be exact I should say that the skeleton is partly sketched out and enveloped in a shroud that allows the viewer to guess its shape.

Would you believe that I've already read three times, line by line, the whole of the catalog for the sculpture section and that I'm completely unable to find anything at all corresponding to that piece? Truly the wretch who made that lovely statue must have called it *Love and Fricassee* or some completely unconnected title, in the style of Compte Calix, for me to be unable to find it in the catalog. Do try to find out for me: the subject and the sculptor's name.

Concerning the two portraits of the Duchess of Alba, I repeat, if you weren't in great financial difficulty, it would be good to seize them at a low price.

Since you thought it fitting to throw a little politics into the end of your letter, I'll do likewise. I've convinced myself twenty times that I'm not interested in politics anymore, yet every time a serious matter arises, I'm seized yet again with passion and curiosity. I've long been watching and expecting this Italian question to surface. Long before the Orsini adventure. And on that head, it would be unjust to say that Napoléon is executing Orsini's testament. Orsini was an honest man, in too much of a hurry. But the Emperor had been thinking of the matter for a long time and had made various promises to all the Italians who came to Paris. I admire the docile way he obeys fate, but that very fate saves him. Who, today, still thinks of Morny and the Grand Central, or of Beaumont-Vassy and of the 40,000 dirty tricks that occupied our thoughts such a short time ago? [31] Now the Emperor has been washed clean. You'll see, my dear friend, that the horrors committed in December will be forgotten. In a word, he's stolen from the Republic the honors a great war should have brought it. Have you read the admirable speech Jules Favre [32] made at the Legislature in the last days of last month, or in the first days of May? He expressed with great clarity the revolutionary necessity, the revolutionary fatality. The president and the ministers let him speak without interruption. He seemed to be speaking in the name of the Emperor. And when, in reference to Garibaldi, a certain vicount de la Tour, a stupid, bigoted Breton, declared that France very much hoped not to dirty itself through such alliances, President Schneider stopped him, saying that a deputy had no right to slander the allies of France, wherever they may come from.

Politics, dear friend, is a heartless science. That's what you refuse to recognize. If you were a Jesuit or a Revolutionary, as every true politician should be, or is forced to be, you'd not feel such regrets for friends thrown aside. I know I horrify you, but tell me, did you even notice just how appropriate was the publication by M. de Cavour of the *Diplomatic Letters of Joseph de Maistre* [*Lettres diplomatiques de Joseph de Maistre*], letters in which, be it said in passing, the pope is treated as a puppet? What an

31. Monry and Beaumont-Vassey were both involved in scandalous speculations.

32. Jules Favre, who had acted as lawyer for Napoleon III's would-be assassin, Orsini, was elected deputy of Paris in 1858. He was the most remarkable representative of the Republican Party.

indictment of Austria. Piedmont kept those letters in reserve and launched them at the right moment.

I only believe that the best that can happen is that, if the Emperor is covered with glory and universally acclaimed, the problem will be finding a use for the victory.[33]

For all your personal disappointments, dear friend, resign yourself, resign yourself.

When I visit you, I'll tell you about my own disappointments, which pile up one on the other, and you'll pity me. I sincerely believe that with the exception of a small number of young men, intelligent, rich (and *without families*!), who don't know what to do with their good fortune, life must be perpetual suffering.

All yours.

POSTSCRIPT: Now, if you want a laugh, read, as I did, Limayrac, Vitu, and Granier de Cassagnac. It seems we're off to Italy to quell the revolutionary monster. Now there, to talk seriously, is an example of useless hypocrisy.

107   TO EUGÈNE CRÉPET
4 August 1859

My dear Crépet,

I've finished your seven articles, all conceived in the style and following the method requested.[34] As you know, I had promised to wait for you, but I learn that you'll be absent for another eight days or so. So I'm requesting your permission to ask M. Gide[35] to pay me for the articles. Altogether they make up, as far as I can tell, slightly more than a sheet. Be kind enough to send me a note that will allow me to present myself to him. I would have waited for your return, were I not being pestered for an amount, half of which would be covered by this manuscript. So this would give me a brief respite. I'll leave the manuscript with M. Gide and on your return we'll collect it to read together. It's true that we've already discussed all this. Please don't see in my letter anything but a sign of deference toward you. How kind you'd be to let me have your reply on the day after tomorrow, the 6th! It is possible.

33. The end of the Italian war was indeed to pose problems for Napoleon III. Not only did it make an enemy of Piedmont, but the clergy and those who followed them withdrew support for the government.

34. These are the reviews of contemporary writers that Baudelaire was preparing for Crépet's collection *The French Poets* (*Les Poètes français*).

35. The publisher of *The French Poets*.

[23?] September 1859

Dear Sir,

I have the greatest need of you and implore your kindness. A few months ago I wrote a fairly long article about my friend Théophile Gautier. This article sparked off such a shout of laughter from the idiots that I thought it would be a good idea to turn it into a little pamphlet, if only to prove that I never repent. I'd asked the people at the paper to send you a copy of the relevant number. I don't know whether you received it but I learned through our mutual friend M. Paul Meurice that you'd been good enough to write me a letter, which hasn't yet been found, since *L'Artiste* took it into their heads to send it to an address I left long since, instead of redirecting it to Honfleur, my real home, where nothing goes astray. I can't possibly guess whether your letter explicitly mentioned the article in question but whatever the facts were I bitterly regret its loss. A letter from you, sir, whom none of us here have set eyes on for such a long time,[36] whom I've only ever seen twice and then almost 20 years ago, is something really pleasant and really valuable! But I must explain to you why I've committed the enormous impropriety of sending you a printed paper without including a letter or some form of homage, some expression of respect and loyalty. One of the aforementioned asses (in this case someone with too great a dose of wit, I mean corrosive wit) said to me: "What! You'd have the nerve to send that article to M. Hugo! Don't you see it's sure to displease him?" Now there's a highly stupid remark! Well, sir, although I know that genius contains by its very nature all the critical faculties and all the indulgence needed, I felt intimidated and I didn't dare write to you.

So now I owe you some explanations. I know your works by heart and your prefaces show me that I've overstepped the theory you generally put forward on the alliance of morality and poetry. But at a time when society turns away from art with such disgust, when men allow themselves to be debased by purely utilitarian concerns, I think there's no great harm in exaggerating a little in the other direction. It's possible that I've protested too much. But that was in order to obtain what was needed. Finally, even if there were a little Asiatic fatalism mixed up in my reflections I think that would be pardonable. The terrible world in which we live gives one a taste for isolation and fatality.

What I wanted to do above all was to bring the reader's thoughts back to that wonderful little age whose true king you were, and which lives on in my mind like a delicious memory of childhood.

36. Victor Hugo was living in exile on the island of Guernsey.

Regarding the writer who is the subject of this article and whose name serves as a pretext for my critical opinions, I can admit to you in all confidence that I know the gaps in his amazing talent. Many times, in thinking of him, I've been distressed to see that God was not willing to be absolutely generous. I haven't lied, I've sidestepped and dissimulated. If I were summoned to bear witness in a court in circumstances where to tell the truth and nothing but the truth could harm a being favored by Nature and beloved of my heart, I swear to you that I'd be proud to lie. I need your help. I need a greater voice than my own and that of Théophile Gautier. I need your dictatorial voice. I want to be protected. I'll humbly print whatever you deign to send me. I beg you not to stand on ceremony. If you find something to blame in these proofs, be assured that I'll reveal your criticism docilely, but without feeling too much shame. Isn't criticism from you still a kind of caress because it's an honor?

The lines I enclose with this letter[37] have been knocking around in my brain for a long time. The second piece was written with the *aim of imitating you* (laugh at my absurdity, it makes me laugh myself) after I'd reread some poems in your collections, in which such magnificent charity blends with such touching familiarity. In art galleries I've sometimes seen wretched art students copying the works of the masters. Well done or botched, these imitations sometimes contained, unbeknownst to the students, something of their own character, be it great or common. Perhaps (perhaps!) that will excuse my boldness. When *The Flowers of Evil* reappears, swollen with three times as much material as the Court suppressed, I'll have the pleasure of inscribing at the head of these poems the name of the poet whose works have taught me so much and brought such pleasure to my youth.

I remember you sent me, when this publication appeared, a remarkable compliment on the *stigma* that you defined as a *decoration*.[38] I didn't understand very clearly as I was still overwhelmed with rage at the loss of time and money. But now, sir, I understand *very well*. I feel very comfortable under my *stigma* and I *know* that henceforth, whatever kind of literature I embark on, I'll remain a monster, a werewolf. Recently the announcement of the amnesty put your name on everyone's lips.[39] Will you forgive me for having been worried for just a quarter of a second? I

37. The two poems entitled "The Seven Old Men" and "The Little Old Ladies."

38. In his letter of 30 August 1857, written when he heard of the *Flowers of Evil* trial, Hugo said: "You have just received one of the rare decorations that the current régime can accord."

39. As a result of his victory over the Austrians, Napoleon III had pronounced an amnesty for his exiled adversaries. Hugo refused to return until, as he said, liberty itself had returned.

heard people all around me saying: "At last, Victor Hugo will come back!" I felt these words reflected honorably on the hearts of these good folk, but not on their judgment. Your note came and set our minds at rest. I knew full well that poets were *worth* all the Napoléons, and that Victor Hugo could never be less great than Chateaubriand.

I am told you live in a high, poetic abode that resembles your mind and that you're happy in the roar of the wind and the water. You'll never be as happy as you are great. I'm also informed that you feel regret and nostalgia. That information may be wrong. But if it is true, a single day in our sad, boring Paris, our Paris–New York, would achieve a radical cure. If I didn't have some tasks to perform here I'd go to the ends of the world. Farewell sir, and if my name were occasionally mentioned benevolently in your contented family, I'd be deeply happy.

109   To Caroline Aupick

1 November 1859

I'll certainly write to you in detail about my affairs and I even believe that I'll soon have good news for you. As for the tea, you're mistaken. I sent you that sample, which is a *highly renowned* tea, not for you to blend it as a kind of seasoning with *inferior teas*, but to take on its own. Then, from what you tell me about it, I'll know whether this tea lives up to its reputation. Have no fear that I'll be cruel enough to let you spend the winter all alone.

My heartfelt thanks for the warm curiosity you show for my affairs. I'm now convinced that if I've often been unhappy, the fault was by and large my own. If I can only have the good health and the *patience* to prove my worth! The word you couldn't decipher was *tea*. It seems that there is another high-quality tea, but that one costs 600 francs per pound. What on earth can it be? Perhaps that's just a joke to arouse my curiosity. The one I sent you, which is very modest in price (48 francs a kilo, 30 a pound) is called Caravan tea and according to one of my friends it's sometimes good, sometimes bad. The merchant himself may have been wrong. On the basis of what you tell me I'll see if I should buy any more of the same kind.

Before leaving Paris I'll be very careful to get the exact address of the man who sells straw mats and oriental rugs, and to ask him for his prices.

Now, I've a few pieces of advice for you: MY BOXES AND PAPERS *must stay in the state in which I left them*. I'm terribly afraid of the stupidity of the servant girls. There is only one wall (the one in my study backing on to the courtyard) on which nothing must rest because of the damp. You must be very careful to collect together and *not to destroy* everything I send you connected with literature, pamphlets, reviews, newspapers, *proofs*. I very often find I have no copy of my own. For instance, I have no copy of my *Salon* (the last articles went to Honfleur after I left, some in the final pamphlet form, the last one in *proofs*), and no copy either of my poems in *La Revue contemporaine*.

Finally, it's essential that you find in the *right-hand* part of my shelves, where the paperbound books are kept, a very small *brochure* (*Bertram*, by *Maturin*, in English) and another, bigger *brochure* (*Bertram*, by *Maturin*, translated into French by Nodier and Taylor). Please put *each* of these brochures (not in an envelope) but under a *band* wide enough to cover *almost* all the jacket. That will cost you much less than if you stamped them at letter rate. Send them to me at the Hôtel de Dieppe. (Be careful not to slip a letter in with them. That would send us to the dock.) Your maid will have the sense to get them sent at printed paper rate.

Now, I hug you with all my heart, and thank you.

POSTSCRIPT: Although you're getting short-sighted, please be good enough to put all the other brochures back without tearing them. Forgive this request.

110　TO VICTOR HUGO

7 December 1859

Dear Sir,

Herewith some lines written for you and with you in mind.[40] Judge them, not with your oversevere eyes, but with your paternal eyes. I'll touch up the imperfections later on. What mattered for me was to express quickly all the suggestions sparked off by an accident, an image, and to show how the sight of a suffering animal pushes our thoughts toward all those who love, who are absent, who suffer, toward all those deprived of something they will never find again.

Please accept my little symbol as a very weak expression of all the sympathy and admiration I feel for your genius.

POSTSCRIPT: A highly excusable feeling of vanity drives me to make a small request. I learn that M. Meurice is sending you a copy of the *Revue indépendante* in which there is an article on *The Legend of the Ages* [*La Légende des siècles*]. In the same number there is a shred of a poem by Poe, on the creation and destruction of worlds.[41] I'm horribly afraid you'll take it into your head to read that. It's printed with numerous errors and will

40. "The Swan," which Baudelaire later dedicated to Hugo.
41. The article on Hugo's volume *The Legend of the Ages* is by Edmond Delière. The fragment of Poe is Baudelaire's translation of part of *Eureka*.

give you a despicable idea of Poe and of his translator. I needn't tell you that when the printers have it reprinted a copy will be reserved for you. I have a horrible feeling of almost personal vanity where this poet is concerned and I have no wish that both he and I should be dishonored in your eyes by a printer's stupidities. Forgive these trembling professional vanities.

III   To Auguste Poulet-Malassis

15 December 1859

I've received a letter from my mother who has, naturally, paid the 1,500 francs but who doesn't give any indication (her letter is dated 14; I've no idea at what time she wrote it) about whether or not she's received the 500 francs for the 15th (today). I've just sent a letter to Pincebourde explaining what's happened, and I gave him the new address of the House of Gélis, Didot and Co. 12, rue des Sainte-Pères. Pincebourde has simply sent word (it's now 10:30) that he'll look into this.

Of the whole packet of poems I gave him, Calonne rejected the gallant *ex-voto*,[42] as capable of scandalizing his readers. I sent him "The Swan" ["Le Cygne"] and I'm also sending him some new lines, entitled "Skeleton at Work" ["Le Squelette laboureur"]. When I've done "Dorothée" (a memory of L'Ile Bourbon), "The Wild Woman" ["La Femme sauvage"] (a sermon delivered to a minx) and "The Dream" ["Le Rêve"], and finally the prefatory letter to Veuillot, which we must talk about together, *The Flowers of Evil* will be ready.

I'm going to send you almost the whole of my literary reviews, which we can't print immediately because of the Gide company, which is to publish some of them in its modern anthology. The book is composed in the following way:

I Edgar Poe, his life and works.

II New Notes on Edgar Poe

III Final Notes on Edgar Poe (the manuscript of this is still at Honfleur)

(These three pieces are at the center of a discussion with the infamous Michel. Nevertheless, my contracts mention only a specific amount of original matter and make no reference to critical opinions on the author. Moreover, good sense would indicate that I can reprint in my own works the critical and biographical sections.)

(And then there's a further argument concerning *The Raven*, etc.)

IV Théophile Gautier (published)

42. "To a Madonna."

V   Théophile Gautier II x
VI   Pierre Dupont I (published by Houssiaux) x
VII   Pierre Dupont II x
VIII   Leconte de Lisle x
IX   Desbordes-Valmore x
X   Auguste Barbier x
XI   Hégésippe Moreau x
XII   Pétrus Borel x
XIII   Gustave Levavasseur x
XIV   Rouvière (printed in *L'Artiste*)

I've had copies made for you of all the articles I've marked with a little cross—be sure to tell me what you think of them. DON'T EVER LOSE ANYTHING I SEND YOU. (That will be the true copy.)

When we've reached the stage of preparing the *Flowers*, I want everything possible to be done to attract attention to this new edition, so we'll follow Hugo's lead: the day before it goes on sale *all the newspapers* with which we have connections must each quote a bit chosen from the previously unpublished poems.

The Opium study is so long it will be published in two sections: the first on 31 December.[43] *Give some thought to the letter I sent you last night.*

What is it that's upsetting you? You must find me tiresome with my bedeviled literary nature at a time when misfortune has struck you.

112   TO JEANNE DUVAL
                                                                    17 December 1859
My dear girl,

You mustn't bear me a grudge for having left Paris so abruptly without having called on you to entertain you a little. You know how exhausted I am with all my worries. Moreover, my mother knew that, of that terrible sum of 5,000 francs I owed, 2,000 were payable at Honfleur, and so she was tormenting me terribly. Everything has worked out well: but just imagine that the day before it was due, 1,600 francs of it still had to be found. Calonne behaved most generously and rescued us. —I promise you I'll return in a few days time as I have to reach an understanding with Malassis, and besides I've left all my trunks at the hotel. Henceforth I don't want to make any more of these lengthy stays in Paris, which cost me so much money. It's better for me if I come often and stay only a few days. Meanwhile, since I may remain away for a week and since I'm unwilling, given your state, for you to remain without money, even for a

43. It did not appear until 15 January.

day, go to M. Ancelle. I'm aware that I've made a few inroads into next year's money, but you know that despite his hesitations he is pretty generous. That small sum will suffice until I return and around New Year I'll get some money. So put this letter in a new envelope and since you haven't found the courage to write with your left hand, have your servant address the letter. Don't forget to put "Avenue de la Révolte, opposite the Duke of Orleans's chapel." You know he's always rushing about the place. So there's no point in sending someone to his house unless it's very early. You'll get this on Sunday, but it's advisable not to send anyone to him until Monday, because of mass and because he goes out with his family on Sundays. I know Malassis will be in Paris on Wednesday. So I've not much time. I found my lodgings transformed. My mother, who can't stay still for a minute, rearranged, embellished (or so she thought) my lodgings. So I'm going to return and if, as I think likely, I'm given some money I'll try to entertain you. As I lack paper I'm adding here directly a word for *Ancelle.* —I've leafed through the catalogs of the exhibition and I've not yet found HIS PAINTER'S address. If you don't want him to read all this, tear it in two and leave only the receipt.[44] I don't care either way. Given the slippery condition of the roads, don't go out unaccompanied. *Don't lose my poems and articles.*

Received from M. Ancelle the sum of 40 francs for Mme Duval.

113   TO ALPHONSE CALONNE

5 January [1860]

My dear Calonne,

I hesitated a long time before going to see you this evening. My horror of arguments held me back! I want to write to you frankly and I want you to believe me when I confirm to you that I'm now writing with no sense of rancor.

Nothing in the friendship I believe you've inspired in me will be diminished, but I warn you that however gracious and cordial you may be I'll no longer submit to your discipline, except for the changes we've already agreed to. For it is of course my duty to deliver to you the final pages of *Opium*.

I'll continue, it's true, to obey the contract in offering you up to 12 sheets (if *Opium* is taken to be complete, I'll have given you almost 8 sheets already) of everything I do. But these indecisions, these castrations, these changes will no longer take place. By that I mean that once

44. Jeanne did not bother to do this. As a result, Ancelle kept both the receipt and the letter, thus preserving the only letter so far found from Baudelarie to his mistress.

I've offered you those 12 sheets' worth, I'll see myself as free, whether you accept them as they stand or whether you reject them.

Consider again how carefully I express even those things I find disagreeable to say. My name and my talent should protect me, and have generally protected me, from those little persecutions practiced by the classical chief editor, and I give you my word of honor that you're the first to whom I've shown such deference.

And this morning too! The beginning of a discussion had been thought out and prepared over a long period. At last I found an opening whose solemnity resembles the opening bars of an orchestra. But smack! You think it would be more judicious to introduce as an opening the obituary notice.[45]

And that on a man ten of whose volumes I'm familiar with and who has written perhaps 30. On a man who is one of the main figures of a school. A 20-line notice! Choose whomever you like to be judge of this!

To sum up, I repeat: there is a degree of age and knowledge where one obviously escapes such schooling. You're harming me and naturally you're harming yourself. I've promised to abridge in the second section two pieces I consider to be the essential pieces the man's written. I'll do it. And after that, I'll rebel. Show my letter to any one of your friends (someone who is intelligent, of course) and you'll see what he'll have to say to you about all this.

All yours, moreover. Of that you mustn't doubt.

If such a rupture had to take place and if I found myself in debt for something, you can rest assured that I'd be able to acquit that debt.

114   To Auguste Poulet-Malassis
Sunday evening, 8 January 1860

What I'm going to tell you this evening is worth the telling. M. Méryon sent me his card and we met each other. He said to me: "You live in a house whose name must have attracted you, because of the connection I presume exists with your tastes." —At that I looked at the envelope of his letter. He'd written: Hôtel de *Thèbes*, and despite that his letter had reached me.[46]

In one of his large plates he substituted for a little balloon a cloud of predatory birds, and when I pointed out to him that it was implausible

45. The reference is to the brilliant opening section of Baudelaire's version of the *Confessions*, which Baudelaire chose to begin with De Quincey's invocation: "O just, mighty and subtle opium. . . ."
46. Baudelaire was actually living in the Hôtel de Dieppe.

that so many eagles could be found in a Parisian sky, he answered that it wasn't without a basis in fact, since *those men* (the Emperor's government) had often released eagles to study the presages according to the rites, and that this had been reported in the newspapers—even in *Le Moniteur*.

I have to say that he makes no secret of his respect for all superstitions, but he explains them badly and sees cabals in everything.

In another of his plates he pointed out to me that the shadow thrown by one of the pieces of masonry on the Pont Neuf onto the side wall of the quay made a perfect profile of a sphinx—and that that had been absolutely involuntary on his part and that he hadn't noticed that extraordinary fact until later when he remembered that the drawing had been made shortly before the coup d'état. Now, the Prince is the person who, in our days, most resembles, in features and acts, a *sphinx*.

He asked me if I had read the stories of a certain Edgar Poe. I told him I knew them better than anyone and had good reason for doing so. Then he asked me, in a very emphatic tone, if I believed that this Edgar Poe actually existed. *I* of course asked him who he thought wrote all the stories. He answered: *"A club of very clever, very powerful writers, who know everything that's going on."* This is one of the reasons he gave. "The *Rue Morgue*. I've made a drawing of the Rue Morgue. An *Orangutan*. I've often been likened to a monkey. This monkey kills *two women, a mother and her daughter*. I've always taken this novel as an allusion to my misfortunes. You'd give me a lot of pleasure if you could find the date on which Edgar Poe (supposing he wasn't helped by any third person) wrote this tale, to see if the date coincides with what happened to me."

He talked to me admiringly of Michelet's book on Joan of Arc. But he's convinced this book isn't by Michelet. One of the subjects that most preoccupies him is cabalistic science. But he interprets it in a very strange way, that would make a member of the cabal burst out laughing.

Don't laugh about all this with unkind wretches. I have absolutely no desire to harm a man of talent . . .

After he left me, I wondered how it was that I, who have always had the mind and the nerves to go mad, have never actually gone mad. In all seriousness I gave heaven a Pharisee's thanks for this.

Guys and I are fully reconciled. He's a charming man, very witty, and he's not ignorant, as all literary men are.

115   TO AUGUSTE POULET-MALASSIS

16 February 1860

[. . .] I *cannot* share your illusions that it will be child's play to make 350 pages with the 3 sheets of the *Revue contemporaine*. May I remind you that you have in the past made pamphlets out of much bulkier scripts. In parentheses, I'll tell you that I would have liked to hear your impression of the general physiognomy of the book, particularly of the *Opium* section. De Quincey is an author who is terribly conversational and digressive, and it was no small matter to give this résumé dramatic form and introduce a bit of order into it. Moreover, I had to blend my own personal feelings into the author's opinions and make an amalgam in which the different parts would be indiscernible. Have I succeeded? My question isn't prompted by childish vanity; it arises from the solitude in which I live, because I've reached such a pitch of sensitivity that the conversation of almost everyone is intolerable to me, and on the other hand I admit I'm always anxious to know if this work that progresses so slowly, sometimes through my own fault, sometimes because of circumstances, is solid enough to be offered to the general public.

Calonne and I are cold-shouldering each other. All in all I owe him 200 or 300 francs, but he has a packet of poems to publish. What's more, I told him very calmly that the pieces I'd promised would appear in *La Presse* and that, at my age and with my name, I could no longer put up with wearisome and pointless pedagogy, and that, after all, the director of a literary collection had no right to intervene, except in cases where he could be compromised by a religious or a political statement.

I've kept three passages of the first text, for our republication. What a lot of problems I have! I'm without a cent, and I'm also at odds with my mother. The indiscretion of people who owe me something, or who make me fine promises without keeping them, has made it necessary for me to get my mother to pay back bills due at Honfleur. This fills me with shame. I owe my mother 10,000 francs, which I borrowed from her at the time when she was well off, and it's not fitting for me to torment her now that she's poor. I may perhaps have recourse to you, to bring the *de Rode* business to an end. When you fall out with people, you pay them what you owe. Well, I haven't been paid. I'm still owed 400 francs that I'd very much like to send on to Mme Aupick. And—take good note that I've been INSULTED by those asses who can't even spell. If I weren't overwhelmed by things that have to be done, I'd have struck that ill-bred pedant in his office. I'm very much afraid that M. Zacharie Astruc, who was present at my thoughtless conversation in the railway buffet, is not unconnected with this quarrel. Moreover—and this is really horrible!— they've lost pages of the manuscript and I'm forced to begin all over again. (Keep my suspicion about Astruc under your hat.)

What a morass of bothersome matters! And now Guys, who really is a bizarre character, has taken it into his head to do something on the *Vénus de Milo*! And he writes to me from London asking me to send him all the

studies and hypotheses made about this statue. I introduced Champfleury and Duranty to Guys, but they declared him an unbearable old
man. Truly the *Realists* are no observers—they don't know how to amuse
themselves. They lack the essential philosophical patience.

And then there's Méryon! Now this is really intolerable. Delâtre begs
me to write something for the album. Good! That gives me an excuse to
write some reveries of 10, 20, or 30 lines, inspired by beautiful engravings, the philosophical reveries of a stroller in Paris. But Méryon comes
butting in—he doesn't see things that way. What is required is: On the
right we have this, on the left that. I'd have to seek out notes in old
books. I'd have to say: here there were originally 12 windows, reduced to
10 by the artist, and finally I'd have to go to the Town Hall to find out the
exact date of the demolitions. M. Méryon speaks with his eyes on the
ceiling without listening to a word anyone says.

You can laugh a little, but keep this secret for me: our good, our
admirable Asselineau told me when I upbraided him, given his knowledge of music, for not going to the Wagner concerts, first that it was such
a distance, *such* a distance from his place (The Italian theater!)[47] and
second that he had moreover been told that Wagner was a REPUBLICAN!

I told him I'd have gone even if he had been a royalist, for that was no
guarantee against either stupidity or genius. I no longer dare speak of
Wagner—people have mocked me too much. That music was one of the
great experiences of my life—it's at least 15 years since I've felt such
exaltation.

Syphilis—you wouldn't believe the extent to which you are deluding
yourself. It's almost complacency. Syphilis was made for everyone and
you're not exempt. You tell me of thrush, of constrictions in the throat so
painful you can't eat without it hurting, of startling feelings of weariness,
a lack of appetite. Answer yes or no: are all those recognizable symptoms
or aren't they? The fact that you haven't had fainting fits and a loss of
suppleness in the calves and elbows, with tumors around the neck and
near the head, doesn't prove anything, except that the beneficial results of
using sarsaparilla and potassium iodide may have prevented these symptoms. You say that the internal wound was not venereal. What proof do
you have? As for the external ulcers, I saw them myself and you know
what my immediate response was. In general terms, remember that all
antivenereal treatments are excellent and rejuvenating by their very
nature and that there is no antivenereal treatment that doesn't use
mercury.

47. The Théâtre italien was on the right bank of the Seine: Asselineau lived on the
other side of the river.

What would be the latest date at which you'd want to show *The Flowers of Evil* at your industrial exhibition? The *Flowers* were mentioned again in the *Salut public* in relation to *Humorous Sonnets*. I haven't seen the article. You missed a fine sale of engravings printed in color. Among them was a large engraving of Lafayette by Debucourt, as lovely as a Reynolds.

116   To Richard Wagner
17 February 1860

Dear Sir,

I've always imagined that however used to glory an artist might be, he would not remain unmoved by a sincere compliment, when that compliment resembled a cry of thanks. I believe, too, that this cry could have *special* value coming from a Frenchman, that's to say, from a man poorly suited to outbursts of enthusiasm and born in a country where there is almost as little understanding of painting and poetry as there is of music. Above all, I want to say that I owe you *the greatest musical pleasure I've ever experienced*. I've reached an age where one hardly enjoys writing to famous men anymore and I would have hesitated much longer to express my admiration to you through a letter had I not day after day set eyes on unworthy, ridiculous articles where all possible efforts are made to defame your glory. Yours is not the first case where my country has caused me suffering and shame. In short, it's indignation that has led me to express my gratitude. I said to myself: "I want to be distinguished from all those jackasses."

The first time I went to the theater to hear your works I was pretty ill-disposed toward them. I admit I even had a lot of bad prejudices. But I had an excuse, for I've so often been a dupe. I've heard so much music by charlatans making great claims. I was instantly won over. What I felt is beyond description, but if you'll deign not to laugh, I'll try to convey my feelings to you. At first it seemed to me that I knew your music already, and later, in thinking it over, I understood what had caused this illusion. It seemed to me that the music was *my own*, and I recognized it, as any man recognizes those things he is destined to love. For anyone who isn't a man of intelligence such a claim would seem ridiculous in the extreme, above all when it's written by someone who, like me, *does not know music* and whose entire musical education extends no further than listening (with great pleasure admittedly) to a few fine pieces by Weber and Beethoven.

Then the element that struck me above all was the grandeur of your music. It represents the heights, and it drives the listener on to the

145

heights. In all your works I've found the solemnity of Nature's great sounds, her great aspects, and the solemnity, too, of the great human passions. One instantly feels swept up and subjugated. One of the strangest pieces, one of those that aroused in me a new musical emotion, is that designed to depict religious ecstasy. The effect produced by "The Introduction of the Guests" and "The Marriage Feast" is immense. I felt all the majesty of a life greater than the one we lead. And another thing, too: in hearing it, I frequently experienced a rather odd emotion, which could be described as the pride and joy of comprehension, of allowing myself to be penetrated and invaded—a truly sensual pleasure, recalling that of floating through the air or rolling on the sea. And at the same time the music occasionally expressed all the pride of life. Generally those deep harmonies seemed to me comparable to those stimulants that speed up the pulse of the imagination. Finally, I experienced in addition—and I beg you not to laugh—feelings that probably stem from my particular cast of mind and my frequent preoccupations. Your music is full of something that is both uplifted and uplifting, something that longs to climb higher, something excessive and superlative. To illustrate this, let me use a comparison borrowed from painting. I imagine a vast extent of red spreading before my eyes. If this red represents passion, I see it change gradually, through all the shades of red and pink, until it reaches the incandescence of a furnace. It would seem difficult, even impossible, to render something more intensely hot and yet a final flash traces a whiter furrow on the white that provides its background. That, if you will, is the final cry of a soul that has soared to a paroxysm of ecstasy.

I had begun to write a few meditations on the pieces from *Tannhäuser* and *Lohengrin* that we heard, but I realized that it was impossible to say everything.

I could continue my letter in this vein interminably. If you've been able to read this, accept my thanks. I've only a few words to add. Since the day I heard your music, I've been repeating to myself over and over again, particularly in hours of despondency: "If only I could hear some Wagner tonight!" No doubt there are others like me. All in all you must have been satisfied with the general audience whose instincts were far above the poor science of the journalists. Why don't you give some more concerts, adding new pieces? You've given us a foretaste of new joys; do you have the right to deprive us of the rest? Once more, sir, my thanks. You recalled me to myself and to what is great, in bad times.

I am not including my address, for that might make you think I had something to ask of you.

146

18 February 1860

Dear Sir,

Your articles [48] and your letter obviously demand a reply. First of all, on a personal level, accept my thanks. You've already spoken of me several times and you've always done so *very well*, by which I mean in a way that is at once most flattering and with a sagacity that surprises me. On rereading that sentence I find it impertinent, even laughable. It seems to be saying that the sagacity comes from paying me compliments. In your article on Hugo, you appear to have been intimidated and worried. You didn't draw a sharp enough line between the dose of eternal beauty in Hugo and the comic superstitions that have crept in as a result of circumstances—that is to say, modern folly or *wisdom*, belief in progress, the salvation of the human race through balloons, etc. As it stands, your article is still the best and the wisest I've read. Generally Hugo's friends are as stupid as his enemies, and the result is that the truth will never be said. Here, apart from Villemain, my friend d'Aurevilly sometimes, and M. Renan, no one has any critical wisdom or insight. I've heard only one clear, just assessment of *The Legend* [*La Légende*] and that was by M. Gautier, at a supper. Never have the most problematic aesthetic questions been so well clarified. Never have what are called qualities and failings been so well defined. But because of the bad times we're going through and the unfortunate circumstances, such statements will never get into print. I'm handing *Le Salut public* to M. Paul Meurice who'll get it to Guernsey without fail. That's all the more probable as Mme Hugo is at present in Paris.

To return to M. Soulary. Your study is excellent and full of charm. Your response to poetry is that of the true *dilettante*. That's exactly how it should be felt. The italicized word will let you know that I was rather surprised to see your admiration for Musset. Except at the age of taking our First Communion, which is when anything concerning girls of easy virtue and silken ladders affects us like a religion, I've never been able to bear *this master of dandies* with his spoiled-child impudence, calling on heaven and hell for matters concerning his bed and board, his muddy torrent of grammatical and prosodic errors, finally his complete inability to understand the work that transforms reverie into art. One day you'll come to admire perfection alone and you'll scorn all these outpourings of ignorance. Forgive my speaking of certain things with such passion, but

48. Fraisse had reviewed the *Flowers of Evil* in 1857 and had paid homage to Baudelaire in an article on Soulary's *Sonnets*.

incoherence, banality, and negligence have always irritated me, perhaps too intensely.

There's a truly remarkable passage in your article. It's the one where you speak of those vigorous temperaments that impress into works of intelligence, composed as circumstances dictated, a predestined and involuntary unity. That M. Soulary is a great poet is obvious today to everyone and it's been obvious to me from the first time I had the opportunity to read his poems. So who is the idiot (perhaps he is a famous man) who treats the Sonnet so lightly and doesn't see its Pythagorean beauty?[49] Because the form is constricting, the idea bursts forth all the more intensely. Everything is appropriate to the sonnet, buffoonery, gallantry, passion, reverie, philosophical meditation. It possesses the beauty of well-wrought metal or mineral. Have you noticed that a section of the sky seen through a ventilator or between two chimneys, two rocks, or through an arcade, etc., gives a more profound idea of the infinite than a great panorama seen from a mountain top? As for long poems, we know what to think of them—they're the resource of those who can't write short ones.

Everything that exceeds the attention span that mortal man can devote to poetic form is not *a* poem.

Permit me to tell you that you didn't understand what I wrote to you about the resemblance that aroused in me such a sense of vanity. Everything you've told me on that score I'd already thought and known myself. Otherwise, where would there be any piquancy, curiosity, or amusement? I can point out to you something stranger, indeed almost incredible. In 1846 or '47 I came across a few fragments of Edgar Poe. I experienced a singular shock. His complete works were not assembled into a single edition until after his death, so I had the patience to make contact with Americans living in Paris to borrow from them collections of newspapers edited by Poe. And then—believe me if you will—I found poems and short stories that I had thought of, but in a vague, confused, disorderly way and that Poe had been able to bring together to perfection. It was that that lay behind my enthusiasm and my long years of patience.

When you do your article on Poe, I'll send you the volumes again. The first has been reworked, although the electros had already been taken. A few terrible errors eliminated—that at least is something. Those horrible volumes at one franc apiece are bulging with errors, and it distresses me to think that I may never be able to make a truly worthy edition of them.

49. An allusion to Enfantin, the founding father of the Saint-Simonian sect.

Eureka will come out this year with Michel Lévy. It's a really tough read, and may make you give up. A few fragments of it have been published in a review I shan't name, with sentences left out, passages cut about, misinterpretations made by the printer, and as many printing errors as there are fleas in the dust of a Spanish river. So if you find them, don't read them. I've made the same plea to all my friends.

Before the *Flowers*, very much increased, Malassis is publishing the *æsthetic curiosities* and the *artificial paradises*. They are all ready to run.

Apart from two or three friends who are very busy I so rarely have the chance to discuss literature that you'll forgive my chatter. And you won't take it amiss that I ask you, since you are in Lyon, who M. J. Tisseur is, and if M. Janmot's compositions (*Story of a Soul* [*Histoire d'une âme*]) have been photographed. I have to do a piece of work into which I'll put Kaulbach, Alfred Rethel, Chenevard, and Janmot and I wouldn't be exactly displeased to have as many documents as possible in front of me. Give M. Soulary my compliments and if you speak to him of the remark you and I made simultaneously, don't fail to add what I meant by it. I'd blush if it were construed otherwise.

118   TO JOSEPHIN SOULARY

23 February 1860

Dear Sir and friend (you'll allow me to use this title which I begged you to use in addressing me),

I'd certainly not have waited for a letter from you to thank you for your volume if I'd known where to send my thanks. I've reread it for the third time, as I don't need to tell you that you're an old acquaintance of mine and that as soon as your work came out I was able to relish its quite unique flavor, all its *vinosity*.

It was with the greatest pleasure that I found in that new edition pieces I hadn't known, among them the sonnet addressed to a proof corrector, which I consider a real marvel. But on that score allow me (since you're willing to be friends with a pedant, you've only got yourself to blame) to make a few remarks.

You give your readers a presentiment of perfection—and a taste for it, too. You're one of those highly privileged people who have the gift of feeling *art* in its furthest quests. And that's precisely why you have no right to disturb our pleasure with bumps and jolts. —Well, at the end of that sonnet there is the following sentence (which I'm translating into prose): "In another world you must have committed a very great sin of pride for God to have condemned you here, etc." You've left out "for" in the poetic version of this. It may not be a grammatical error, strictly speaking, but that's the sort of French that M. Soulary, to whom meter can't pose any problems, ought not to allow himself.

Since I'm such a careful reader, you won't bear me any grudges, will you? Moreover, there are such a lot of flattering things I could say to you. You're able to imitate the soul's upward flights, the music of meditation. *You love order*. You dramatize your sonnet and give it a conclusion. You know the power of rhetoric. And so on. All these fine skills arouse the admiration of all your readers who can *meditate or dream*; but since you seem to want me to treat you with perfect frankness, I'll tell you that you (like me) should go into mourning for your popularity. That's a bad expression, since one can't be widowed of something one never possessed. It's true that we could console OURSELVES by saying with certainty that *all great men are stupid*—that is, all the representative men, those who represent the masses. It's a punishment God inflicts on them. Neither you nor I are *stupid* enough to earn universal approval. There are two other marvelously gifted men who are in the same case: M. Théophile Gautier and M. Leconte de Lisle. One can also say that we will enjoy very powerful and very subtle pleasures that the crowd will never know.

119   TO APOLLONIE SABATIER

[4 March 1860]

If I tell you I have great sorrows, that never before have I gone through a storm to equal this one, that I need solitude, you'll not believe me. But if I say my nose is as round, fat, and red as an apple, and that in such a case I don't even see men (let alone women) I'm sure you'll believe me.

The great difficulty had been removed, for I met Feydeau, who wasn't going to let drop such a fine chance to hear himself discussed and to talk about himself. Fortunately, as I'd foreseen that possibility, I'd prepared myself quietly for it. I took all my courage in my hands and said to him: "Your work is sublime, etc., but etc." He made it very clear to me that with him "buts" are not well received. In all sincerity, I find him more problematic than Victor Hugo himself and I'd be less embarrassed to say to Hugo: "You are stupid" than to say to Feydeau: "There are moments when you are less than sublime." And then, that evening (this will figure among my misfortunes), in the middle of a crowd where I thought I was quite safe, *a Jew*, someone you know, M. Heilbuth, buttonholed me and forced upon me a workshop discussion with such intensity that I thought I'd either faint away or fling myself at him.

You see that I love scandalmongering with you. If it's true to say that one should always spare one's accomplices, I'd be happy to be overly unkind about everyone when talking to you, so that *I'd be incapable in future of leaving you.*

I'm very pleased you noticed the line about your eyes, for the fact is that they can be very ugly (when you want them to be). I believe in all sincerity that I'm about to enter into happier climes and that this coming week I'll come in person to ask your forgiveness for *having pretended* to forget you. I'll probably bring the album with me.

All yours, with all my heart.

The enclosed 8 francs are those I've been forgetting for too long—for the carriage.

120   To Alphonse Calonne

[mid March 1860?]

Dear Sir,

You guessed correctly the reason why I hadn't been to see you. I was justified in believing, until I'd received word from you, that we were no longer on good terms or that you had suppressed my poems. [50]

Alas! Your criticisms fall precisely on those words, those *intentions*, those sallies that I considered among my *best*. It will be enough for me to tell you briefly what I intended. (Movement generally implies noise, to the extent that Pythagoras attributed music to the *moving* spheres. But dream, which separates things and breaks them down, creates the *new*. —The word *royal* will help the reader understand the metaphor, which transforms memory into a crown of towers, like those that weigh down the brows of the goddesses of *maturity*, of *fecundity*, of *wisdom*. Love (feeling and intellect) is stupid at 20, *knowing* at 40). All that, I assure you, was devised over a long period of time.

On the other hand you'll see that I've corrected several deplorable imperfections that had been much tormenting me. I add a sonnet which I hope will please you. [51] After you've cast an eye over my corrections you'll understand why I request a second proof.

POSTSCRIPT: Let me add that the proofs are very poorly composed.

50. The poems that were to appear in the *Revue contemporaine* of 15 May: "Parisian Dream," "Love of Deceit," "The Dream of a Curious Man," "Semper eadem," and "Obsession."
51. Probably "The Dream of a Curious Man" or "Semper eadem."

151

[about 10 April 1860]

My dear Crépet,

You're tormenting me horribly, and it's all pointless. For your sake as much as for my own I put an enormous amount of application into those essays. *What I've done is good and irrefutable.* Nevertheless, because I wanted to be obliging and deferential, I have already promised you that I'll rework several passages. *I've already done so*, in the essay on *Barbier*, for example. Now how on earth can I correct anything at all when I have no page proofs? How do you expect me to begin again, *for the third time*, the passage about that ass Laprade, when I don't have the proofs before me?[52] Yet you know full well that I asked for a second copy of the proofs, which, according to the letter you wrote me, implied on my part the desire to oblige you again by trying yet another transformation.

As for taking advantage of my absence to change what I've put, you won't do it. First, because it would be dishonest. Second, because we agreed that if I refused to make certain changes, Boyer would do the work. Finally, because it behooves you first to give me a text of my Essays as they were originally written.

(On this score, I'll point out that I'd be very happy to receive the *Gautier* and the *Barbier*, which have probably been corrected and may already be set.)

There's another way of getting over all our problems. What money have I received from you and Gide? Despite all the expenses piling up on me, I'd be able to repay you that sum, or provide you with the means of getting it back.

I beg you not to interpret as impertinence this extreme suggestion. I myself would resort to it only if things were utterly desperate.

122   To Auguste Poulet-Malassis

[about 20 April 1860]

You're right. Strictly speaking, willpower is not an *organ*.[53] And yet I chose to violate language in that way to put across a particular idea. If I said it was a *fluid*, you'd accept that. Nevertheless, I take your side here—the public's habits of thought mustn't be teased. Likewise, for the same reason, I accept your point of view on "These *are*" instead of "it is"

52. The passage on Laprade was probably initially included in the article on Barbier. Crépet insisted it be removed.

53. In *Artificial Paradises* Baudelaire had written: "The will power is attacked, that most precious of all our organs." He changed the word "organs" to "faculties."

followed by a plural noun—which, whatever you say, is a purer style (Pascal, Bossuet, La Bruyère, Balzac, Honoré de Balzac, etc).

Thus, as Champfleury says, we have idiosyncratic habits that push us to talk differently from those of our age.

I've just scrounged *La Raison d'Etat* from Michel.[54] Although the Italian *brio*, the abundant improvisations, sometimes lead to a careless, hustled style, in general it's very fine. The preface in particular (you really must look at that) has a certain airy, fatalistic, resigned eloquence that recalls the best passages from the purest, classical French beauty. The chapter on Machiavelli, from whom nevertheless Ferrari takes his distance, is also astounding. In a word, throughout the work genius makes a pact with Destiny: "Let me understand your *laws* and I'll let you off the vulgar pleasures of life, the empty consolations of Error (sic)."

I'm checking my accounts and I'm sending you this résumé which will enable you to check your own. [. . .]

So, we must move quickly on the *Flowers*, even if it means bringing out a book in mid-summer. I ought to set out for Honfleur immediately. First I want to get hold of 1,000 francs. I'm convinced it will come. If things come to *the worst*, I'll leave at the end of the month, and if necessary sacrifice the *preface* and the three pieces I've just begun, and the question of putting things in order which so preoccupies you can be done in an hour. [. . .]

123   TO AUGUSTE POULET-MALASSIS

[23 April 1860]

What a distressing letter. The *Revue indépendante* itself humiliated me less with *its stupidities* than you have with *mine*. I'll go through your letter point by point.

1. About the feminine world, the *mundi muliebri*.[55] How on earth can you attribute this bizarre genitive to me? Remember the *Sultan*, whose function was to express admiration for an adorably thin woman who had a Florentine kind of beauty. How could you have failed to guess that Calonne, *who is a pedant*, must have said to himself (after I'd given the go-ahead to print): "What an ignoramus that Baudelaire is! He thinks the ablative plural (*bonis*) is that of the genitive singular, which is always i." As for the rest of your criticism, my answer is provided by the work of the

54. By Giuseppe Ferrari.

55. This expression is in *Artificial Paradises*. In Latin the term *mundus* has a very general meaning, including that of ornaments, dress, adornments of a woman, but by extension referring to that which is adorned, the universe and its inhabitants.

imagination I've done and that the intelligent reader must also do: What is it that the child so loves in his mother, his nurse, his elder sister? Is it simply the being who nourishes him, combs his hair, washes him and rocks him to sleep? It's also the caresses she gives and the sensual pleasure she provides. For the child, this caress is bestowed unbeknownst to the woman, through all her feminine graces. So he loves his mother, his sister, his nurse for the pleasant tickling of her satin and furs, for the perfume of her breast and her hair, for the sound of her jewels, the play of her ribbons, etc., for all that *mundus muliebris* that begins with the shift and expresses itself through the very furniture on which the woman places the imprint of her femininity. *So*, I'm right. *So*, I haven't made a mistake in my Latin. "But," you say, "You're making a mistake in your French with your 'feminine *world*.'" That's true enough, and to show you that I'm doing it deliberately and consciously I underline the word *world*. As there is, in truth, some justice in your criticism, I'm attempting to satisfy you with a revision of my text, and I beg you to let me know if you're pleased with it.

(Could you let me have a second proof, to give me time to check with Sasonoff, Fowler, or anyone else, that I've got things right in my obituary notice on De Quincey? Tomorrow I'll do the pharmaceutical note and I'll be able to tell you what happened about the copies I'm allowed to take.)

To come back to that so-called error, it's not really in *mundi*, which is very well translated by the preceding lines in the words atmosphere, odor, breast, knees, hair, clothes, *balneum unguentatum*; the error lies more in *world* as an interpretation of *mundus*.

2. As for the rest, [56] that's really serious. It's really hard for me to accept that I've said a *pasture* could slake a *thirst*, and that "I am a God who has" instead of "have." I feel that everyone will see that, and that *Le Figaro* will seize on that pasture and romp about in it, and that I'll never be able to open the book without finding those very errors leaping out of the page at me. Are you fond enough of me to do two cards? If you do, be very careful that new errors don't slip into the four pages of those cards.

Herewith the cover.

I'm writing to Guys to ask him for a note of the English newspapers which discuss French literature.

Send me a word in reply.

POSTSCRIPT: So: "God who have" and "implacable appetite" if that fits in with the rest of the sentence. On the back of the cover, Charles or at least Ch. You understand, of course, that these two cards,

56. These remarks refer to *The Poem of Hashish*.

if you agree to do them, and the second proof, won't slow down the publication. The word is "tincture," not "tint."

124   To Gustave Flaubert

26 June 1860

My dear Flaubert,

Many thanks for your excellent letter. I was struck by your observation[57] and, having very sincerely descended into the memory of my reveries, I realized that I've always been obsessed by the impossibility of understanding certain of man's sudden thoughts or deeds, unless we accept the hypothesis that an evil force, external to man, has intervened. Now that's a great admission that the whole of the nineteenth century couldn't conspire to make me blush at. Note well that I'm not going to renounce the pleasure of changing my mind or contradicting myself.

One of these days, with your permission, I'll stop at Rouen en route to Honfleur; but I presume that like me you hate surprises, so I'll let you know some time in advance. —You say I work hard. Is that a bit of cruel mockery? Many people, myself included, think I don't do much at all. Work means work without stopping; it means rejecting one's senses, refusing reverie, and then you become pure willpower continuously functioning. Perhaps I'll get there.

All yours. Your very devoted friend.

POSTSCRIPT: I've always dreamed of reading (in its entirety) the *Temptation* and another extraordinary book, of which you've published no fragments at all (*November*). And how is *Carthage* coming on?[58]

125   To Alfred Guichon

13 July 1860

Sir,

Telling me you love Edgar Poe so much amounts to paying me the gentlest of compliments, since it's telling me that you are like me. So I'm replying in all haste. I think you were wrong to buy the pieces you mention. I've long been at work on a beautiful edition. It won't include

57. In his letter of 25 June, Flaubert, in thanking Baudelaire for *Artificial Paradises*, wrote that in this work Baudelaire had "on several occasions insisted too much (?) on the Spirit of Evil" (*Lettres à Charles Baudelaire*, p. 155).

58. Reference to *The Temptations of Saint Anthony*, fragments of which had appeared in *L'Artiste* in December 1856 and January and February 1857; to an early novel, *November*, published only after Flaubert's death; and to *Salammbô*, published in 1865.

the work of philosophy, *Eureka*, which is to appear in Lévy's collection at 3 francs the volume. I am, however, going to include the unpublished pieces. Moreover, I'd warned you that they were very poorly printed, particularly *The Angel of the Odd*, in which not only the figurative spelling, which is intentionally absurd, was not followed, but in which whole lines and words were skipped, making sentences meaningless. There are, too, errors in *The Philosophy of Composition*.

If I succeed, and I have every reason to hope I will, in getting this affair underway, we'll get onto it next winter. It will probably make a large in-octavo of 800 pages. There will be two portraits. One of them serves as the frontispiece to the posthumous edition of Poe's works (published by Redfield, New York), and is a reproduction of a painting that Griswold owned. This Griswold is the American author who was given the task of putting Poe's papers in order and who not only performed his task so badly but also defamed his dead friend in the preface to his edition. The other portrait embellishes the big illustrated in-octavo edition of the poems published in London. My collections are not in Paris and I no longer remember the editor's name.

There are other editions and other portraits, too, but invariably they are merely a more or less altered reproduction of these two typical portraits. If my enterprise were successful, I'd have them reproduced with the utmost care. The one from the American edition represents Poe with the well-known physiognomy of a gentleman: no moustache; sideburns; high collar. Tremendously distinguished. The other (from the London edition of the poems) is based on a daguerrotype. Here he is very French: moustache; no sideburns; collar folded down. In each, his brow is enormous both in breadth and height; he looks very pensive and his mouth is smiling. Despite the immense masculine force of the upper part of his head, it is, all in all, a very feminine face. The eyes are vast, very beautiful and abstracted. I think it would be delightful to reproduce them both.

126   To Auguste Poulet-Malassis

[late August 1860]

That frontispiece is again looming up on the horizon. I'm lost. How can you still have confidence in *any* artist's interpretation of *any* idea? Bracquemond will be determined to conserve what he can of his plate. Those flowers are ridiculous. He should at least have consulted books on the analogies and the symbolic language of Flowers, etc. Would you be willing to accept some good advice, offered in all seriousness? If you really want a frontispiece, cut out carefully the image Langlois made and ask Bracquemond to do a copy, exactly, adding nothing at all and removing nothing at all. The skeleton, the branches, the snake, Adam, Eve, everything should stay as it is. That is the only way to get something done. *Don't let him add anything at all.* This frontispiece is no longer ours, but it suits the book as it stands. It has the advantage of being able to adapt to any book at all, since all literature derives from Original Sin. —I'm speaking in all seriousness. —If you don't do this you'll only get ridiculous images.

Instead of that, what do you take it into your head to do? You put into Bracquemond's mind a mixture that will always baffle him. You expose yourself again to the same danger, that of not being understood (it's obvious he has no idea what's meant by: arborescent skeleton, since he wasn't even willing to stick to your sketch). He'll never be able to represent sins in the form of flowers.

Believe me, cut the page out of your book, and you can stick it back in again later. Insist absolutely on this: that he must copy exactly the whole image, adding nothing and changing nothing. He'll want to keep part of his skeleton, with its horrible proportions, its legs which are striding out (why striding?) and its pelvis which is partly hidden by the flowers. Finally, he'll never be able to fit branches onto the arms, because the hands reach the very edge of the page. Take it from me: either *nothing at all*, or a *servile copy* of Langlois's macabre image. I'm convinced that even now Bracquemond hasn't succeeded in understanding what you mean.

For the book of critical reviews. Yes, certainly. The last two sections, *Guys* and *The Philosophical Painters* [*Les Peintres philosophes*] are going to be published. *I was expecting* your final hypothesis about the philosophy of history.[59] I know your mind, as if it were my own child. I think that there is in you some old remains of the 1848 philosophies. First, can't you see, through an effort of imagination, that whatever transformations there are in the races of mankind, and however rapid destruction may be, there will always remain a need for antagonism, and that relationships, even if the forms and colors are different, will remain essentially the same? If you'll agree to accept the formula, it's a question of achieving eternal harmony through eternal struggle.

Second, I believe (because of the absolute unity that exists in the creative cause) that where your hypothesis is concerned, you'd have to consult a naturalist who was also a philosopher, my cousin for example. Do you think that any race of animals could absorb the other races? And even in your idea of absorption of all human races into a single one, can't

59. C. Pichois suggests that Malassis, in commenting on Ferrari's work, made some comments of a virtuously republican nature.

you see that man, the supreme animal, must himself absorb all the animals? Finally, if it's true that many races (of animals) have disappeared, it's also true that others have been born, destined to eat their neighbors or be eaten by them. And it's true, too, that if races of men have disappeared (in America, for example), other races of men have been born, destined to continue the struggle and the antagonism, according to an eternal law of numbers and proportional forces. You know Saint Augustine's dictum, which has now been adopted by those scientists who profess the spontaneous creation of animalcula: *God creates at every second of time*. From that one must draw the conclusion that the struggle continues at every second of time.

So you are forcing me to go into publishing and throw myself into questions I have not examined.

To return to the *Flowers of Evil*. *Please* GIVE ME THICKER CHARACTERS THAN BEFORE. And to go back again to that terrible Bracquemond. I've given him *carte blanche* within these limits: I want an *arborescent skeleton*, the tree of the knowledge of good and evil, in whose shade flourish the seven deadly sins in the form of allegorical plants. I recommended him to refer, for the tree, to the *excellent engraving that you and I know about*. He's already had explained to him what an arborescent skeleton is, and just look at how he understood it! "The Tree of the Science of Good and Evil" holds for him no meaning that is clear in plastic terms. You and I have both already urged him to refer to the *excellent engraving* mentioned above, but what use has that been?

He must trace it and imitate it, copying it in its *totality* and in its *tiny details*.

POSTSCRIPT: And you give him carte blanche!

I met Ferrari, who had taken advantage of a period of leisure to leave the parliament and come here. It seemed to me that he was more interested in the sale of his books than in the unification of Italy. I also felt he was ready to accept any plan and enter willingly into a ministry headed by Cavour, Garibaldi, or Mazzini.

I myself advised him to make himself emperor of Morocco. That made him laugh a great deal, but you take my word: the idea is not far from his thoughts.

127   TO CAROLINE AUPICK

11 October 1860

I can only, alas, give you two words in reply: *my debts have doubled through the necessity of doubling all debts at the end of a period determined by all* those who have worked out such questions. I owed M. Arondel 10,000 francs; for several years I've owed him 15,000. I borrow in order to pay. And to give you a further example, every penny of the money I've received from the reproduction of my works over the last 16 months goes to cover the interest of the renewal of a debt of 3,000 francs, which I contracted in order to install myself at Honfleur. Moreover, the total sum has swelled because of the difficulty of working in the midst of such agonies, while my expenses continue unabated. You rack your brains over this, making a thousand assumptions in order to understand, instead of simply saying to yourself: "Le Conseil Judiciaire." It's that shocking error that ruined my life, withered all my days, and gave all my thoughts the colors of hatred and despair. *But you don't understand me.*

Now I'm going to voice seriously, without exaggeration, some very somber thoughts. I may die before you, despite the diabolical courage that has hitherto supported me so often. What has restrained me over the last 18 months has been the question of Jeanne. (How would she survive after my death, since you'd have to pay all my debts from the money I'd leave?) There are other reasons, too: leaving you alone! and leaving you the horrible problem of sorting out a chaos I alone can understand!

The mere thought of the preparatory work I'd need to perform to facilitate an understanding of my affairs is enough to make me constantly renounce performing the act which I consider to be the most reasonable a human being can perform. To confess everything, what supports me is my pride, and my savage hatred of all mankind. I still hope I'll be able to dominate, to avenge myself, to reach the stage of being impertinent with no fear of punishment—and other such childish dreams. Finally, although I neither wish to frighten you with the aim of attaining some sort of end, nor to hurt you, nor make you feel any remorse, I've every right to think that some fine morning a crisis could destroy me—given that I'm really very weary and have never known joy or security. After your death, one thing is clear and beyond all doubt, since the fear of harming you, during your lifetime, can still make me stay my hand. But once you are dead, nothing will stop me. Finally, since I'm making a clean breast of things, and want to give everything its proper emphasis, what prevents me from acting are two charitable thoughts: you and Jeanne. It's absolutely certain that you couldn't say I live for my own pleasure. I'm coming to the point. Whatever destiny may befall me if, after having drawn up a list of my debts, I were to disappear suddenly during your lifetime, you'd have to do something to support that aged beauty who has now become an invalid. All my literary contracts are in order, and I'm convinced that a day will come when everything I've done will sell very well. Social conventions oblige me to make you the beneficiary of my will. Moreover, the Conseil Judiciaire did not, thank God, deprive me of my right to make a will. I repeat that if through illness, accident, despair, or any other cause I were freed of the boredom of living, you must devote to the relief of that woman, after the most reasonable and sordid payment of my debts, all that may remain, plus the income, however small, from the sale of my poems, my translations, and my prose works. But you have no head for business.

I've rediscovered my brother and *seen him*, talked with him, and of course he'd also be of assistance. He owns nothing but he earns money.

I've reread everything I've written and frankly, considering your weakness, it's abominable of me to send this. Yet I have the deplorable courage to do so. *It will at least serve to show you what thoughts habitually come to me and have done throughout my existence.*

Some positive news.

NO news of the play. And yet I'm *at least pleased with my plan.* I wouldn't have believed that I could overcome difficulties of such a new order. I utterly despise all those banalities, but I do think that at the end of a work like this, I could perhaps earn 50,000 francs. And to think that a simple letter of satisfaction from the director of *Le Cirque* would allow me to borrow 3,000 francs in a month! My dream, as you know, is to blend literary qualities with the tumultuous stage settings of the street theater.

My biography is to appear, together with a portrait of me. More problems. What information can I provide that isn't odious? You know how little I value *public esteem*, as you call it, but I've still got to appear, like an actor, in a decent attitude. To pay him homage and as a gesture of friendship I sent my *Paradise* to the excellent M. Cardine.

I've rented a small apartment at Neuilly, so I wouldn't have to have any more truck with hotels. I've moved my furniture, which is in poor condition, and I confess that I'd counted on a last obliging act on your part to restore it and to add a bed and a table, etc. . . .

But I'm still at the hotel.

The Flowers of Evil is in the process of being printed. It's a terrible business. It's a book that will always sell, unless the law interferes again. The poems have been increased by 34 new pieces, almost all of which you've seen. The rest will be published in *L'Artiste.* But I'm in a state of *great perplexity.* There's a preface in prose, a bit of violent buffoonery. I'm hesitant about publishing it and yet I'll never have my fill of insulting France. —I'm abandoning M. de Calonne, at the risk of incurring a law suit. M. Buloz has invited me to return to him, even if he has to pay a few debts, if I've run up any with Calonne (and I have).

There's been more talk of that ridiculous Cross of Honor. I truly hope the preface to the *Flowers* will make it permanently impossible. Moreover, I courageously replied to one of my friends who was making overtures about it: "*Twenty years ago* (I know what I'm saying is absurd) it would have been a good thing! Today I want to be an *exception*. Every Frenchman can be decorated *except for me*. I'll never change my morals or my style. Instead of the cross, they should give me money, money, nothing but money. If the cross is worth 500 francs, let them give me 500 francs! If it's only worth 20 francs, then let them give me 20 francs." In a word, I answered those louts like a lout. The more unhappy I become, the more pride I have.

I send my love sadly, very sadly. I love you with all my heart and you've never known it. Between you and me there is this difference that I know you by heart, and you've never been able to decipher my miserable nature.

POSTSCRIPT: I read carefully everything you told me about the land slip in the garden. It's very sad. Poor little house! If I have sufficient strength and health to survive all my torments I promise faithfully not only never to sell it, but even never to mortgage it.

You didn't even deign to read attentively the second part of my last long letter. And yet the ideas I suggested to you were ones I had measured, meditated, and weighed carefully. —I'm speaking of the letter in which I admitted to you that creditors had snatched from me money that someone had entrusted to me for a particular purpose.

My love once more.

128   TO ALPHONSE CALONNE

3 December [1860]

It won't be until tomorrow evening that I'll be completely free of the musician[60] (it's been a great disappointment for me) and then I'll at last devote to you a whole string of days. You'd make me very happy if, despite the absence of a manuscript, you could pay me the first of two bills; as for the second, it will be renewed. The first piece I'll send you will be the *painters*. The second will be *Dandyism*. Sainte-Beuve's book will, I think, provide me with an excuse to look at Chateaubriand from a fresh angle, as *the father of Dandyism*.[61] If therefore, as is likely, you ask one of your writers for a review of the Sainte-Beuve, that shouldn't prevent me from taking it up again as the starting point for my own piece.

I'll come round and see you this evening.

60. Stoepel had set to music Longfellow's *Hiawatha*. He asked Baudelaire for a translation of the text into French, which he provided but for which he was never paid.
61. Sainte-Beuve had just published his *Chateaubriand and His Literary Circle under the Empire* (*Chateaubriand et son cercle littéraire sous l'Empire*).

[about 20 March 1861?]

Dear friend,

I didn't need your letter, since for several days I've been meditating on that subject, and I'd already visited Hetzel. So I was about to write to you. I'm very sorry to cause you pain and despite that terrible and oft-repeated statement, "We're going to go under," I'm forced to ask of you something that may be impossible and which in any case would be a great act of devotion, *with the reservation nonetheless that after payment I'll go on the great expedition of errands and within a couple of days I'll close either partially or completely the hole made in your private affairs*. You can be the judge:

25 March	1,000	Tenré (impossible)
25 March	500	Schwartz (impossible)
25 March	350	Gélis (impossible)
1 April	500	Lemercier (impossible)
10 April	1,100	Hetzel

So our shuttle is impossible since all the moneylenders appear this time in the total. You could perhaps, at Lemercier's or Gélis's, get a note accepted if it's signed by someone other than me, for I must tell you that, to crown my misfortunes, I'm at present being sued for 1,900 francs' worth of disputed IOUs (of which only 600 concern me *directly*). Schwartz and Gélis are mixed up in that so you can see the danger.

Now, Hetzel. Hetzel's banker has suspended payments. He's now using (once a month) the discount bank—once a month, that's to say from the 25th to the 30th. I've had a chat with him. He'll willingly take your notes but I know that the first time he did so the discount bank refused them and finally it was his banker who accepted them. He offered to let me use them in Belgium but I think the company he was going to use there has just gone bankrupt as a result of the Mirès affair.

Moreover he told me that in a few months' time he'd willingly take (if you agree) the *Reflections on Some of My Contemporaries* [*Réflexions sur quelques-uns de mes contemporains*]. As for the *Curiosities*, he urges us insistently to change the title, which, according to him, *smacks of remaindered works*, even if the substance itself is highly amusing.

I want to add a word or two, the sort of thing I can say to you alone. For a pretty long time I've been on the brink of suicide. What holds me back has nothing to do with cowardice or even regret. It's my sense of pride, which prevents me leaving my affairs in a mess. *I'll leave enough to pay my debts*. But I still need to make careful notes so that my executor can sort everything out. You know I'm neither a sniveler nor a liar. For the last two months in particular I've fallen into an alarming listlessness and despair. I've felt myself attacked by the kind of illness Gérard[62] had, that is, the fear of being incapable either of thinking, or of writing, a single line. It's only in the last 4 or 5 days that I've been able to prove that I wasn't dead from that point of view. That's a great step forward.

A fine edition of Edgar Poe and probably the theater will pay my debt, although it's constantly increasing, and at far too fast a rate. But I return incessantly to my obsession: that of letting the debt lie by paying regular interest. Do you know that every two months, or two and a half months, I have a flood of errands, a forced delapidation of time and money, a palpitation of all my willpower, a real anguish every time I turn a door handle? Moreover, this debt, which I incurred essentially to install myself at Honfleur, now prevents me from doing so, as I have to be in Paris and always on my guard.

I've the greatest desire to see you here. It's not a question of the pleasures of comradeship, but of yourself and your interests. For several years now the book trade has been going badly, including your own. Add to that the nullity of the excellent de Broise and you can guess what your future will bring. Everyone—and I don't mean those who are hostile to you but those who are attached to you—says of you: "Those men know absolutely nothing about publicity." Sainte-Beuve said to me the day before yesterday: "Where's Malassis?" "In Alençon." "But he's *mad*!" "It's so he can finish the Hatin book." "What's the use of a foreman then?" he added finally.

Mad as you are, you ask me what stage my book is at! How can I worry my head about it? De Broise's presence in Paris is a deathblow both to me and to it. I know Buloz and Montégut have promised a big piece of work, but when will it come? Montégut prefers to be several months behind. Sainte-Beuve has given his promise, but when will he come up with the goods?

To sum up: I think Lemercier and Gélis are possible for you but they won't be possible *for me* until later on. The 25th or later I'll see Hetzel again. I think Gélis will help you provided that *he doesn't have much at present* and that he doesn't feel he's dealing with accommodation bills.

POSTSCRIPT: The portrait and the advertisement haven't even appeared in *L'Artiste*.[63]

---

62. Gérard de Nerval.

63. The portrait of Baudelaire by Braquemond included in the second edition of *The Flowers of Evil*, which Baudelaire wanted *L'Artiste* to publish: it never did.

Oh, my dear mother, is there still *enough time* for us *both* to be happy? I no longer dare believe so. I'm 40, there is the Conseil Judiciaire, enormous debts, and finally, worse than all this, my willpower is lost, destroyed! Who's to say that my mind itself is not impaired? I don't know, I can't judge anymore since I've even lost the ability to make an effort.

First of all, I want to tell you something I don't tell you often enough and that you are perhaps unaware of, and that is that the tenderness I feel for you increases constantly. It fills me with shame to confess that this tenderness doesn't even give me the strength to pull myself together. I contemplate the years that have passed and spend my time reflecting on the brevity of life. Nothing more. And my willpower is constantly rusting away. If ever there were a man who knew, in his youth, spleen and hypochondria, then I'm that man. And yet I want to live and I long to know some degree of security, of glory, of contentment with myself. Something terrible says to me: *never*, and yet something else says: *try*.

Of so many plans and projects accumulated in 2 or 3 boxes I no longer dare open, what will I carry out? Perhaps nothing at all, ever.

1 April 1861

The preceding page was written a month ago, or six weeks or two months, I no longer know when. I fell into a kind of constant nervous fear: sleeping and waking were equally awful; action was impossible. My copies lay on my desk for a month before I summoned the courage to wrap them up. I didn't write to Jeanne, I didn't see her for nearly three months. Naturally, since there was no possibility of doing so, I didn't send her a cent. (She came to me yesterday. She's just left the hospice and her brother, whom I believed to be supporting her, sold in her absence part of her furniture. She's going to sell the rest to pay off a few debts.) In this horrible state of mind, with its powerlessness and its hypochondria, the thought of suicide returned. I can tell you now it's over. At every hour of the day that thought persecuted me. I saw in it the absolute escape, escape from everything. At the same time, *for three months*, through what seems on first view a particular contradiction, I prayed! Constantly I prayed (to whom? to what particular being? I have absolutely no idea) to obtain two things: for myself, the strength to go on living; for you, long life. May I say in passing that your desire to die is most ridiculous and highly uncharitable, since your death would be the last straw for me, and would make any happiness I might have utterly impossible.

At last the obsession disappeared, driven out by a violent and unavoid-able task, my article on Wagner, improvised in three days in a printing office. But for the obsession of the printing works I'd never have had the strength to do it. Since then I've again fallen ill from listlessness, horror, and fear. I was physically ill two or three times, and pretty badly, but one of the things I find particularly unbearable is that when I fall asleep, and even in my sleep, I hear voices very distinctly, whole sentences, but very banal, very dull, and with no relationship to those things that concern me.

Your letters came. They were hardly calculated to bring me solace. You're always armed to stone me along with the crowd. All that has been going on since my childhood, as you know. How on earth do you succeed in always being for your son the very opposite of a *friend*, except in matters of money, and even then provided—and this is what reveals what an absurd, and yet at the same time generous, character you have—that such matters do not affect you. I was careful to indicate for you in the table of contents all the new bits. It was very simple for you to verify that they were all written to fit into the framework. A book I've been working on for 20 years and of which, moreover, I'm not even entitled to prevent subsequent reprints.

As for M. Cardine,[64] that's a serious matter, but in an entirely different way from that you imagine. In the midst of all my sorrows, I don't want a priest to come and struggle against me in the spirit of my old mother, and I'll put that to rights, if I can, if I have the strength to do so. The man's conduct is monstrous and inexplicable. As for burning the books, no one does that any more, except for the idiots who enjoy seeing paper burst into flames. And to think I stupidly deprived myself of a precious copy, to please him and to give him something he'd been requesting for the last three years! And now I have no copies left for my friends! You've always had to make me kneel to someone or other. At one stage it was M. Emon. Do you remember? Now it's a priest who hasn't even enough delicacy to hide from you a hurtful thought. And, finally, he didn't even see that the work set out from a Catholic idea! But that's an entirely different consideration.

What particularly saved me from suicide was two thoughts that will seem very childish to you. The first is that it was my duty to provide you with detailed notes of all my debts, so you can pay them off, and that meant that first I'd have to go to Honfleur where all my documents are filed, since I alone can make head or tail of them. The second—shall I confess it?—was that it was very hard to make an end of myself before having published at least my critical works, if I renounced the plays (and

64. Mme Aupick's spiritual advisor.

I'd planned a second), the novels, and finally the great book I've been meditating over the last two years: *My Heart Laid Bare*, in which would be accumulated all my rage. Oh, if ever that sees the light of day, Jean-Jacques's *Confessions* will seem pale. You can see that I'm dreaming again.

Unfortunately, to create this exceptional work, I'd have had to keep masses of letters from all and sundry, letters that over 20 years I've burnt or given away.

Finally, as I told you, a violent task tore me out of my torpor and my illness for three periods of 24 hours. The illness will return. With regard to the Conseil Judiciaire, your remarks about it set me musing again. I think that I've at last hit on a *combined* means that would only half ruin me, would give me a vast amount of free time, and would therefore enable me to *enrich your revenue*, since however little I earned I'd only need half of it at the very most.

I'll explain that to you. What a damned invention that was! The motherly invention of a mind too preoccupied with money, an invention that dishonored me, drove me into constant debts, killed any amiability I had, and even hampered my artistic and literary education, which has remained incomplete. Blindness creates greater scourges than malevolence. What is certain is that the present situation can't go on much longer. I don't believe I can go mad but I could become sufficiently antisocial to pass for a madman.

As soon as I'd read your letter I wrote to Ducreux, saying that I didn't want him to torment you and that I alone had to pay and that he would moreover hear from me at the end of the month. Now the new month has begun and I have nothing. I really don't want anything at all from you (the 25,000 francs! I often think about them) but today I have to beg from you 200 francs. I confess to you in all frankness that I'll extract from that sum 50 or 60 francs for my hotel (which I'll have to go on keeping on good terms with until the day when a break in the clouds lets me go to Honfleur without fearing that my peace of mind, on which yours depends, might be disturbed) or else for a few personal items I can't do without.

I beg you to send the money: and use the railway (opposite the steamboats) or a registered letter. I believe the real figure is 190 francs but I think that the administrative staff (of the post office at least) don't take fractions into account. If you can, arrange for it to reach me the day after tomorrow. It's always dangerous for you to pay any of my bills at all—you can guess how that might encourage people. As for me, I'm being sued for 2,000 francs in IOUs, 1,300 of which should be the responsibility of M. Calonne. I'm on bad terms with him. He behaved shamefully toward me. Those IOUs were advance payments. Now the price of everything I produce and am to produce for the *Revue européenne* goes to Calonne. I don't get any of my rightful payment. Concurrently with that, the sum of 700 francs doesn't directly concern me. You see how I need to be in good heart. I don't have the right to use any of it for my own benefit. Amusement and pleasure are closed worlds for me these days. And to be able to return to Honfleur I'll need at least a month, 30 days, of ceaseless work. Do you think I'm paying dearly enough for the follies of my early years?

I had a lot of other things to tell you. But I have neither paper nor time. Be kind to me. Remember that you're often unjust to me without suspecting that you are being so, particularly when you accuse me of not feeling enough affection for you. It was because I wanted to prove my affection that I kept the beginning of this letter, written at a time when I hadn't received your reproaches.

You can't imagine how often in my plans for the future I've linked my life to yours. Did you get *La Revue contemporaine?* I'll send you the *Revue européenne.* I don't have time to reread my letter.

131   TO CAROLINE AUPICK

[6 May 1861]

My dear Mother,

If you really possess maternal genius and are not still weary, come to Paris, come and see me, and even bring me back to Honfleur. For a thousand terrible reasons I can't go to Honfleur just now in search of what I most need, which is a little encouragement and a little loving. At the end of March I wrote to you asking: "Will we never see each other again?" I was in one of those crises where one sees the terrible truth. I'd give anything to spend a few days with you, you are the only being from whom my life is suspended, a week, three days, a few hours.

You don't read my letters carefully enough. You think I'm lying or at least exaggerating when I speak of my despair, of my health, of the horror I feel for life. I tell you I'd like to see you, and that I can't rush up to Honfleur. Your letters contain numerous errors and false ideas that a conversation could set right and that volumes of writing couldn't eradicate. Every time I take up my pen to tell you about the situation I'm in, I'm afraid. I'm afraid of killing you, of destroying your weak body. And I for my part am constantly, unbeknownst to you, on the verge of suicide. I believe that you love me passionately. Your intelligence may be blind but your character is so great! I myself loved you passionately in my childhood. Later, under the pressure of your unjust acts, I didn't show enough respect—as though the injustice of a mother could authorize lack of respect in a son! I've often repented, although, in my usual way, I

167

said nothing. I'm no longer the violent, ungrateful child. Long meditations on my destiny and your character helped me understand all my faults and all your generosity. But, to put it in a nutshell, the ill is done, done through your imprudence and my failings. We're obviously destined to love one another, to end our lives as honestly and gently as possible. And yet, in the awful circumstances in which I find myself, I'm convinced that one of us will kill the other, and that the end will come through each of us killing the other. After my death, you won't go on living: that's clear. I'm the only thing you live for. After your death, especially if you were to die through a shock I'd caused, I'd kill myself—that's beyond doubt. Your death, which you mention too often in tones of resignation, wouldn't correct a single aspect of my situation. The Conseil Judiciaire would be maintained (why would it not be?), nothing would be paid, and to crown my grief, there'd be *the horrible sensation of absolute isolation*. For *me* to kill myself would be absurd, wouldn't it? "So you're going to leave your old mother utterly alone?" you'll say. Indeed yes! If I don't exactly have the right to do so, I believe that the amount of suffering I've undergone for nearly *30 years* would excuse me. "And God?" you'll say. With all my heart (how sincerely no one but I can know!) I long to believe that an external, invisible being takes an interest in my destiny. But what must one do to believe it?

(The idea of God makes me think of that damned priest. In the pain and sorrow this letter will bring you, I don't want you to consult him. That priest is my enemy, through pure stupidity perhaps.)

To return to that suicide, which is an idea that isn't obsessive but returns periodically, there's one thing that should reassure you. I can't kill myself without having put my affairs in order. All my papers are at Honfleur, in great confusion. So I'd have a lot of work to do at Honfleur. And once I was there I couldn't tear myself away from you. For you must realize that I wouldn't want to sully your house through a detestable act. Moreover it would drive you mad. And why suicide? Because of the debts? Yes, and yet the debts could be overcome. It's above all because of a horrible fatigue that stems from an impossible situation that has persisted for *too long*. Every minute proves to me that life no longer has any savor. You committed a most imprudent act in my youth. Your imprudence and *my former faults* weigh heavily on me and envelop me. My situation is atrocious. There are people who salute me and pay me homage, there are perhaps some who envy me. My literary position is more than good. I can do as I please. Everything will be published. As I have a cast of mind that is not popular, I won't earn much money, but I'll leave behind a very famous name, that I know—provided I have the courage to go on living. But my spiritual health is terrible—gone

168

forever, perhaps. I still have my projects: *My Heart Laid Bare*, novels, two plays, including the one for the *Théâtre français*, but will all that ever get done? *I can no longer believe it.* My situation as regards my honor, frightful—and that's the greatest evil. Never any rest. Insults, outrages, affronts you can't imagine, which corrupt the imagination and paralyze it. I earn a little money, it's true. If I didn't have debts, and if I no longer had a fortune, I'D BE RICH—now just give that a moment's thought! I could give you money, and there'd be no danger in my acting charitably toward Jeanne. We'll speak of her again in a moment. It's you who have provoked these explanations. All that money flows away in an expensive and unhealthy existence (for I live very badly) and in the payment or rather the insufficient redemption of old debts, in legal costs, documents, etc.

In a moment I'll come to positive matters, I mean current ones. For to tell you the truth, I need to be saved, and you alone can save me. Today I want to tell you everything. I'm alone, I have neither friends, mistress, dog, nor cat to whom I can complain. I have only the portrait of my father, which remains mute.

I'm in that horrible state I experienced in the autumn of 1844. A resignation worse than fury. But my physical health, which I need for your sake, for my duties—that's yet another matter! I must talk to you about it, although you take very little notice of it. I don't mean to talk of those nervous disorders that destroy me day by day and nullify my courage, the vomiting, the insomnia, the fainting fits. I've told you about them far too often. But there's no point in having any shame with you. You know that when I was very young I had a venereal disease, which I later believed totally cured. At Dijon after 1848 it exploded anew. It was again brought under control. Now it has returned and has taken on a new form, spots on the skin, an extraordinary weariness in all my joints. You can believe me: I know all about it. Perhaps in the sorrow I'm plunged in, my terror is aggravating the malady. But I need a strict diet and the life I lead makes it impossible for me to follow such a diet. I'll put all that aside and go back to my dreams. Before coming to the project I want to tell you about, I'm taking a very real pleasure in confessing. Who knows if I'll ever again be able to reveal to you the very depths of my soul that *you've never appreciated or even known.* I've no hesitation in writing that, so surely do I know it to be true.

In my childhood I went through a stage when I loved you passionately. Listen and read without fear. I've never told you anything about it. I remember an outing in a coach. You'd just come out of a clinic you'd been sent to, and to prove that you'd given some thought to your son, you showed me some pencil sketches you'd done for me. Can you believe what a tremendous memory I have? Later, the square of Saint-André-des-Arts and Neuilly. Long walks, constant acts of tenderness. I remember the quays, which were so melancholy at evening. Oh, for me that was the good age of maternal tenderness. I beg your pardon for describing as "a good age" one that for you was doubtless a bad one. But I lived constantly through you, you were mine alone. You were both an idol and a comrade. You may well be surprised to hear me speak with passion of a time so far in the past. I myself am astonished. It's perhaps because I've conceived once again a desire for death that the old things are so vividly painted in my mind.

You know what a horrendous education your husband inflicted on me later on. I'm 40 years old and it's still painful for me to think of the colleges, and of the fear my stepfather inspired in me. Yet I loved him and moreover I'm now wise enough to render him due justice. But all in all he was pigheadedly clumsy. I want to pass over this rapidly, for I see tears in your eyes.

Finally I fled and henceforth was completely abandoned. My sole love was pleasure, perpetual excitement. Travel, fine furniture, pictures, girls, etc. Now I'm being cruelly punished for that. As for the Conseil Judiciaire, I've only one comment. I now know the immense value of money and understand the seriousness of everything connected with it. I can understand how you could believe you were being clever, how you could think you were working for my welfare. But there is nevertheless a question that has always obsessed me: how is it that the following thought never entered your mind: "It's possible that my son will never have as good a sense of the proprieties as I do, but it's also possible he may become a remarkable man from other points of view. In that case, what will I do? Will I condemn him to bear the brand of shame into old age, a brand that harms, a cause of impotence and sorrow?" It's clear that if there had never been a Conseil Judiciaire I'd have spent every penny. I would have had to conquer my distaste for work. The Conseil Judiciare was formed, everything was spent, and now I'm old and unhappy.

Is rejuvenation possible? That's the whole question. All this return to the past had no aim other than to show you I have some excuses to put forward, if not a complete justification. If you feel I'm reproaching you in what I write, let me at least assure you that that in no way changes my admiration for your great heart, my thanks for your devotion. You've constantly sacrificed yourself. Your only genius is for sacrifice. Less reason than charity. I'm asking more of you. I'm asking you to give me some advice, to support a complete understanding between us, to get me out of my difficulties. I beg you, come, come. I'm at the end of my nervous strength, at the end of my courage, of my hope. I foresee unending horror. I foresee my literary life shackled forever. I foresee catastrophe. You can easily ask friends, Ancelle for instance, to put you up for a week. I'd give anything to see you, and hug you. I foresee a catastrophe and can't go to you just now. Paris is bad for me. Twice already I've committed a seriously imprudent act that you may well judge severely. I'll end by going out of my mind.

I ask you, for your happiness and mine, insofar as we can still experience such a thing. You gave me permission to discuss with you a plan I have, and this is it: I'm asking for a half-measure. The alienation of a large sum, limited say to 10,000—2,000 to liberate me immediately, 2,000 to be paid to you to cover unforeseen or predictable expenses, the essentials of life, clothing, etc. . . . for a year (Jeanne will go into an establishment where only what is strictly necessary will be paid). Moreover, I'll discuss her case with you in a moment. Again, it's you who have incited me to do so. Finally, 6,000 would go to Ancelle or Marin, to be paid out slowly, successively, prudently, so as to pay off perhaps more than 10,000 and prevent any shock or scandal at Honfleur.

That would give me a year's peace. I'd be a really great fool and a great rascal if I didn't take advantage of it to rejuvenate myself. All the money earned during that period (10,000 or perhaps only 5,000) would be paid to you. I wouldn't hide from you any of my business affairs or any benefits I received. Instead of filling in the gaps, that money, too, would go to pay off debts. And so it would continue in the subsequent years. So I could *perhaps*, through a rejuvenation that would take place before your very eyes, *pay for everything*, without my capital being whittled away by more than 10,000, although it's true that that leaves aside the 4,600 of former years. And the house would be saved. For that's one of the considerations I bear constantly in mind.

If you were to adopt this blissful project, I'd want to be reinstalled at the end of the month, perhaps immediately. I give you permission to come and get me. Of course you understand that there's a mass of details a letter can't include. In a word, I'd like the whole sum to be paid only with your consent, after a full debate between us. In fact, I'd like *you* to become my Conseil Judiciaire. Is it possible to be forced to associate such a loathsome idea with so gentle a concept as a mother?

In that case, unfortunately, we'd have to bid farewell to the little sum, the little gains, 100 here and 200 there, necessitated by life in Paris. It would be a question of big speculations and big accounts, the payment of which would be slow in coming. —Consult yourself alone, your conscience and God, since you're lucky enough to believe. Reveal your thoughts to Ancelle only very slowly. He's a good man, but narrow-minded. He can't believe that someone who has chosen to be a rascal and whom he's had occasion to haul over the coals can be an important man. He'll let me kick the bucket through sheer pigheadedness. Instead of thinking only of money, give a bit of thought to fame and repose and *my life*. In this case, as I say, I wouldn't be coming for periods of two weeks or a month or two months. I'd be coming to stay permanently except when the two of us went to Paris.

Work on the proofs could be done via the post. There's another wrong idea of yours that I must put straight, an idea that constantly enters your letters. *I'm never bored in solitude and I'm never bored when I'm with you.*

I only know that your friends would make me suffer. I agree to accept that.

Occasionally I've had the idea of summoning a family council or going before a tribunal. Do you know I'd really have some good things to tell them, even if it were only this: "*I've produced 8 volumes in horrendous conditions. I can earn my livelihood. I'm being assassinated by the debts of my youth!*" I haven't done so through respect for you, to protect your dreadful sensitivity. Please be grateful to me for that. I repeat that I've made myself pledge to seek help from you alone.

Beginning next year, I'll devote to Jeanne the revenue of my remaining capital. She'll withdraw somewhere where she's not completely alone. This is what has happened to her. Her brother bundled her into a hospice, to get rid of her, and when she came out she discovered he'd sold some of her furniture and clothes. In four months, since my flight from Neuilly in fact, I've given her a mere seven francs. I beg you for repose, give me repose, work, and a little tenderness.

Obviously, given the current state of affairs, some things are horribly urgent. As a result, with all this inevitable fiddling with banks, I've committed yet again the fault of using for my personal debts several hundred francs that don't belong to me. *There was absolutely no other way out.* Of course I'd thought I'd be able to repair the damage immediately. Someone who's in London is refusing to pay me 400 francs he owes me. Someone else who was to give me back 300 francs is traveling. It's always the unexpected that happens. Today I found the *terrible courage* to confess my fault to the person concerned. What's going to happen? I really don't know. But I wanted to clear my conscience. I hope that respect for my name and my talent will prevent a scandal and that he'll be willing to wait.

Farewell. I'm exhausted. A few details about my health: I've neither slept nor eaten for three days, my throat feels tight. And yet I must work. No, I take back the "farewell," since I'm hoping to see you. Oh, read this very attentively, and try to understand me properly. I know this letter will cause you pain, but you'll certainly find in it accents of gentleness, tenderness, and even hope that you've heard all too rarely.

And I love you.

132   To Léon Cladel

[30 or 31 July 1861]

Dear child,

It would be a good idea for us to get together to revise one last time your *Everlasting Love* [*Amours éternelles*],[65] which you were kind enough to dedicate to me. The ninth proof was sent to me yesterday by the *Revue fantaisiste*'s printer; there were half a dozen unsuitable terms and a few phrases from the far side of the Loire[66] which are more Roman than French and which I consider too heterodox, so that in my opinion they detract from your interesting work. Come quickly, very quickly, to my place where I'll wait for you, if need be, the whole afternoon.

133   To Mario Uchard

[November 1861]

Sir,

First of all, my thanks for the pleasure your book *Raymon* gave me. But since you asked me to be utterly frank with you, I'll take full advantage of your request, without fear of angering you.

The novel seems to me to be divided into two quite distinct parts: the first, *Passing Fancies* [*Les Amourettes*] (I wasn't very affected by this section); the second, which I find as powerful and rousing as one of Godwin's conceptions (an intense compliment, as you see) is the *drama* that takes place between father and son.

These two parts are completely separate and each is even treated in a different manner. The first is full of digressions and sidetracks, and moves forward slowly. Moreover, some of the digressions I find rather disagreeable (for example, the jibes at Byronism. Why come to the aid of the Pecksniffs? They're strong enough as it is). The second part is solid, suggestive, and as tightly constructed as a play. So it's the *harsh, bitter* parts in the theme that most aroused my sympathy. In the *flippant* parts I almost felt hurt. Moreover, those digressions have the inevitable result of

65. A short story dedicated to Baudelaire, who had written a preface to Cladel's novel *The Ridiculous Martyrs* (*Les Martyrs ridicules*).

66. Cladel was born in Quercy.

destroying a book's *magic*, the reader's belief and the plot's verisimilitude. You say *I* too often and when you say *I* (other than in a book that is about the self), you turn your reader away from the pleasure of taking an interest in your book.

The English type is excellent and completely likable. The story of the abandoned mother's sufferings (a form of widowhood, with poverty into the bargain) is very fine. As for the recognition scene of father and son, the father's dejection, the immediate change in his character—all that is marvelously well done. But I emphasize again the bizarre aspect of a book that seems to be two juxtaposed books. Now for another nasty comment: when your characters speak they too frequently use expressions that belong to men of the world. I'd prefer them to use a less true, less *worldly* speech.

You see that I've obeyed your instructions even to the point of risking your displeasure. My thanks again (and my excuses).

134   TO ALFRED DE VIGNY

[about 16 December 1861]

Dear Sir,

For a great many years now I've wanted to be introduced to you, as one of our dearest masters. My candidature for the French Academy provided me with a pretext to present myself at your home a few days ago. But I learned that you were unwell and thought it more discreet not to do so. Yesterday, however, M. Patin told me you were feeling distinctly better, and so I've decided to come and weary you for a few moments with my presence.

I do beg you to send me away immediately and without standing on ceremony if you fear that a visit, however short, might tire you, even if the visitor were one of your most fervent and devoted admirers.

135   TO ALFRED DE VIGNY

[about 16 December 1861]

Dear Sir,

I returned home quite overwhelmed by your kindness and as I'm eager to allow you to get to know me I'm sending you something in addition to what you requested. In the two pamphlets (*Richard Wagner*, *Théophile Gautier*) you'll find a few pages that will please you. Here are my *Artificial Paradises*, which I'm weak enough to consider of some importance. The first part is mine alone. The second consists of the analysis of De Quincey's book, to which I've added here and there a few ideas of my own, but with great modesty. Here are the *Flowers*, the last copy I possess on fine paper. The truth is that this copy was earmarked for you a very long time ago. All the old poems have been revised. All the new ones I've indicated in pencil in the table of contents. The only praise I ask for this book is that readers recognize that it's not a mere album, but has a beginning and an end. All the new poems have been written to fit into the strange framework I chose.

I've added an old issue of a review that contains the beginning of a new experiment that may interest you.[67] Jules Janin and Sainte-Beuve found in it a certain relish. As for my articles on fine arts and literature, I don't have a single copy at hand. If I can dig up a copy of the old edition of the *Flowers*, I'll send it to you. Finally, there are the poems of Poe. I won't make any recommendations—they're all equally interesting. Don't return this volume: I have another copy.

My thanks again for the charming way in which you welcomed me. However lofty the image I had of you, I didn't expect the reality. You are yet another proof that a vast talent always involves great kindness and exquisite indulgence.

136   TO VICTOR DE LAPRADE

23 December 1861

I'm so rushed and overwhelmed with business that I've not yet found time to tell you, as I'd initially planned to do, how hurt and offended I am as a poet at the ministerial violence that recently attacked you, one of our best and most serious poets. I'm all the more sincere in saying this because I feel that in the eyes of superficial people this severity will ricochet back on the man who'll be called your accuser.[68] And he is one of my oldest friends. The minister who strikes you, compromises him in doing so. And yet the violence that may appear in a piece of literary criticism does not imply a categorical desire to harm. He is both innocent and punished. I've had the chance over the last few days to discuss this affair with MM. Patin and de Vigny and saw that their main feeling about it was a sense of sorrow. Despite the minister's theory, we in France will never grow accustomed to considering a teacher as if he were a servant, and our entire education sytem prevents us from doing so.

I recently met M. Paul Chenavard and begged him to write to you in

67. A reference to the prose poems.
68. Laprade, who was hostile to the Empire, had responded to an attack launched by the progovernment Sainte-Beuve, in a satire entitled "The Muses of the State." As a result, the minister for education fired him from his position as professor of French literature in Lyon.

my favor. You may perhaps not know that I've taken it into my head to apply for the Academy—as though I haven't had enough painful experiences in my life, which is already so complicated, and as if I hadn't already suffered enough insults. Oh what a job I've taken on! I'm told: "Most of those gentlemen don't know you, and a few *unfortunately* do know you." Had I dared I would have opted for Father Lacordaire's chair, because he's a man of religion and a *Romantic*, but I was told that my candidature was already enough of a scandal without adding to it that of wanting to succeed a monk, so I stifled my admiration for Lacordaire and I'm pretending to aspire to Scribe's chair.

Chenavard did what he could to turn me aside from such a mad course, but as I've already started I have to persevere. He also told me that you belong to a party (I don't know what the parties are that divide the population of Parnassus and even if it makes me appear an ass, I don't want to find out). However, I told him I fully believed you to be a royalist and that I was unfortunately at the very antipodes of your point of view, but that I make strict use of my right to be absurd, and that, although every republican is under the apparent obligation of being an atheist, I'd always been a fervent Catholic, which forges a link between us—in addition to that of rhythm and rhyme. At that I have to confess that Chenavard burst out laughing. The philosopher, the subtle reasoning mind had never detected the Catholic in *The Flowers of Evil*. Yet even if the work were diabolical, is there, can one say, any one more Catholic than the devil?

But seriously, I've committed a real piece of stupidity and I'm persevering in it to make it seem a wise act. Reduced to speaking of qualifications, I present myself with the first three volumes of my Poe translation; the fourth (pure sciences under the monstrous title *Eureka*) is currently awaiting publication; then there is my deplorable *Flowers of Evil* (you may perhaps not have the second edition, which is revised and augmented with 35 new poems designed to fit into the general framework. I'll try to send you this.) There's also my treatise on stimulants (*Artificial Paradises*), which earned me this enormous piece of stupidity from M. Villemain, enunciated with indescribable solemnity: "Toxicology, Sir, is no morality!" Just so; absolutely; but if one speaks of stimulants, isn't one obliged to talk of morality? There's also a very considerable number of studies on contemporary men of letters, painters, sculptors, engravers, musicians, etc.

I confess that all that is little more than nothing, particularly in comparison with my dreams. Forgive me sir, for writing to you at such length, but in talking to someone I don't know but whose sympathy I sense, I'm seeking solace for the fatigue caused me by my first visits. To tell the truth, they shattered my nerves. I've been well punished for my ill-timed ambition. Perhaps I shan't have the pleasure of seeing you when you come to Paris. I may well escape to the seaside after having been lectured at or insulted by all the Academicians whom decorum obliges me to see. (However, I'll not go without having paid court to Monseigneur d'Orléans. I want to carry out my folly minutely and conscientiously.) So I beg you to accept this letter as the equivalent of an official visit. If there is a case where republican formulas are free from ridicule, it's surely between poets. As such, Sir, please accept my fraternal greetings.[69]

POSTSCRIPT: If you have connections with M. Joséphin Soulary and M. Armand Fraisse, please give them my regards. If you know M. Janmot, tell him I've long desired to render to him what is due, and that I'm preparing a big study called *The Philosopher Painters, Painters Who Think*, or something along those lines. The atmosphere of Lyon is perfectly known to me and it's a very special one.

137   TO CAROLINE AUPICK

25 December 1861

My poor dear mother, left so much on her own! Your last letter caused me much pain and yet anyone would think, given the long time I've let pass before replying, that I wasn't much affected by it, isn't that so? What! That wretched little trip to Paris affected you so much that now you're bored, you who never used to be bored at all. I was very surprised by your letter because I'd grown used to thinking of you as endowed with a vast store of energy, so much so that I can say my affection contains much admiration. I'm not seeking to flatter you, but, like all men, I admire above all the qualities I don't possess. Moreover, I'm not capable of feeling affection for those whom I can't admire at least to some extent. (That's why, in parentheses, there's little love lost between my brother and me. Quite apart from my numerous bones of contention with him—for unlike you he made no attempt to soften the rancor I felt against him through immense devotion.) [. . .]

If you ask why I could be so barbaric as to leave you such a long time without news or consolation, I who mean everything to you and who have no other way of thanking you and amusing you than by speaking of myself, I'll answer first that I've been ill on several occasions, and then (this is the great and deplorable reason) that when I'm unfortunate

69. Predictably, the flippant tone of this letter and the combination of apparent sympathy and overt self-seeking infuriated Laprade.

enough to neglect a duty, the following day it's even harder to perform that duty, and it becomes daily more and more difficult until that duty ends by seeming impossible to perform. That's connected with the state of anxiety and nervous terror I'm perpetually living in and my remark holds good for all possible duties, even that very pleasant and natural one of writing to my mother. The only way I ever get out of difficult situations is through an explosion—but what I suffer in my existence is beyond expression, believe me! Finally, in November, two catastrophes hit me, one after the other.[70] And now, as if I didn't have enough problems stored up I've just added another, that of my candidature. Oh if I'd known what torment it would be! And how tiring! You'd never guess what problems, what letters, what chores this strange fantasy necessitates. I've only seen a few Academicians and already my nerves are shattered. Nevertheless, there's one happy outcome of this episode, which is that it has aroused my interest. One cannot live without some mania, some *hobbyhorse*. And I constantly see suicide as the sole and above all the simplest solution to all the horrible complications in which I've been condemned to live for so many years. [. . .]

The only thing that interests *me* is the small emoluments linked to the position—I don't even know exactly how much is involved. For you'll certainly guess that in my conscience I feel no need for the approbation of *all these old fools* (I'm using the very expression that some of them use to describe others). But I told myself that you attach great importance to public honors and that if by a *miracle*, and that's what it would need, I were to succeed, it would give you immense joy. It's true that I also said to myself: "If for a wonder I did succeed, my mother would perhaps understand at last that I can't bear to remain in a dishonorable position. Perhaps then we'd find a solution." One of my great preoccupations was the following: "People hate me so much and there are so many evil people that one fine morning I'll find in one of the minor papers a sentence like this: 'Since when have convicted men had the right to take part in government?' Or: 'It's perfectly natural for a convicted man to want to sit among all these old men enjoying their second childhood.'" Thank God that hasn't yet happened. That cursed Conseil Judiciaire has always made me timid and clumsy. I feel as if I had a shameful sore that everyone could see. Just think what I've endured for 17 years.

When I see you perhaps I'll be able to make you laugh with the tale of some of my visits. But it would take a whole volume to write it down. Lamartine wanted to dissuade me, by saying that at my age one shouldn't

70. Two reviews favorable to Baudelaire and willing to publish his work had collapsed: the *Revue fantaisiste* on 15 November and the *Revue européenne* on 1 December.

run the risk of being snubbed (it seems I look young). De Vigny, whom I hadn't known before, closed his door to all comers to be alone with me, and kept me for three hours. He's the only one so far who has taken an interest in my cause and the proof is that he sent me word yesterday to come back in ten days, after I'd seen a few other members, to let him know my impressions. Like Lamartine, he tried at first to dissuade me, but when I told him that, following Sainte-Beuve's advice, I'd begun by declaring my candidature officially to the secretariat, he said that since the harm was done, it was essential to persevere. Mérimée, with whom I have connections, avoided having to see me. (It's obvious he has his own candidate and is working for him. Linked as he is with the court he has an imperialist candidate in mind.) My visit to M. Viennet was a comedy that needs a whole volume to itself. M. Villemain is a pedant and a fool, a solemn old ass, and if God grants me life, I may well make him pay very dearly for the way he received me. M. Patin, whom I'd been warned against, was charming. From the beginning I was already so discouraged, disgusted, and enraged that I had an idea I considered brilliant. Given that I was wasting so much time, I wanted my visits to be paid for, as those of doctors are, not by my *patients* but by the public. That is, I conceived the project of writing my impressions day by day and thus to make a comic work that would have been published plumb in the middle of the discussions about the election or afterwards. You can guess what the result would have been: first the Academy would have been barred against me for ever, and then I would have been accused of having introduced myself into people's homes with the preconceived plan of making them strike comical poses for me. Alfred de Vigny, to whom I had the effrontery to reveal this fine project, told me I was not the first inventor of the idea. Victor Hugo had had the same temptation in the past, but when his election eventually came through he didn't publish his book. [. . .]

Christmas 1861

My dear Houssaye,

You who manage to look as though you've nothing to do still know how to fill your day sensibly. So take a few moments to run through this selection of prose poems. I'm embarking on a long-term experiment in this genre, and I intend to dedicate it to you. At the end of the month I'll send you everything I've completed for it (a title like *The Solitary Promenader* or the *Parisian Prowler* would perhaps be better). You'll be indulgent for you, too, have on several occasions attempted to write pieces of this sort and you know how difficult it is, particularly if you're going to avoid giving the impression that it's merely the plan of something to be put into verse.

I thought it appropriate to commit an enormous piece of stupidity—I mean my candidature for the Academy. I've been told that you've also been through all that so you'll know what a horrible odyssey it is, an odyssey with neither sirens nor lotus. I'd be very grateful if you could announce this extraordinary candidature in your gossip column of *L'Artiste* or in your Pierre d'Estoile.[1] Perhaps you're also a candidate.[2] But I swear to you that you can be generous toward me without running any risks. Moreover, I know you'd be generous to me even if there were risks involved. What's more, you won't have any problem understanding me when I tell you that as I have no hope at all I'm enjoying acting as fall guy on behalf of all the ill-starred men of letters.

I had intended to bring you two manuscripts: one for *La Presse* (which we've discussed), and one for *L'Artiste*, the latter being the nearer to completion. I've been meditating about my prose poems for several years. I'll ask you at the same time to pay me for the part I've already *completed* or for the whole lot *completed*, for the sudden and coincidental collapse of both the *Revue fantaisiste* and the *Revue européenne* has reduced me to bread and water, but since it's New Year, and you may be hard up,

1. Houssaye's pseudonym in *La Presse*. Houssaye announced Baudelaire's candiature in *L'Artiste*, using his other pseudonym Pierre Dax.
2. Houssaye was not a candidate.

and moreover since one's not allowed to fall on other people without warning in this way and since, finally, I'd like to find a way of reconciling my immediate needs with your comfort—if money is out of the question, let me have a written note promising to publish my poems. In those conditions I have a friend's purse that is always at my disposal.

The good thing about this book is that you can cut it wherever you want. I have a notion that Hetzel will take it as the basis for a romantic volume with illustrations. My departure point was Aloysius Bertrand's *Gaspard de la nuit*, which you doubtless know, but I soon realized that I couldn't persevere with mere pastiche and that the book couldn't be imitated. I'm now resigned to be myself. Provided I amuse you, you'll be pleased, won't you?

I've been wanting to give you this little volume for some time and I've just learned that you're performing a miracle, or at least want to perform one, in rejuvenating *L'Artiste*. That'll be really fine; it will rejuvenate *us* at the same time. Finally, whatever happens, and however little help you can give me, my thanks in advance.

139   To Gustave Flaubert

[24 January 1862]

My dear Flaubert,

I've had a rush of blood to the head and done something utterly mad that I'm transforming into an act of wisdom by my persistence. Had I enough time (and it would take a great deal of time) I'd entertain you greatly by telling you about my visits to Academicians.

I'm told you're a close friend of Sandeau (who a little while ago said to a friend of mine: "Does M. Baudelaire write in prose then?"). I'd be infinitely grateful to you if you could write to him, telling him what you think of me.[3] I'll go and see him and I'll explain to him what's behind this candidature which so surprised some of these gentlemen.

I've long been wanting to send you a pamphlet on Wagner and something else as well, but stupidly enough for a candidate I don't have any of my own works at hand. Last Monday in *Le Constitutionnel* Sainte-Beuve wrote an article about candidates which is a real masterpiece—the sort that makes you die laughing.

All yours, your very devoted.

3. Flaubert wrote to Sandeau on 26 January 1862 urging him to support Baudelaire, if only for the pleasure of seeing him in company with his archenemies Nisard and Villemain. Sandeau professed admiration for Baudelaire but felt the candidature rushed and ill-prepared.

[24 January 1862]

Yet another service I owe you![4] When will it end? And how can I thank you? I'd missed the article, which explains why I've been so long in answering. A few words, dear friend, to let you know the particular kind of pleasure you gave me. I was deeply hurt (but I didn't say anything about it) by hearing myself described over several years as a werewolf, an impossible and rebarbative man. Once, in a malicious paper, I read a few lines about my repulsive ugliness, calculated to drive off all sympathy (that was hard for a man who has so deeply loved the perfume of woman). One day a woman said to me: "It's odd, you're very respectable. I thought you were always drunk and smelled bad." Her words were based on the legend about me.

At last, my dear friend, you've put all that to rights and I'm deeply grateful to you for it—for I've always said it's not enough to be erudite, the important thing is to be amiable. As for what you call my *Kamchatka*, if I often received encouragements as vigorous as that, I think I'd have the strength to build them into an enormous Siberia, but one that was warm and well populated. When I see how productive you are, how vital, I'm filled with shame. Fortunately, I have leaps and crises in my character that—however insufficiently—make up for the action of constant willpower.

Must I now—I who am the incorrigible admirer of the *Yellow Rays* [*Rayons jaunes*] and *Pleasure* [*Volupté*],[5] of the Sainte-Beuve who is a poet and novelist—must I compliment the Sainte-Beuve who is a journalist? What do you do to have that sureness of expression which lets you say everything and allows you to turn all difficulties into games? That article wasn't a pamphlet: it was a piece of justice. One thing struck me: I found in your article all the eloquence you have in conversation, with your good sense and your liveliness.

Truly, I'd have liked to work on it with you a little (forgive this arrogance!): I could have given you two or three horrors that you were unaware of. When we next have a good chat I'll tell you all about it.

Oh—and your utopia! The perfect means of removing from the elections that *vagueness, beloved by the great*![6] Your utopia fired me with new

4. Sainte-Beuve's article on the candidates for the Academy in which he mentioned Baudelaire as having created a "bizarre kiosk" in the "farthest reaches of Romanticism's Kamchatka."

5. "Yellow Rays" was a poem in Sainte-Beuve's collection entitled *Joseph Delorme; Pleasure* (*Volupté*) is the title of his confessional novel, admired by Baudelaire as an adolescent.

6. In his article Sainte-Beuve proposed that the Academy be divided into sections for theater, novel, poetry, etc.

pride. I, too, have created a paradise, a reformed society. Could it be an old store of revolutionary spirit that drives me to it, as, a long while back, it drove me to dream up new constitutions? The great difference is that yours is perfectly viable and may in the near future, perhaps, be adopted. Poulet-Malassis is fired with the desire to print your admirable article as a pamphlet—but he can't find the courage to go and see you. He thinks you'd resent such a request. Please promise me that you'll find a few minutes to answer the following points:

A great sorrow, the need to work, physical pain, caused in part by an old wound,[7] have interrupted my campaign. I've at last got hold of 15 copies of my main books. My distribution list—highly selective—is completed. I think it's a good plan to go for Lacordaire's chair. There are no other writers running for it. That was my original plan and if I didn't carry it out at first it was becaues I didn't want *to disobey you*, or to appear too eccentric. If you think this is a good idea, I'll write to M. Villemain before next Wednesday, telling him briefly that I feel a candidate's choice shouldn't be governed merely by the desire to succeed but should also be a sympathetic homage to the memory of the deceased. Lacordaire, moreover, is a Romantic priest and my heart goes out to him. Perhaps I'll slip the word *Romanticism* into my letter, but I won't do it without consulting you.

That terrible orator, that highly serious and most unlikable man *must* read my letter. He's a man who preaches when he chats, assuming the physiognomy and solemnity (but not the good faith) of Mlle Lenormant. I've seen that woman in professorial robes, hunched in her chair like Quasimodo and she still had an advantage over M. Villemain because her voice is so likable.[8]

If by chance you're fond of M. Villemain, I immediately withdraw everything I've just said and because of my love for you I'll work at finding him likable. But I can't help thinking that, as a Papist, I'm worth more than he is—and yet I'm a suspect Catholic.

Despite my balding pate and my white hair I want to talk to you as if I were a little boy. My mother, who is very unhappy, is constantly asking me for *news*. I sent her your article. I know how much maternal pleasure it will bring her. Thank you, for her sake and mine.

7. An allusion to the renewed attacks of syphilis.
8. Mlle Lenormant was a well-known fortuneteller and medium.

[30 January 1862]

Herewith Sainte-Beuve's terrific article, his manifesto. I'm also including two verses from excellent ballads by Théodore de Banville that will certainly interest you. It's an easy and far from shameful matter for me to put some sonnets in *Le Boulevard* if a poet like Banville is willing to keep me company there. All the terrible compliments you were good enough to pour on my poems give me cause to fear for my elucubrations in prose. But you've made me long for your sympathy.

It's so easy to forget the time in your company that I forgot to tell you yesterday about good ale and bad ale. Since you want to give this diet a try, shun any bottle labeled *Harris* as if it were the plague (that's no exaggeration—it really did make me ill). He's a frightful poisoner. Although *Allsop* and *Bass* are good brands (particularly *Bass*), you must be careful about their labels, too, for there are counterfeits around. The best course is to go to one of the honest suppliers I've mentioned below and to take their ale in all confidence. [. . .] You don't take it amiss, do you, that I'm meddling in the little details of your personal health and let you share in my experience of Paris?

Your devoted and grateful,
Charles Baudelaire.

142   To Gustave Flaubert

31 January 1862

My dear Flaubert,

You're a true warrior. You deserve to be a member of the holy battallion. You have the blind faith of friendship which implies true politics. But, perfect hermit that you are, you've not read Sainte-Beuve's famous article on the Academy and its candidates. It fed conversations for a whole week and must have set up violent reverberations in the Academy.

Maxime du Camp told me that it dishonored me, but I'm persisting with my visits, although certain Academicians have declared (but is my information correct?) that they won't so much as receive me in their homes. I've had a rush of blood to the head, but I don't regret what I've done. There's an election on 6 February, but it's in connection with the last chair (Lacordaire's, 20 February) that I'll try to extract two or three votes. I'll be on my own (unless a reasonable candidate crops up) opposing the ridiculous little Prince de Broglie, a duke's son, a living Academician. Rumor says his election is a forgone conclusion. Those people will end up fixing the election of their doormen, provided the doormen are orleanists.

We'll probably see each other soon. I'm still dreaming of solitude and if I were to leave before you come back I'd pay you a visit of a few hours—over there.

How could you have failed to guess that Baudelaire meant: Auguste Barbier, Théophile Gautier, Banville, Leconte de Lisle, that is to say, pure literature? That was fully understood instantly by some of my friends and it earned me the sympathy of a few.

POSTSCRIPT: Have you noticed that writing with an iron pen is like walking with clogs on rocking stones?

143   TO CHARLES-AUGUSTIN SAINTE-BEUVE
[3 February 1862]
My dear friend,

I'm trying to guess which hours you have free and I'm not succeeding in picking them. I've followed up your advice and haven't written a word but I'm proceeding patiently with my visits, to make it fully understood that, as regards the election to replace Father Lacordaire, I want to pick up the votes of a few *Men of Letters*. I believe Jules Sandeau is to discuss me with you. He said to me most graciously: "You've caught me too late but I'll try to find out if there is something I can do for you." I've seen Alfred de Vigny twice and each time he kept me for three hours. He's an admirable and delightful man, but he's not suited to action and even talks himself out of taking any action. Nevertheless, he displayed the warmest sympathy toward me. You won't know that the month of January was for me a month of disappointments and bouts of neuralgia, accompanied by a wound. I'm telling you this to explain why I've interrupted my program. I've seen

Lamartine,
Patin,
Viennet,
Legouvé,
Villemain (horrors!),
De Vigny,
Sandeau.

Indeed, I no longer remember the others! I could find neither Ponsard, nor M. Saint-Marc Girardin, nor de Sacy.

I've at last sent copies of some books to *ten* of those whose works I know. This week I'll see a few of those people. I've published in the *Revue anecdotique* (without signing it—infamous conduct isn't it?) an analysis of your excellent article, just as my thoughts occurred to me. As for the article itself, I sent it to M. de Vigny, who hadn't read it, and who told me he'd like to see it. As for the politickers in whom I detect no signs of warmth, I'll visit them in turn by cab. They can have my card but not my face. I read your *Pontmartin* article this evening. Forgive me if I say: "What a waste of talent!" There's something in your prodigality that sometimes shocks me. It seems to me that if it had been I, then as soon as I'd said, "the most noble causes are sometimes supported by noodles," I'd have considered my task completed. But you have a particular gift for suggesting and making your reader guess your meaning. Even toward the most guilty fools you are deliciously courteous. This M. Pontmartin is a great hater of literature. (Do you know he's said to be the son of a man who got rich by buying up the possessions of émigrés? That may be a slander but if it's true it makes his theory much more comical.)

I've sent you a little packet of sonnets and I'll soon send you several parcels of *Reveries* in prose, not to mention an enormous work on the Painters of Human Behavior (pen, watercolor, lithographs, engravings). [. . .]

144   TO CAROLINE AUPICK

29 March 1862

I assure you that my life is not disorderly. Each day order assumes a greater role for me. I'm sad, resigned to everything, even to suffering right to the end of my life, resigned to the Conseil Judiciaire and determined simply to do all I must to get it destroyed. I'm going to have four volumes to publish this year. I'd be willing to bet that these four volumes will pass *unnoticed*. There's no justice for me in this world. As soon as I've concluded negotiations for these volumes and have found journals to take the articles—some of which are finished, others of which have still to be completed—which are the last pieces needed for the volumes, I'll return to you. I don't even need to have the money from these negotiations to go there. I'll give someone power of attorney to draw the money for me and to pay my creditors.

The *Prose Poems* [*Poèmes en prose*] are to appear in *La Presse*. A thousand francs! But, alas, *they are not finished*. The *Literary Dandies* are to appear in *La Presse* and, perhaps, too, the *Philosophical Painters*. I'll have to stay in Paris to complete all that. And then to clinch it all. I think Hetzel will buy from me the reprint rights, to publish the prose poems in the form of a book. The money from all that has already been distributed.

I've two further resources, but they are less certain than work. It takes years of exhaustion and punishment to learn the simplest truths, for example, that work, which seems so disagreeable, is the only way to avoid suffering from life, or at least to suffer less from it. [. . .]

This letter will strike you as less despairing than the others. I don't know how my courage has returned. I certainly don't have any reason to take a delight in life. Recently I read at Flaubert's place a few chapters of his next book.[9] It filled me with a fortifying envy. Hugo is to publish his *Les Misérables*, a novel in 10 volumes. Yet another reason why my poor volumes, *Eureka, Prose Poems*, and *Reflections*, won't be noticed.

To be more than 40 years old, paying off debts and trying to make a fortune through literature in a country that loves nothing but vaudeville and dancing. What an atrocious destiny!

You reproached me for not having shown you any tenderness in my last letter. But, dear mother, you should have given some thought to the way in which your questions about Jeanne would revive unbearable memories for me. Always be indulgent and rest assured your indulgence won't be granted in vain. [. . .]

145   TO ARSÈNE HOUSSAYE

15 May 1862

My dear Houssaye,

Although, when all is said and done, you've just made me very happy, by provoking a decisive explanation, I'm still sufficiently affected to want to repeat *in writing* what I said to you. I hope you'll pay my letter the honor of keeping it. You spoke to me of many things that don't concern me, such as the ingratitude of the young. Just one of those topics interests me because it touches one of our intimate friends, Banville, who himself told me how displeased you were. To tell the truth, I thought you were being unfair. I think he meant: *"All controlling boards* of the *Comédie française* are *powerless* to do things well, because . . ."* (the reason isn't important). He did not say "There have been boards that were bad and now there is a good one"—which in any case would have been absurd. So if Arsène Houssaye were ineffectual (and that wasn't even stated), he was neither more nor less so than any director caught up in a despicable situation.[10]

Now I want to talk to you about myself and matters that concern me. This morning you provoked me into making an utterly pointless declaration of friendship. It would have been far more reasonable to have given me an opportunity of being agreeable to you. I've frequently longed for such an opportunity but fate failed to provide it. I beg you once again to believe me.

This brings me to the question of Crépet's anthology, for I can see that

9. Chapters from *Salammbô*, which Flaubert completed on 20 April.
10. Houssaye was the director of the Comédie française from 1849 to 1856.

it weighs on your mind. All in all, I think you're perfectly right to be offended by Crépet's uncertainty. (My name, too, was almost cut out.)

This is what happened. When Crépet, three years ago I think it was, told you of his plan, a list of names was drawn up; Philoxène and I, and Asselineau (Banville was away at the time) drew up a preparatory list for the 16th, 17th, 18th, and 19th centuries. Boyer didn't leave out a single name. You know what an astounding memory he has. And that was why, when it came to the modern writers, I suggested your name, saying that as we were being so generous toward forgotten poets we must be *very accurate* and *very complete* for the ROMANTIC SCHOOL. Philoxène was in complete agreement. *Crépet wouldn't have a bar of it.* Don't hold it against him—he's an excellent lad who knows nothing about anything and who, just because he is irresolute, always wants to show how much *character he has*.

Nevertheless, just in case he changed his mind, I prepared an article about you, which moreover would not have been accepted any more than my Hégésippe Moreau and Auguste Barbier. These were refused because they contain *a few adverse criticisms*. Crépet, who didn't want to have your name mentioned, would have said to me, if he had changed his mind: *"We can't publish an article that is not utterly agreeable for the poet concerned."*

Do you see now how bizarre all this is? Philoxène and I defended you staunchly, Crépet rejected our arguments in his own way and since then has changed his mind, which is always the case with him.[11]

It's likely that I won't have any more business relationships with this nice chap whom I like very much, but who has finally irritated me with all his beating around the bush, his timidity, his horrible fear of appearing dependent on anyone. Only keep my secret about these frivolities.

There's better to come, dear friend. I still remember the general tone of my article. I spoke of the penetrating character of your poems, of my initial emotions on reading them; I emphasized their melodious nature and the absolute sincerity of tone. I also spoke of the intimate link between your poems and some of your first short stories. I even recall daring to say of your poems what I think, in fact, of those of several other writers and particularly of my own, that however much they may please and delight, they make one want to rewrite them—which is both to praise and to censure them. Finally, I lamented a number of little errors, the fact that they are too brief, that the inspiration is, so to say, cut short, etc.

It may be that in attempting to convince you I cause you a little more

11. *The French Poets* contains an article on Houssaye but it is by P. Malitourne, not Baudelaire.

offense, but I prefer to justify myself in my own way. Let's leave all that behind us. Promise me, dear friend, not to speak of this again. For my part, I promise you to seize the next opportunity to do you a favor, since you're like St. Thomas, and you like to put your fist into proof. That will be the real benefit (for me) of this morning's little crisis.

Now, as we spoke horribly fast, let me repeat what I said about my concerns. I didn't come to ask you for money this morning, I don't even need any, apart from a small sum at the end of the month to enable me to go away. I came to ask you to do your best to fill *L'Artiste* and *La Presse* with me for a little while. *Guys, Villemain, Mercier, Literary Dandyism* [*Dandysme littéraire*], *Didactic Painting* [*Peinture didactique*] will be first-rate pieces. The prose poems likewise. You'll do them as quickly as you can, but I'm not asking for the impossible. I thought I could be—not agreeable—but less disagreeable by speaking to you of your tickets. I also thought it would give you an easy way of being useful to me. But you let me know that that would complicate your life—so reject the whole idea. But take as many pieces as possible. [. . .]

Read my *Guys, Painter of Modern Life* [*Guys, peintre de mœurs*] and you'll see why I attach so much importance to it.

146   TO THÉOPHILE GAUTIER

4 August 1862

My dear Théophile,

It would be delightful if you were to say a few kinds words about the venture undertaken by the Etchers.[12] It's surely a good idea and there will be works in the collection that will charm you. We must support, of course, this reaction in favor of a genre that is opposed by all the fatheads.

By the way, I owe you my thanks, with all my heart, for your article about me in the Crépet collection. It's the first time in my life that I've been given exactly the praise I longed for.

147   TO CAROLINE AUPICK

[10] August 1862

Dear Mother,

You're unhappy aren't you, very unhappy? I'm going to come. I've already taken the necessary steps, by which I mean I've made it impossible for me *not* to leave at the end of the month. I think there can be few

12. Gautier did publish an article on the work of the etchers. Baudelaire himself supported them by devoting two articles to them.

examples of a life as delapidated as mine, and that's really odd as I take no pleasure in such delapidation.

I don't want to tell you (and anyway I don't have the time) the extraordinary battles I've had with myself, the despair, the reveries. Nor do I want to tell you for the hundredth time that you are the sole living creature who interests me. It seems to me that given that I've made such a confession to you, you ought to believe me. I feel I'm in a crisis, in a phase where I'll have to take a decisive step, that is, do just the opposite of everything I've done so far—love glory alone, work incessantly, even *without hope of payment*, suppress all pleasure, and become what's called a great example of grandeur. And last try to make a *small* fortune. I despise those who love money but I've a horrible fear of servitude and poverty in old age. So I'll arrive at your place, or rather our place, the 31st, 1st, 2nd, or 3rd. Since you love me so much, and since you are willing to apply yourself only to the things that interest me, I'll know how to make it up to you and to prove to you that I know and love you, that I'm capable of assessing and valuing a mother's heart.

At last! At last I think that at the end of the month I'll be in a position to flee the horror of the human face. You wouldn't believe the depths of degradation that exists in Parisians. It's no longer the charming and amiable world I knew in the past. The artists know nothing, the writers know nothing either, not even how to spell. They've all become abject, perhaps inferior even to the socialites. I'm an *old man*, a mummy, I'm despised because I'm less ignorant than the mass of men. What decadence! Apart from D'Aurevilly, Flaubert, Sainte-Beuve, I can't get on with anyone. Gautier alone can understand me when I discuss painting. *Life fills me with horror.* I repeat: I'm going to flee the human face, but above all the French face.

I've a very beautiful book to bring you, but I'm preparing a lengthy study on the subject: *Second Tableau of Paris by Sebastien Mercier, Paris during the Revolution of '93, up to the Time of Bonaparte*. It's marvelous.

You've no doubt received *Les Misérables* that I sent you (I deliberately waited until after Easter) imagining (wrongly, perhaps) that you wouldn't want to read books at Easter. There were also two articles, one by me and one by d'Aurévilly. The book is disgusting and clumsy. On this score I've shown that I possess the art of lying. To thank me he wrote an utterly ridiculous letter. That proves that a great man can be a fool.

Your Chateaubriand (a Belgian edition) is held up in the offices of the minister for the interior. [. . .] I love you and embrace you. Tell me that you're well (if that is the case) and that you'll go on living for a long time for me, and me alone. You can see how ferocious and self-centered my affection is.

148 TO MICHEL LÉVY

In the third edition,[13] which I'll call the *Definitive Edition*, I'll include a further 10 or 15 pieces, plus a long preface in which I'll explain my tricks and my method and where I'll teach all and sundry the *art of doing as I do*. And if I should lack the courage to write this serious tomfoolery, I'll simply add, as a preface, Gautier's excellent article on *The Flowers*, which is published in the 4th volume of Crépet's anthology, *The French Poets*.

149 TO CAROLINE AUPICK

13 December 1862

How can it be that I find it so hard to write to my mother and that I do it so rarely? Such a simple matter and one that ought to be very pleasant! But it's also very difficult to do anything at all that is both a pleasure and a duty. And the mass of cares that grow as I get older prevent me carrying out satisfactorily anything that can be seen as a duty, and particularly an agreeable duty.

Anyway, dear mother, before everything else, before everything else, *how are you?* If you could hear my thoughts from afar, you'd often say to yourself: "That's my son thinking of me." But that's just a lot of words and poetic reverie. You'd prefer me to prove my zeal. How harsh you were to me in one of your letters! That cruel sum of 500 francs. The only serious thing that struck me in your letter was *the cliff*.[14] But I always imagine that you guess a lot of things. How could I foresee that such a misfortune would befall me at the very moment when I planned to leave? For example, Malassis's bankruptcy, which you surely heard about—in which I was very nearly compromised and which in any case threw my life into great disorder. I owe 5,000 francs. I've decided to hide them from the law to attempt to give them to Malassis and his mother later on. And then *The Flowers of Evil* and *Paradise* abandoned to their fate in the sale. But you don't have the slightest understanding of such matters.

I've absently begun my letter by writing on a sheet of paper that was upside down, so I'll have to number the sheets so you can read this easily. Any one who was superstitious would see that as a bad omen.

I sent you some books to take your mind off things—they're good books. The *Letters on Animals* (written, apart from the preface, by a

13. That is, of *Flowers of Evil*. The third edition did not appear until after Baudelaire's death. The preface exists only in note form.

14. The cliff at Honfleur was subject to landslides. The 500 francs refers to a loan Mme Aupick had made Baudelaire.

doctor) and *Rameau's Nephew*, which you've probably read before, are marvels.[15] But you didn't guess at all why I sent you *The French Poets*. It certainly wasn't, as you thought, to show you some old things of mine, but to let you read Gautier's article about me, that is, the role he attributed to me in the history of poetry. Perhaps you didn't notice this.

And your spies? What are we to say of them? What asses! They told you I was happy. —Never. —Could that be possible? —Or else I'm terrifyingly happy to get rid of people quickly. —They told you I was well dressed? —It was only a week ago that I set aside my rags. They told you I was well? None of my infirmities has gone—neither the rheumatisms, nor the nightmares, nor the bouts of anxiety, nor my unbearable capacity for feeling all noises strike me in the stomach; —and above all my fear has not left me, the fear of dying suddenly, the fear of living too long, the fear of seeing you die, the fear of falling asleep, the horror of waking up—and that prolonged lethargy which makes me put off the most urgent matters for months. Bizarre infirmities that somehow intensify my hatred of everyone.

But tell me of yourself, in minute detail, above all of your health.

A very long time ago, *at the time of the 500 francs*, I went, *all alone of course*, to Versailles. I adore Versailles and the Trianons. The solitude there is delicious. I couldn't help thinking of you all the time I was going there, because some years ago we went along the same route together from the rue d'Amsterdam to Saint-Cloud, I think it was. It was at the time when you were returning from Madrid or Constantinople. I recognized the viewpoints at which you cried out with your usual exaggeration: "How beautiful that is!" and then you added: "But you don't respond to Nature's beauties: you're not at the right age for that." For that's how you talk. The flowerbeds of the Trianon positively dazzled me and I imagined that you were with me. I saw you, I really saw you, making the sort of grimace I know so well and saying to me: "It's *all very fine*, but you see, my dear child, I prefer my own garden." Dear mother, I wanted to make you laugh.

Finally, dear mother, let me hear about you.

I'm plunged in a most important affair, but I won't be able to bring it to a good conclusion. Everyone knows I'm overwhelmed with debts. I'll be slaughtered. If in a week I write to you saying: "It's done and well done," you'll be able to count on my presence and a more pleasant life.

And if your imagination lets you guess what I endure, *think of the Conseil Judiciaire. Do you want me to die under its regime?*

I embrace you.

15. *The Letters on Animals* (*Lettres sur les animaux*) was written by C. G. Leroy; the second title is a work by Diderot.

150 To Champfleury

[4 March 1863]

My dear friend,

I'm very fond of you, but you're so stubborn! I knew full well the letter would be shown around.[16] So you really do want to compromise my dignity in a social set in which you've compromised your own? I'll do my utmost to *please you*, but that utmost won't amount to very much.

When I wrote to you, I'd already sought information on the matter. You know how much I love loose women and how much I hate *philosophizing women*. As for lunch, yes, but *at my place on Sunday at noon*.

151 To Champfleury

6 March 1863

My dear friend,

The Sphinx and the bizarre man—that's still what you are, and you're bizarre *entirely naturally*, for art wouldn't dream up your bizarreness. What! You write me a letter that you try to make unpleasant, just because I tell you I don't like bad company. Dear friend, it's always filled me with horror—filth and stupidity, and crime, have a relish that may offer a temporary pleasure, but bad company, that sort of foamy ripple found on the edges of society, why that's impossible! You claim my letter has a *hidden* meaning. I'll explain that meaning, which in my opinion ought to leap out at you from the page.

Champfleury's joyous nature, his delight in hoaxes, —I have a little in common with that. Champfleury has discovered an amusing world, full of husbandless women and young, unmarriageable girls looking for husbands, together with some pedants who claim to love philosophy. Champfleury knows, as I do, that a woman is incapable of understanding so much as two lines of the catechism. But he writes to me to share his joy, and he also wants the fun of watching me clash with that fool of a woman. (And I told you I was ready to do anything to please you, but that that particular episode bored me.)

Now that's the hidden meaning. As for your little sermon on virtue at the end of your letter, in which you include such splendid praise of yourself, I've nothing to say on that head, except that when you have such a high opinion of yourself, it's not very charitable to overwhelm others with it. It's clear that you're a happy man, *happy through your own exertions*, and that I am not, for I'm always displeased with myself.

Let me tell you that your letter also has a teasing, vengeful tone that,

16. The letter in which Baudelaire refused Champfleury's request to be allowed to introduce him to the portrait painter Mme O'Connell.

coming from you to me, at our age, is inappropriate. What! The word *dignity* stirs you as much as that, where it concerns an old friend? Come and see me, I beg you, on Sunday at noon; if you don't come I'll believe you bear me a grudge.[17]

POSTSCRIPT: You love the comic, so read Lamartine's last *conversation* (on the subject of *Les Misérables*). That's a funny bit of writing for you. And as you're too eager to seek hidden meanings, can I beg you not to see any link between it and my letter. [. . .]

152   To Caroline Aupick

3 June 1863

[. . .] As soon as you have the time, send me by *rail*, in a single parcel, the three other volumes of Edgar Poe, in the striped binding, with the spine in green morocco. You must know where they are in my library, since you've already sent me one volume. You know the enormous price I paid for it, so wrap it up very carefully so that the binding can't be damaged in any way. [. . .]

You must have been racking your brains to understand why I didn't write you any more letters. The true, the only reason was my discontent with myself. You guessed it to some extent. I'd promised myself that I'd write only when I'd shaken off the weight of lethargy that has crushed me for so many months. How I came to feel so low, reaching such depths that I thought I'd never pull myself up again, and how I was able to *cauterize* my illness suddenly, by a furious burst of activity, without either respite or weariness, I haven't the faintest notion. *I know I'm completely healed*, and that I'm a miserable creature composed of laziness and violence, and that habit alone can offset all the vices of my temperament. Idleness has become such a violent source of pain, the wild idea of my literary powerlessness has terrified me so much, that I've flung myself into work. That revealed that I've lost none of my skills. But it's very dangerous to let them lie dormant like that. There are people who damage me more than they realize by saying: "When is your next book coming out?" or "So you're not doing anything anymore?"

This is the point I've reached—it's all the more necessary that you understand me well in that I'm absolutely obliged to ask Ancelle (with your support) for the sum of 1,000 francs, as a temporary aid, so that I can have peace of mind while coming to the moment when I'll change my way of life completely, for I can't return to Honfleur without having

17. Champfleury refused and it was not until May 1865 that the two writers patched up their quarrel.

194

acquitted my literary debts, or at least having reestablished the habit of permanent work. I can be lazy there as I have been here, and the fear of boredom wouldn't drive me any more at Honfleur than it does here, where I have been bored for months, as no one was ever bored before. So this is the current state of my literary affairs. Some pretty good things completed for some time haven't appeared, thanks to the stupidity of editors of journals and reviews, but at least they're done and that's what matters.

I haven't been able to find a buyer for my collected critical articles (on *painting and literature*). I'll have to wait until my next volumes have made their mark. Those will pull the others along with them. If everything that's currently underway had been completed by October, I'd have got everything published this winter. Now I'll have to finish everything at once, to appear in September or October, the usual time for books to be published. I've sold the Hetzel firm *The Flowers of Evil* for five years, a third, augmented edition. And *The Spleen of Paris* [*Le Spleen de Paris*] for five years, 600 francs per volume at a print run of 2,000 copies. They're certain to do five editions for each in five years.

The Spleen of Paris is incomplete, and it wasn't delivered on time. I only need two weeks' work to finish it, but two weeks of vigorous work. I made the mistake of allowing the activity that had sustained me to subside. But I'm very pleased with all that I have done for it. It'll be a remarkable book.

I've sold the Lévy publishing house two new volumes to increase the Edgar Poe collection. The 4th is almost finished. There's only a few pages needed, 2 or 3 days of courage. The 5th needs 10 days or so, no more.[18]

I've not yet found another buyer for *Artificial Paradises*.

A few months ago I said to myself, I don't want to hear anything more about those little author's rights, which are paid only at intervals of several months. And I had the idea of asking from anyone at all a sum of several thousand francs, in exchange for the authorization to draw all my rights until they'd been fully paid. I told Ancelle of my plan, to get his advice on this kind of mortgaged loan. I needn't tell you he thought it an abominable scheme. He finds it very odd that I don't calmly wait for payments and that I'd consent to pay interest in advance to get my hands on several thousand at once. The good soul would be right if he were dealing with a rich writer, who was in a position to wait.

Two or three people came forward. There's always lots of people willing to earn money through a writer. Finally a real banker, who has some knowledge of the publishing trade, said to me: "I'll lend you what you

18. *Eureka* and *Histoires grotesques et sérieuses*.

want, but I insist you show me all your contracts (there are some at Honfleur; I'll have to go and get them)—that your publishers show me the accounts of what they've given you over the last few years, so I can see what your books bring in—and finally they'll have to provide a guarantee that all the volumes are completed and delivered." That's the sticking point at present. But what I need is an immediate alleviation. For the *Edgar Poe* he offered me not merely a loan but an absolute and permanent alienation of all my rights in exchange for a set sum. It's clear that this man knows his literary values. I confess I'm tending toward the absolute transfer—but not for my own personal works. [. . .]

For you summer has come, the garden season. I'll go and see it in July. If I go this month I'm afraid it will only be to collect some papers. You were kind enough to remember my nightmares—you think of everything, and forget nothing. It's true that you live in solitude, which increases one's lucidity of mind and character. Well, that unbearable illness is over. When I examined it, I realized that it had two causes, one, a terrible irritation of the stomach, the other, a psychological cause, a kind of intellectual illness, a constant fear, increased by imagination, the result of having delayed and neglected important matters.

That's as clear as mud, isn't it?

My love to you, and a thousand apologies for wearying, irritating, and worrying you, the very person to whom I'd like to give pleasure and rest.

153   TO GERVAIS CHARPENTIER

20 June 1863

Dear Sir,

I've just read the two extracts (*The Temptations* and *Dorothy*) included in *La Revue nationale*. I find they contain some extraordinary alterations brought in *after* I'd given my permission for it to be printed. That, Sir, is the reason why I've avoided so many newspapers and reviews. I told you: suppress a *whole piece*, if a single *comma* displeases you, but don't suppress the comma—it's there for a reason.

I've spent my whole life learning how to construct sentences, and I can say without fear of being laughed at that what I hand over to the press is *perfectly complete*.

Can you really think that "the shapes of her body" is an equivalent expression to "her hollow back and her thrusting breasts"? Especially when it concerns the black race of the eastern shores. And can you believe it *immoral* to say that a girl is "ripe" at the age of 11, when it's well known that Ayesha (and she wasn't even a negress born in the tropics) was even younger when Muhammad married her?

Sir, I sincerely wish to thank you for the pleasant welcome you've given me, but *I know what I write* and I tell *what I've seen*. If I'd been warned in time, at least, I'd have been able to suppress the whole piece.

154   TO ETIENNE CARJAT

6 October 1863

My dear Carjat,

Manet has just shown me the photograph, which he was taking to Bracquemond; my congratulations and thanks. It's not perfect, *because that kind of perfection is impossible*, but I've rarely seen anything as good as that. I'm ashamed to put so many requests to you and I don't know how I'll be able to thank you, but if you haven't destroyed the negative, make me *a few* copies. *A few*, that means as many as you can. And if this seems indiscreet to you, I really want you to tell me so, but not too harshly, all the same.

Manet has just told me the most unexpected piece of news. He's leaving for Holland tonight and will return with *his wife*. He does have some excuse, however, for it seems she's beautiful, very kind, and a very great pianist. So many treasures in a single female, isn't that rather monstrous? Send an answer, if this reaches you.

155   TO ALGERNON SWINBURNE

10 October 1863

Dear Sir,

One of my friends, indeed one of my oldest friends, is going to London—a M. Nadar, whom you'll no doubt have some pleasure in meeting. Please be kind enough to do for him everything you would probably have done for me, had I gone to give public lectures in your country. Information, advice, publicity—he needs a lot of things.

I'm infinitely grateful to M. Nadar for having asked me for letters to the very few acquaintances I have in London, since he thereby obliged me to repay a very great debt that has long been overdue. I'm referring to the wonderful article you published in the *Spectator* of September 1862 on *The Flowers of Evil*.

One day M. Richard Wagner flung his arms around my neck to thank me for a pamphlet I'd written on *Tannhäuser*, and said to me: "*I'd never have thought that a French writer could understand so much with such ease.*" As I'm not exclusively patriotic I extracted from his compliment all the graciousness it contained. Allow me, in my turn, to say to you: "*I'd never have guessed that an Englishman could penetrate so deeply into French beauty,*

French intentions, and French prosody." But after reading the poem published in the same issue ("August") and finding it imbued with an emotion at once so real and so subtle, I no longer felt surprised in the slightest: it takes a poet fully to understand a poet. Nevertheless, allow me to say that you take my defence rather too far. I'm not such a *moralist* as you obligingly pretend to believe. I believe simply (as no doubt you do yourself) that every poem and every work of art that is *well made* naturally and perforce suggests a moral. It's up to the reader. I even feel a very decided hatred toward every exclusively moralistic *intention* in a poem.

Please have the goodness to send me your publications—it would bring me great pleasure. I have several books to publish. I'll send them to you as they come out.

156   To Caroline Aupick

25 November 1863

My dear Mother,

I've been wanting for ages to set aside 2 or 3 hours to write to you at length and properly. But the days are so short: I suffer terribly after lunch, and after dinner I feel such boredom in my unlit room, I suffer so much from the lack of any *friendship* or *luxury*—I'm so crushed by my solitude and my loneliness that I constantly put off all my duties, even those I most want to fulfill.

From time to time, several times a day, morning and evening, I say to myself: "I wonder how she is? She's unhappy and perhaps she thinks I'm having a good time."

The great aim, the only aim of my life now is to transform work, the hardest, most problematic thing in the world, into the thing I most enjoy, and that's a question of habit. I consider myself terribly guilty, for I've misused life, my faculties, my health, I've lost 20 years through reverie, and that puts me lower than a mass of boors who work every day of their lives.

No; you've no reproaches to make concerning M. Lévy's 200 francs. I won't even take 20 francs of it. Lévy has undertaken to share this money among several of my creditors when he has received the last page of his 5th volume and I'm in the midst of completing it now. The 4th volume has come out, I think, but I don't have the time to go out and distribute the copies.

I'll send you a copy—just to prove to you that this terrible book is completed, for I doubt you could read 2 pages of it without falling asleep. I even doubt that there are 10 people in the whole of France capable of appreciating it.

M. Emon was wrong. I very much hope I won't stay more than 6 weeks in Brussels (and even that is a long time). I'll leave in the first weeks of December. I'll send you a box that will be the signal of my flight. For there's no point in my paying the rent of a room I'll no longer be occupying and I want to take the furniture out of the room.

I predict my trip will not be a success. I'm confident I'll be well paid for my readings. But you know my trip has a further aim, which is to sell three volumes of criticism to the firm that bought *Les Misérables*. Well, everyone tells me those people are unintelligent and very avaricious. It could happen that I'll be forced to sell them in Paris when I get back, and at a shameful price. But *the money from the readings is not to be sneezed at*. It seems that newspapers (or gossip) have announced my arrival and I'm expected.

The fragment I'm sending you is taken from the three volumes concerned. The Delacroix[19] whipped up a lot of anger and approval. I'm used to that. I'm sending you the first installment of a work I consider pretty important. I'm most annoyed at the comment (signed G. B.) that accompanies it (our *feuilleton*).

Now, remember that what concerns me most and is always of importance to me is your health. Tell me how you are.

157   TO VICTOR HUGO

17 December 1863

Although I always hesitate over asking anything at all of those toward whom I feel most affection and respect, I'm writing today to request a *great* service, indeed an *enormous* service. My discontent with Parisian editors and my feeling, which is not without a basis in fact, that I'm not given complete justice, have made me resolve to seek an editor abroad, for three volumes, one of which is *Artificial Paradises* and the other two *Reflections* (fine arts and literature). In order to whip up some fierce publicity for these works I decided to give some public lectures in Brussels, with well-chosen extracts—of the best passages of course—for example: *Of the Essence of Laughter,—Eugène Delacroix, His Work, Thought, and Conduct—The Painter of Modern Life—Edgar Poe, His Life and Works—Victor Hugo—Théophile Gautier—Théodore de Banville and Leconte de Lisle—Richard Wagner*—and I'm even going to support my evaluations by quoting passages from the relevant authors, as I'm distrustful of Belgian erudition.

Well, I've heard that M. Lacroix is to pay you a visit. The great service

19. Baudelaire's article on the life and works of Delacroix.

199

you could perform for me would consist in telling him whatever favorable judgments you have of my books and myself, and informing him about my plan to give these lectures. It would, I repeat, be a very great service, for M. Lacroix is sure to have absolute confidence in your judgment and I hope the lectures would be the final touch in persuading him.

I frequently ask after you, and am told you're in admirable health. Genius aided by health! How fortunate you are!

I'm planning to send you in the near future *The Flowers of Evil* further augmented, together with *The Spleen of Paris*, which was written to act as a counterpart to the poems. I tried to include in it all the bitterness and ill humor that wells up in me. A few days ago I was to have sent you *Eureka* (4th volume of my Poe translation), a strange book that claims to reveal how universes are created and destroyed. But M. Lévy is so close-fisted that he decided to remove from the distribution list the name of anyone who couldn't be directly useful to him. I'll make up for *my* (or rather *his*) faults another time.

I'll leave for Brussels a few days before the end of the month. If you can take 10 minutes of your time to write to me you'd make me happy and that would give me confidence for my expedition. But I can imagine what a nuisance letters must often be for you, and I don't have the slightest wish to inconvenience you.

In Paris my address is 22 rue d'Amsterdam. In Brussels I'm not yet sure where I'll be staying.

Farewell. Please accept my expressions of affection and admiration. You're a powerful lord but, as you see, you have to suffer all the inconvenience of sovereignty. Everyone has a request to make of you.

158   To Caroline Aupick

31 December 1863

My dear good Mother,

There's nothing worse than having to write to one's mother with one eye glued to the clock, but I want you to receive this tomorrow—a few words of affection and a few promises, which you can believe or not. I've acquired the detestable habit of putting off until the morrow all my duties, *even the most pleasant of them*. That's how I've come to put off until the morrow so many important things over so many years and that's why I'm in such a ridiculous position today, a position that is both painful and ridiculous, notwithstanding my name and my age. The solemnity of the end of a year has never struck me with such intensity as it does this year. So, despite the massive abbreviations of my thought that I'm committing here, you'll understand me perfectly when I tell you that I beg you *to stay in good health, look after yourself well, live as long as you can,* and *grant me your indulgence a little longer.*

All I'm going to do or all I hope to do in this year (1864) I should and could have done in the year that has just passed. But I'm attacked by a frightful illness, which has never played such havoc with me as in this year—I mean my reveries, my depression, my discouragement, my indecision. Truly, I consider the man who succeeds in healing himself of a vice as infinitely braver than a soldier or a man who defends his honor in a duel. But how to heal myself? How transform despair into hope, weakness into willpower? Is this illness imaginary or real? Has it become real after being imaginary? Could it be the result of a physical weakness, or an incurable melancholy resulting from so many stormy years, years spent without consolation, in solitude and wretchedness? I've no idea, but what I do know is that I feel utterly disgusted with everything and particularly with all kinds of pleasure (that's no bad thing) and that the only feeling that convinces me I'm still alive is a *vague* desire for celebrity, vengeance, and fortune.

But even the little I have done has met with so little justice. I've found a few people who have had the courage to read *Eureka*. The book will sell badly but I should have anticipated that: it's too abstract for the French.

I'm definitely going to leave. I'm giving myself 5 days, a *week* at most, to collect money from three newspapers, to pay a few people, and to pack. I only hope that I'm not seized with disgust for the Belgian expedition the moment I reach Brussels! But it's an important affair. The lectures, which can only bring in a very small sum (1,000, 1,500, or 2,000) providing I've the patience to give them, are only the secondary motive of my trip. You know my real motive. It's a question of selling M. Lacroix, a Belgian editor, three volumes of *Varieties* and getting a good deal for them.

The thought of my life in Brussels makes me shudder. The *lectures*, the *proofs to correct that will be sent from Paris*, proofs from *newspapers*, proofs from *Michel Lévy*, and finally, through all that, I must finish my *Prose Poems*. Nevertheless I have the vague feeling that the novelty of my stay will do me good and prod me into some activity. I've talked too much of myself, but I know you like that. Tell me about yourself, about your state of health and mind.

I want to take Hugo as my accomplice in this enterprise. I knew that M. Lacroix was to go to Guernsey on a certain day. I'd asked Hugo to intervene. I've just had a letter from Hugo. The storms in the Channel upset my plan and my letter arrived *four days after the editor left*. Hugo says he'll fix it up through a letter, but nothing is as good as the spoken word.

9 April 1864

Recently, in a friend's house, I came across your article [20] in *Le Moniteur* of 29 March, of which your father had shortly before sent me the proofs. No doubt he told you of my astonishment in reading it. If I didn't write immediately to thank you, that's only because of my timidity. A man who is not very timid by nature can be ill at ease in the company of a beautiful young woman, even when he knew her as a very little girl—particularly when she's done him a good turn. And he may well fear that he'll either be too respectful and cold, or that he'll thank her too warmly.

My first impression, as I said, was astonishment—an impression that is, moreover, always pleasurable. Then, when I could no longer mistrust my eyes, I felt an emotion that is difficult to describe, half pleasure at being so well understood, half joy at seeing that one of my oldest and dearest friends had a daughter who was truly worthy of him.

In your very accurate analysis of *Eureka*, you did something that at your age I may perhaps not have been capable of doing, and that many a very mature man who calls himself cultured is certainly incapable of doing. Finally, you proved to me something that I would readily have judged impossible, and that is that a young girl could find in books serious amusement, a sort of amusement utterly different from the highly stupid and commonplace amusements that generally fill the lives of women.

If I weren't afraid of offending you again by slandering your sex, I'd say that you've forced me to throw doubt on the nasty opinion I've formed of women in general.

Don't be scandalized by these compliments, which are so oddly mixed with civilities. I've reached an age where one can no longer correct one's personality, even for the best and most charming person.

Believe me when I say I'll always cherish the memory of the pleasure you've given me.

20. Her review of Baudelaire's translation of *Eureka*.

7 · *Poor Belgium!: 1864–1867*

160   TO EDOUARD MANET

27 May 1864

My dear Manet,

My thanks for your affectionate letter. Give my regards to your mother and wife, and if you've good news for me as regards your paintings, write to me. I'm replying now to your congratulations.

The Belgians are fools, liars, and thieves. I've been the victim of the most shameless swindle. Here deceit is the rule and brings no dishonor. I've not yet broached the great matter that brought me here but everything that happens bodes ill—leaving aside the fact that I'm considered to be an associate of the French police by people here. Don't ever believe what people say about the good nature of the Belgians. Ruse, defiance, false affability, crudeness, treachery—now all that you *can* believe.

161   TO THÉOPHILE THORÉ

[About 20 June 1864]

I don't know if you remember me and our former discussions. The years have passed so quickly! I read very attentively everything you write and want to thank you for the pleasure you gave me by taking up the defense of my friend Edouard Manet and giving him a *degree* of justice. The only thing is that there are a few little matters in need of rectification in the judgments you expressed.

M. Manet, who is considered a raving madman, is quite simply a very loyal, straightforward man, doing his best to be reasonable but unfortunately marked by Romanticism from birth. The word *pastiche* is not accurate.[1] M. Manet has never seen any Goyas, M. Manet has never seen any El Grecos. M. Manet has never seen the Pourtalès gallery. That may seem unbelievable to you, but it's the truth. I myself have been filled with wonder and stupefaction at these mysterious coincidences.

In the days when we enjoyed the marvelous Spanish museum that the stupid French republic in its misguided respect for property restored to

1. Thoré's review of the 1864 Salon had accused Manet of creating pastiches of El Greco, Goya, and Velázquez.

the Princess of Orleans, M. Manet was a child and served on board a ship. He's heard so much about his *pastiches* of Goya that he's now trying to see some of Goya's paintings. It's true that he'd seen some Velázquez paintings, but I don't know where.

You doubt the truth of this? You doubt that such amazing geometrical parallels can exist in nature? Well, I myself am accused of imitating Edgar Poe! Do you know why I've translated Poe so patiently? Because he was like me. The first time I opened one of his books, I saw, with horror and delight, not only topics I'd dreamed of, but *sentences* I'd thought of, and that he had written 20 years before.

Et nunc, erudimini, vos qui judicatis . . . ! Don't be angry, but keep a warm memory of me in a corner of your mind. Every time you try to pay Manet a service I'll be grateful.

I'm taking this scrawl to M. Bérardi so it can be sent to you. I'll have the absolute courage or rather cynicism of my desires. Quote my letter, or at least several lines of it. What I'm telling you is the naked truth.

162   TO CAROLINE AUPICK

31 July 1864

My dear Mother,

I'm requesting one more month in Belgium before I settle down at Honfleur. I've begun a damned book and must finish it. I've taken all the notes I need on Brussels; five chapters are written; but I'll have to rush around the provinces. A fortnight should suffice. Liège, Ghent, Namur, Antwerp, Malines, Bruges *above all*, will be a form of relaxation for me. I've calculated that I can do this trip cheaply. A hundred and fifty francs will suffice. The trains are expensive but they cover the distance so quickly!

I'm forced to call on your goodwill again, that is, if it's possible (for I'm still at the stage of the ashamed child in my relationship with you). I'll do *what I can* to bring you in September part of the money from the *letters*.[2] If you can't help me out, I'll think again, and find some other means of continuing with my plans and covering my expenses, however small. My three great needs at present are to give a little money to the hotel, to go to Paris to bring various urgent matters to a conclusion, and to calm down by means of a partial payment a creditor who's martyring me (the thought of going to Paris makes me shudder). I've recently been forced, in order to pay for certain essentials, to make the acquaintance of the Brussels pawnshop and now I need some things; —finally, I must

2. The "Belgian Letters" Baudelaire was thinking of publishing in *Le Figaro*.

make this tour of the provinces, but that's the *least urgent* as I've still got a good 10 days' work on my Brussels notes.

My *letters* can't bring in any money yet because, having weighed everything up very carefully in my own mind and in consultation with a Frenchman, even if the affair does reach a happy conclusion, they won't appear *while I'm here*. These letters will be highly humiliating for Belgium and a man far more famous than I, M. Proudhon, was driven out of here, *under a rain of stones*, because he'd allowed himself a few very innocent jokes in a newspaper. I think it's a good idea for me to spend 24 hours in Paris and throw myself so to speak into the wolf's jaws! Fix up the matter of the letters with *Le Figaro*, find a press that will reprint them in volume form, and find a press to publish the three volumes I'd come to Belgium to sell, that's what matters. Could it be that my name no longer has any value, and that these three volumes are unsellable? No, that's impossible. Yet I'm so discouraged that I'm sometimes inclined to believe it. Oh, if only I could improve my courage and my health I'd revenge myself on this crude race, until the time comes when I have enough authority to say what I think of France itself.

(It was on June 23 that I heard from M. Lacroix's associate that my affair was no longer possible. It was said politely, with a mass of reasons that I later proved to be lies. And then he asked me for a novel. What hypocrisy! He knows I don't have one.)

The thought of going to Paris frightens me and yet it's the bravest thing to do and perhaps the surest, too. I write so many letters that remain unanswered. If you only knew what anger one feels when one is utterly isolated, locked away in a hostile milieu, without any conversation, without any possibility of pleasure, and when none of those one needs replies to letters!

I'm amazed I've been able to do the little I have done (I've taken all my notes and written up the first chapters, and then corrected the proofs of a book that is being published in Paris) in the state of mind and health I've been in for more than two months. I've never felt such despair and weakness. Three months of *continual diarrhea*, broken occasionally by unbearable constipation—hardly the way to strengthen the mind. As for the palpitations and the stomach pains, they're gone, I don't know how. Moreover, there's nothing original in my condition. Several French people have been attacked by this diarrhea, which I attribute to the climate and the use of *faro* (beer).

All return quickly to English beer or French wine. A jug of *faro* costs 2 sous, English beer 3 sous, and Bordeaux 3 francs a bottle. As for me, my misfortune continues, and the only benefit I've got from it is an extreme sobriety. Even if I were well I'd not sit down to table with anything but disgust, so insipid and monotonous is the cooking. I bet you send me a pile of pharmaceutical recipes—I don't want any. I'll cure myself in September.

I think it would be right to find the courage to go to Paris. I've sent articles to *La Vie parisienne*. No answer. To *L'Opinion nationale*, no answer. To *Le Monde illustré*—no answer! Truly people cannot imagine the torment you feel when you're locked away on your own with a boring race and deprived of essential information.

I'll put off the end of this letter until later. Moreover I'm not in a hurry to send it to you. I'd so like to have a pleasant piece of news for you.

I hope I won't be forced to go to Paris. The thought of it fills me with such despair! One of my friends who was passing through has said he'll take it on himself to put the question to *Le Figaro* and even get money, while imposing the condition that the letters aren't published until my return.

163   TO NADAR

30 August 1864

My dear Nadar,

I probably won't still be in Brussels at the period when the celebrations[3] are on, for all my time between 8 and 20 September will be devoted to excursions in the provinces.

Since you'd had the kind intention of offering me a place in the gondola of your balloon, would you allow me to pass this favor on to M. O'Connell, the *best companion*, in my belief, that you could find? You know my distrust of the Belgians. I won't therefore appear suspect to you in praising M. O'Connell (who moreover is not Belgian, as his name goes to show). If you want someone cheerful, nimble in all gymnastic exercises, fairly familiar with all sorts of mechanical devices, and fond of all possible adventures, you'll find every one of those qualities in him. He very naïvely took it into his head to get Arthur [Stevens] to introduce him to you, and Arthur, as you know, passes in France for the king of the Belgians and in Belgium for the emperor of the French, so naturally he boasts that he can have everything done at his bidding in both countries.

I told M. O'Connell that all that was very silly, and that I believed that a word from me to M. Nadar would be much better. I'm going to write to him saying I've written to you and that if I'm away when you come, he can quite simply call on you himself.

Everyone here says: "*I'm going up with Nadar.*" (These people omit the

3. In celebration of Belgium's independence, achieved in 1830.

M., familiarity being the mark of boors and provincials.) But my opinion and that of anyone with any sense is that all the lovers of sky travel will go into eclipse at the last moment. This M. O'Connell really made me laugh a few days back. Would you believe he took it into his head to say very candidly to Arthur, in front of several witnesses: "My poor Arthur, you and I, who are of the race of cuckolds . . ."! —Talking of Arthur, *don't repeat my jokes about him.* That bastard has already all but pulled me into several quarrels—he's keeping a watch on me, even to the point of examining all my papers. (Now, thanks to his researches, he's fully convinced of *your prudence* and the . . . *solidity* of your balloon, so I think he has *more or less made up his mind.*)

Dear friend, you were right. I'm always getting into scraps. Would you believe that *I* could *beat up* a Belgian? It's incredible, isn't it? That I could beat up anyone is absurd. And what was even more monstrous was that I was completely in the wrong. So, my sense of justice taking the upper hand, I ran after the man to give him my apologies. But I couldn't find him.

M. O'Connell's address if Chaussée de Haecht 115. I'm feeling a bit moved, like Hetzel, to no purpose, and I send my love. My regards to Mme Nadar. Perhaps I'll come and bid you good day in Paris in three or four days' time.

164   To Narcisse Ancelle

13 October 1864

My dear Ancelle,

There are several reasons why I've taken such a long time to answer you. The first is that I've been ill again (but don't mention that to my mother if you should happen to write to her). This time, it's no longer my stomach but a fever that wakes me at 1 or 2 in the morning and which prevents me sleeping again until about 7. This daily accident makes me see in the darkness lots of wonderful things that I'd very much like to describe but unfortunately it results in a very great weariness that extends throughout the next day. The second reason is that despite the charming and cordial tone of your letter, and the kindness of your offer *I was determined to do without you.* Today it's clear that that is not possible. —Let me explain. — The fragments I've written are worth a good 1,000 francs but I won't let them be published *while I'm in Belgium.* So I'll have to return to France to get money and I need money to go to France, and also to go on another excursion to Namur, Bruges, and Antwerp (it concerns painting and architecture. Six days at most). —So I'm in *a vicious circle.* M. de Villemessant of *Le Figaro* is impatiently awaiting my articles. Were I to ask him for money and to say to him at the same time—"Don't publish yet!"—that would, frankly, be an abuse of his complacency. And then, the 1,000 francs I'm expecting from my fragments will perhaps not be paid until each is actually published. [. . .]

All I've got out of my trip to Belgium is the chance to get to know the stupidest race on earth (at least I presume there's none stupider), a little book that is curious in the extreme and may serve as a bait to tempt a publisher to buy the others; and finally the habit of continuous and complete chastity (laugh, if you like, at this ugly detail)—*a chastity, moreover, that has no merit whatsoever*, given that the sight of a Belgian female repels all thoughts of pleasure.

Finally, I've all but finished my *Histoires grotesques et sérieuses*, which are to be published. How deeply I now repent having renounced, for 200 francs, all my rights on 5 volumes, when I think that Michel will perhaps make yet again a more than modest profit through this constant sale.

So much for my state of mind. I'm now going to supply the material details that you've asked for in utter frankness. But just imagine, dear friend, what I have to endure! Winter is suddenly upon us. Here, you don't set eyes on the fire, for the fire is in an oven. My work—when I do work—is punctuated by yawns. Just think what I endure given that I find Le Havre a black American port and that I first came to know the sea and the sky at Bordeaux and at Reunion Island, at Mauritius and Calcutta, just think what I suffer in a country where the trees are black and *where flowers have no perfume*! As for the cooking, you'll see that I've devoted some of the pages of my little book to it. As for conversation, that great—indeed, sole—pleasure of the intelligent being, you could travel the length and breadth of Belgium without finding a single person who knows how to *converse*. Many people, driven by the rubbernecker's curiosity, crowded around the author of *The Flowers of Evil*. The author of the *Flowers* in question couldn't fail to be a monstrous eccentric. All that rabble took me for a monster and when I proved to be cold, moderate, and polite, abhorring freethinkers, progress, and all modern stupidity, they (so I suppose) decreed that I was not *the author of my book* . . . What a comic confusion between author and subject! That damned book (of which I'm very proud) is, therefore, highly obscure, highly unintelligible! I'll long be made to suffer for having dared to paint evil with a degree of talent!

Moreover, I have to confess that for two or three months I've been letting myself go, taking a particular pleasure in wounding people, in showing myself to be *impertinent*, a talent in which I can excel when I put my mind to it. But here, that's not enough. If you want to be understood you have to be downright rude.

What a mob of riffraff. I, who considered France an utterly barbaric country, am now forced to recognize that there exists a country that is more barbaric still.

Well, whether I'm obliged to stay here with my debts or whether I flee to Honfleur I'll finish this little book which has at least forced me to sharpen my claws. I'll use them later against France. It's the first time that I've forced myself to write a book that is completely humorous, simultaneously comic and serious, and where I have to talk about *everything*. It's my break with modern folly. In the end, perhaps I'll be understood.

Yes, I need to return to Honfleur; I need my mother, my room, and my collection. What is more, my mother has been sending me deeply depressed letters in which, with a degree of moderation that hurts me, she refrains from making any criticisms, as if she were afraid of abusing the authority she's attained during the last few years, for fear of leaving a bitter memory. —That wrings my heart. —At Honfleur I'll finish a whole mass of things that are now half-done. *The Spleen of Paris* (which has been interrupted for such a long time), *Poor Belgium!* [*Pauvre Belgique!*] and *My Contemporaries*. [. . .]

165   To Narcisse Ancelle

13 November [1864]

My dear friend,

Don't forget the very important date of next Sunday, 20 November. So that I can have your 600 francs on Sunday at 8 A.M. you must post them off on Saturday earlier than you would in Paris, because you live in the suburbs. There's a difference in the postal collections that you need to bear in mind. If I get your 600 francs on Sunday morning I'll be in Paris at 9 in the evening. I beg you not to mess up my plans this time. — Please don't see any form of criticism in that last comment. [. . .]

Simon Raçon throws me into the wildest rages through the constant interruptions in his proof service.[4] Likewise the *Opinion nationale*. Likewise *all and sundry*. It is, I think, true to say that all men obstinately put off what they have to do until the assigned hour. This criticism of the world at large rings oddly in my mouth, since I myself am one of the worse offenders in this area. —But every day I struggle to overcome this tendency. I'm convinced that if an idiot is rich it's because he has this quality and that if a genius is poor, it's because he lacks it.

4. For *Histoires grotesques et sérieuses*, which were supposed to appear in the *Opinion nationale* but never did.

I've tried to put this last month to good use by going further into certain questions (for example, public education) and I've made the most amusing discoveries. Napoleon I, Louis-Phillipe, and above all Duruy, esquire (who wants to turn France into a kind of Belgium), still hold sway here. —If I can find a courageous editor in Paris (for *Le Figaro won't dare* publish my book in its entirety) I'll say some amusing things. The ministers, the deputies, the men who deal with the gravest matters have no understanding either of the meaning of words, or of spelling, or of the logical construction of a French or Latin sentence. —It's true that in France people know hardly any more about it.

To sum up, I'm not completely pleased with myself. The shock your delay caused me has forced me to put off until spring the analysis of certain aspects of the provinces. But for 4 or 5 months I'll enjoy the pleasure of getting two-thirds of my book published.

I've a score of visits to do in Paris. I think I can do them all in a week. This book on Belgium is, as I've told you, a means of trying out my claws. Later I'll use them against France. I'll patiently explain all the reasons for my disgust with mankind. When I'm *utterly alone* I'll seek out a religion (Tibetan or Japanese), for I despise the *Koran* too much, and on my deathbed I'll foreswear that last religion to show beyond doubt my disgust with universal stupidity. You can see I haven't changed and that Belgium itself hasn't succeeded in stultifying me.

If I leave on Sunday at 3, which depends on my getting your 600 francs, I'll be in Paris toward 9 P.M. So I won't have the pleasure of seeing you until Monday morning. All yours. My regards to Mme Ancelle.

166   TO CAROLINE AUPICK

1 January 1865

My dear Mother,

I have no need of the solemnity of this day, so sad a day among all the days of the year, to lead my thoughts back to you and to think of all the obligations and all the responsibilities I've acquired over so many years. My main obligation, my sole obligation even, would be to make you happy. I think of that constantly. Will I ever be allowed to do it?

I sometimes think with a sudden shudder that God could abruptly take that possibility out of my hands. I promise you first that this year you won't be forced to accept any request for aid on my behalf. I blush when I think of all the privations I've forced upon you. I'll even try to repay some of that money to you this year. I also promise you that no day this year will go by without my doing some work. Such a program must infallibly end in reward.

My mind is full of morbid imaginings. How difficult it is to do as one ought *every day* without a single interruption. How difficult it is, not to dream up a book, but to write it without lassitude—in a word to be in good heart day after day. —I've calculated that everything I've had in my head for a long time would have cost me a mere 15 months' work, if I'd worked assiduously. How often I've told myself: "Despite my nerves, despite my terrors, despite the creditors, despite the horrors of solitude, I must pull myself together, take heart! This may well bring rewards." How often God has already granted me 15 months. And yet I've often interrupted the work, I've interrupted too often up to now the execution of my projects. Will I have the time (even if we take my courage for granted) to make up for everything I have to make up for? If I were at least sure of having 5 or 6 years ahead of me! But who can be sure of that? For me, that thought has now reached the proportions of an obsession, the thought of death—I don't mean that it is accompanied by stupid terrors. —I've already suffered so much and been punished so much that I believe many things can be forgiven me—but the thought of death is nonetheless hateful because it would reduce all my plans to nothing and because I haven't yet carried through a third of all I want to do in this world.

You've no doubt guessed how much I stand in terror of going through Paris without any money, of having to spend in Paris, my personal hell, a mere 6 or 7 days, without being able to offer some guarantees to some of my creditors. I don't want to return to France until I can do so in *glory*. My exile has taught me to do without all the distractions that exist. I lack the energy needed to work without interruption. When I have it I'll be bold and calmer. My hopes are high. I've given someone in Paris responsibility for my literary affairs—I think I'll soon have cause to write to you on that score.[5] —I believe I'm in people's thoughts. You know all the things I have to publish—alas, how many of them are overdue!

1. *Histoires grotesques et sérieuses* (That will come out after the tumult of New Year. Michel will send you a copy.)

2. *The Flowers of Evil*. (Augmented)

3. *The Spleen of Paris*. (I've gone back to that, as you'll have realized because of the issue of the *Revue de Paris* I sent you.)

4. *Artificial Paradises*.

5. *Contemporaries*

6. *Poor Belgium!*

(It's in regard to these last three works that I'm ardently awaiting replies

5. There seems to be no proof that Baudelaire had transformed this project into a reality at this stage.

from Paris.) As for a series of *Tales* and *My Heart Laid Bare*, I'll do them at Honfleur. Those will be the great days of maternal love. I hope they won't be the days of precocious old age!

Tell me in great detail about your health, I beg you. Your colds? What are these weaknesses in your legs and back that you mentioned recently? Tell me about them. It seems that they struck you as new developments since this is the first time you've mentioned them. Are you still pleased with Aimée?

I send tender hugs, with all the effusion of a child who loves only his mother. I'll bring you 2 or 3 little things that will please you.

167　To Mme Paul Meurice

3 January 1865

It would be very unpleasant for me, indeed I'm forbidden, to let a New Year begin without wishing you all joy of it. We all need that wish and for my part I feel a kind of affection for people who give me the season's greetings in an agreeable way.

Need I tell you how fond of you I am? Need I tell you how much I hope you have repose, prosperity, and those calm pleasures that are essential even to the most virile of souls?

Need I say, too, how often I think about you (each time I force a Belgian to play a piece of Wagner's music, each time I have occasion to talk about French literature, each time there arises yet another example of that Belgian stupidity you've so often talked to me about)?

I've been taken for a police spy here (that's a good one!)—thanks to that fine article I wrote about the banquet in honor of Shakespeare; as a homosexual (I myself spread that rumor around and *they believed me!*), then I was taken for a *proof corrector*, sent from Paris to correct the proofs of *infamous works*. Exasperated at being believed all the time, I spread the rumor that I'd *killed* my father and then eaten him; that moreover if I'd been allowed to escape from France it was because of my services to the French police AND I WAS BELIEVED! *I'm swimming in dishonor like a fish in water.*

Dear Madame, don't reply to this letter. You'd be hard put, despite all your intelligence, to answer such a missive. Forgive a mind that occasionally seeks out minds in which it can confide and which has never ceased to think of your grace and kindness. I pray that you may be happy (since I always pray for all those I love) and beg you not to forget me in your prayers *when you have as much humility as wit.*

Please give your husband my wishes for the new year.

3 February 1865

My dear Lemer,

I've been wanting to write to you for a long time, as I told Henry de la Madelène, and, if I've delayed so long, it's not just because of my habitual apathy where my own affairs are concerned, but also because of a certain timidity that makes me constantly procrastinate business matters, probably because I think anything I want is bound to fail.

For many years I've dreamed of finding a man (if he were also a friend, that would be perfect) who would be good enough to concern himself with my literary affairs. As for me, long experience has proved to me that I'm utterly inept in such matters. Why I don't have the intelligence needed for that I don't know, but in this area I've committed so many follies that I've decided not to get myself involved in it anymore.

First of all, would you agree to be this person I'm looking for? It's a step I should have taken years ago, but after all it's never too late. Second, I'm forced to ask what price you'd want to put on your services, that is to say what would be your percentage of the contracts you made on my behalf? I may not take up a lot of your time, but I'd certainly take up a little, and although we've known each other long enough to consider that some kind of relationship exists between us, I'm forced to ask you that stupid question. I've been told that in business modesty is foolishness. I needn't add, my dear Lemer, that whatever you decide will be fine. Only I hope to discover a zealous friend.

I'll explain what's available at present. I hope that next year, perhaps even in a few months' time, if I have a little respite, there will be other works to give you.

I'm appending summaries of four books I want you to sell: *Artificial Paradises* (so badly edited a few years ago that this can be considered an unpublished work. I believe the book to be good as it stands and will neither add nor withdraw anything); *Reflections*, divided into two parts or two volumes. This isn't, as you might believe, a packet of newspaper articles. Although these articles, most of them unknown, were published at long intervals, they're all connected by a single and systematic line of argument. I've a pretty keen desire to show what I've been capable of doing where criticism is concerned. Finally the fourth volume, *Poor Belgium!* in one volume. This last isn't complete. I've been able to profit from my nine months' stay, but I'll have to add 2 or 3 chapters on the provinces, on the old towns, and the weather is too appalling to allow me to dash about again yet.

Now, a few little ideas that I'm just going to suggest to you, for you'll do as you see fit. I would very much like to alienate these four volumes for a specified length of time—2 years, 3, 5 years, or for a considerable number of copies, which, when all is said and done, comes to the same thing. But I feel that will be difficult, because an editor naturally prefers to see a book's fortune first, to avoid the risk of paying out a lot at a time, reserving the right to renew the contract once the first edition has sold out.

Another question: don't you feel there is an advantage, if there is the possibility of doing it, in selling the four volumes to the same printer? In any case I think I shouldn't alienate anything absolutely and finally because I have to make sure of being able, at a future date, to publish my collected works all through the same editor.

The manuscript of *Contemporaries* is at home, at Honfleur. I'll go and get it when I've finished my notes on Belgium. *Poor Belgium!* will be ready for delivery in March. As for the *Paradises*, I have a copy. Do you think it would be a bad idea to send all or part of the book on Belgium to a journal? I know Villemessant would be very pleased with the idea, but I wanted to consult you beforehand. Now for the question of the editors themselves. Michel Lévy bears me a grudge for having given *The Flowers of Evil* and *The Spleen of Paris* to Hetzel. Hetzel is angry with me (and he has every right to be so) because I haven't yet handed over *The Flowers of Evil* and *The Spleen of Paris*, which are finished but which I'm still chewing over. Dentu and Charpentier don't seem to me the right kind of publishers to make my books popular. I may be wrong, but Dentu doesn't strike me as serious enough and Charpentier is too much a part of Louis-Philippe's reign—you'll know what I mean by that. But I don't attach absolute importance to what I'm telling you here. There remain Didier, Amyot, and Hachette, who are first-rate publishers. But doesn't Hachette reveal a fair degree of democratic pedantry? I warn you, *Poor Belgium!* is a book that attacks freethinkers, although it's expressed in highly comic terms.

Scatter the volumes about, if you can do not better. What is the maximum you think you can ask for a volume in-octavo—or for an in-18? But these are secondary questions. Moreover, as I've said, I'll give you complete control over all that and it goes without saying that if you accept the job I'll forbid myself to take any direct steps whatsoever with any editor whatsoever.

In a few days I'll send you two or three articles and a pile of prose poems that you can divide into two or three collections. May this be the last few times I'll have to ask for the hospitality of any newspaper! I recoil from editors-in-chief, even when they're my friends. I've begun to work on two other big works, but I feel I'll complete them only at Honfleur. One is a series of short stories, all interconnected, and the other is a great monster dealing *de omni re* and called *My Heart Laid Bare*. All yours, my dear Lemer, and don't forget me.

Reflections on Some of My Contemporaries is very long. *Reflections on* could be left out. Above all what I wanted to avoid were the words *artistic* and *literary*, which kill a book's sales.

169   TO MME PAUL MEURICE

3 February 1865

When one receives a charming letter, particularly when it is very unexpected and very little merited, one's first duty is to reply straightaway. I'm very much at fault, therefore, for having put off for 30 days the pleasure of answering you and thanking you. I could say to you, and it would be the truth, that I'm very often ill; but that would be a poor excuse, because colds, headaches, and fevers don't last a full 30 days. I prefer to tell you the truth, which is that it's part of my nature to abuse my friends' indulgence. And, too, there is in this odious climate some atmosphere that not only stultifies the mind but also hardens the heart and drives us to forget all our duties.

You'll guess how much pleasure you gave me when I confess I was so deeply ashamed at having written such enormous bits of folly, almost as freely as I'd write to a comrade, that, unable to break the brass cornerpost that held the letterbox, and not expecting any reply, I still used all my ingenuity to dream up ways of earning your forgiveness. So when I read your reply, a reply I'd so little expected, I felt a double pleasure—first the pleasure of *hearing you speak*, and then the *pleasure of astonishment*. So I have to admit that there's not a shadow of a doubt that you possess the finest qualities in the world.

I want to reply immediately to some of the things you said that particularly touched me. I assure you I have no *particular* source of sorrow. I'm always in a bad mood (that's an illness) because I suffer from the stupidity around me and because I'm not pleased with myself. But in France, where there is less stupidity, where stupidity itself is more polite, I still suffered. And even if I had absolutely nothing to criticize myself for, I'd be just as unhappy, because I'd dream of doing better. So, whether I'm in Paris or Brussels or an unknown city, I'm sure to be ill and incurable. There is a form of misanthropy that stems not from a bad character, but from an overresponsive sensitivity and a disposition to allow oneself to be shocked too easily. Why do I stay in Brussels although I hate it? First because I'm here and in my current state I'd be uncomfortable anywhere at all. Second because I've inflicted on myself an act of contrition—I've forced myself to do penance until I'm cured of my vices (it's a slow business) and also until a certain person, whom I've charged with my literary affairs in Paris, has cleared up certain questions.

Since you're pardoning me for everything and allowing me to assume any tone at all, I'll tell you that this highly detestable Belgium has already done me a great service. *It's taught me to do without everything.* That's a great deal. *I've become sensible because of the impossibility of finding satisfaction.* I've always loved pleasure and it may be that that has caused me the most harm. In a little seaport one has the pleasure of studying the movement in the port, the ships arriving and departing, the pleasure of drinking in bars with inferior beings, whose sentiments nevertheless interest me. There's none of that here. Here the poor don't even inspire charity. In Paris, there are dinners and friends, museums, music, women. Here, there's nothing. As for fine eating, that's out of the question. You know there's no Belgian cuisine and that these people don't know how to cook eggs or grill meat. Wine is drinkable only as something rare, precious, marvelous, and kept for special occasions. I believe—God damn me!—that these animals drink out of vanity, to pretend to know something about it. As for young wine, sold cheaply, the sort you drink a full glass of when you're thirsty, that's utterly unknown. Gallantry is even more of a closed book. The sight of a Belgian woman gives me a vague desire to faint. The god Eros himself, if he wanted to freeze all his fires at a single blow, would need only to look at a Belgian woman's face. Add to that the fact that the coarseness of the women, which is equal to that of the men, would destroy their charm, if these unfortunate beings could ever have any charm to begin with. Several months ago I found I'd lost my way at night in a suburb I didn't know. I asked directions from two young women who just answered: "Gott for damn (or domn!)!" I'm transcribing that badly, but no Belgian has ever been able to tell me how to spell the national expletive, but it's the equivalent of "Sacré nom de Dieu."[6] So these lovely maidens answered me in these words: "In God's name, leave us alone!" As for the men, they never fail in their special calling of crudeness. On a day when there was black ice I saw a little actress from the Park Theater slip. She hurt herself badly and as I struggled to lift her up, a Belgian who was passing gave a great kick at her muff which was rolling in the street and said: "Well, and this? Are you forgetting this?" Perhaps he was a deputy, a minister, a prince, perhaps even the king himself. A worker in Paris would have picked it up in all honesty to return it to the lady. As I was telling you, I'd willingly invite all sensual people to come and live in Belgium. They'd

6. "In God's name"; literally, "Holy name of God."

be cured in no time and in a few months *disgust would make them all virgins again*.

Yet another service this land of rogues has paid me.

—You've teased me more than once about my leanings toward mysticism. I assure you that even you would become pious here—out of sheer *amour propre*—out of a need not to conform. The sight of all those atheist apes has fully confirmed my ideas on religion. I don't even have good things to say about *Catholics*. The liberals are atheists, the Catholics are superstitious, they're each as coarse as the other, and each party is dominated equally by hypocrisy.

Two more little anecdotes—profoundly Belgian anecdotes—to amuse you. One day a cafe waiter said to me as he served me: "So you go into churches, sir? You were seen at Christmas in such-and-such a church." I answered: "Don't breathe a word about it." But I said to myself: "They'll talk about it in the Council of Ministers." Two days later I met a Belgian who said to me: "So, you go to mass, do you? Gott for domn! (still the same expletive that I don't know how to spell). What can you be going to mass for, since you don't have a missal?" That's a quintessentially Belgian line of reasoning. You can't pray without a book. You don't think without a set of rules. Yet it falls down on one point for a missal would be of no use to a Belgian, since he wouldn't understand the written prayers.

One day I was led with great pomp and circumstance to a minister who owns an expensive collection of paintings. After looking at the rest, I was led to a Bartolini copied by Ingres. That was where I was meant to fall into ecstasies. But no one had warned me. I said: "It's probably by Ingres. The hands and face are too large. *That* isn't *style*, and besides they're red and dirty. There is a great man who preceded Ingres and who has a great deal more genius. I mean David!" Then the minister turned to my mahout (for I believe that *I* was also on show) and consulted him delicately: "It seems to me, moreover, that David has recently been *rising in value*!" I couldn't control myself. I answered that it was enough that he had never fallen in value for people of intelligence.

There's yet another service I owe Belgium. You can tell Bracquemond. It's destroyed my illusions about Rubens. When I left Paris I had too high an image of that lout. Rubens is the only kind of gentleman Belgium could produce, by which I mean a churl clad in silk. I'd prefer to the best Rubens a little piece of Roman bronze or an Egyptian spoon—made of wood.

My sincere greetings to your husband. Say hello to Fantin and Manet. I'm asked to convey to you M. Charles Hugo's good wishes. It's said that his father is to come and live here. Heavens! I was about to forget the very serious and interesting question of your outfits. You did well to talk to me about them, you know how interested I am in clothes. I'm almost as erudite where clothes are concerned as Malassis is knowledgeable on books or botany. For the poor chap has taken up botany (not entomology, because there are no insects in the woods here, any more than there are birds. Wild creatures flee from the Belgians). I understand all your outfits and they remind me of an age that lives on in my mind. As for the hairdo, I understand that less well, I'm ashamed to admit. Moreover, I've only one comment to make to you. When a highly intelligent woman has white hair, whatever hairdo she tries out, she shouldn't neglect to *show* her white hair. It makes her more beautiful.

I kiss your hands gallantly and shake them vigorously.

170   TO NARCISSE ANCELLE

12 February 1865

[. . .] A thousand apologies for all the trouble I'm causing you. I've never been so furious as in these last ten days, waiting for news, receiving nothing but bad news, and utterly powerless to do anything. For ten days I've been hoping to receive important news about my literary bits and pieces, and there's NOTHING, NOTHING, NOTHING! This morning, for the first time in ages, I ate a solid meal, with the greed of a child. It was too soon. I can feel my migraine coming on again.

A few days ago, I looked through a packet of very interesting letters from Proudhon, addressed to friends from Belgium. Théophile Thoré (you remember him—for several years he's used the pseudonym William Bürger) came to see me recently. We hadn't seen each other for 20 years or near enough. I was immensely pleased to see him again. Moreover, I'm in a mood where any Frenchman would strike me as a genius. Although he is a republican, Thoré has always had elegant habits. He told me he once went on a journey with Proudhon but was forced to abandon him because he was so disgusted by Proudhon's affectation of rustic habits, his affectation of rustic coarseness in everything, and his aping of peasant impertinence. —So one can be at one and the same time a fine mind and a churl, just as one can both possess a *unique genius* and be a *fool*. Victor Hugo has given us ample proof of that. —By the way, Hugo is to come and live in Brussels. He's bought a house in the Leopold quarter. It seems that he and the Ocean are no longer on good terms. Either *he* didn't have the strength to put up with the Ocean, or the Ocean *itself* tired of his company. What a waste of time, carefully arranging a palace on a cliff! As for me, alone, forgotten by all and sundry, I wouldn't sell my mother's little house unless things came to the absolute worst. But I've even more pride than Victor Hugo, and I feel, I know, that I would never be as stupid as he. —You can be comfortable anywhere (provided you're in good health, and have books and engravings) *even looking at the Ocean*.

Proudhon had never read Hugo. He ought to have read the papers. But someone lent him *Les Misérables* (Hugo's disgrace). He annotated the last 2 volumes line by line. That must have been a marvel of comedy— logic correcting the absence of logic. —Well, the Belgian who owned the copy (admire the Belgian!), on finding his copy defaced, carefully erased all the notes. An entire monument lost!

Whoever was it who wrote on the back of your envelope: *Greetings and Brotherhood*! or *Fraternal Greetings*!—words that were soiled by the postmark? That's not the sort of language *your friends* use. But it reminded me of the enthusiasms and jests of February.[7] How old all that is already!

Do you know that the sons of King Leopold receive, with their Papa's approval, an allowance from Emperor Napoleon III, as an indemnity for the part they lost in the (seized) inheritance of the house of Orleans? What base souls! Condemned dynasties. Our emperor may be a great rogue but he prefers glory to gold and that's what makes him interesting. I'll verify that information before I publish it. Not an easy task.

I'm eager to see *The Life of Caesar* [*La Vie de César*] and to know if Napoleon-Louis is a true man of letters.

My compliments to Mme Ancelle.

Regards. Don't forget me.

171   TO MICHEL LÉVY

15 February 1865

My dear Michel,

I'm not a publisher and I think you have no confidence at all in any of my ideas. Yet it is possible that my idea was a good one. In the 9 months I've been here I've never spoken to M. Lacroix,[8] I've never greeted him because of the instinctive horror he inspires in me.

One day I was chatting with Verboeckhoven and, since he was talking to me about foreign writers who would be good to translate, I suggested to him that he publish a new translation of *Melmoth the Wanderer*, a forgotten work, the code of Romanticism, admired by Balzac and Victor Hugo.[9] Where Romanticism is concerned I know what I'm talking about.

I learn that those gentlemen have just commissioned a translation

---

7. The Revolution of 1848 began with demonstrations on February 22.
8. Lacroix and Verboeckhoven was an important publishing house in Brussels.
9. Charles Maturin's Gothic novel.

from Mlle Judith. What a massacre of a masterpiece! I know how those gentlemen get translations done—at 25 francs a page—by people who don't know the language. I got my hands on the translation of Kinglake's *History of the Crimean War* (it doesn't bear Lacroix's name: since he has a publisher's commission in Paris that would be dangerous) and I could devine the mistranslations without even looking at the original.

To commission a true and intelligent translation of *Melmoth* could be a *good deal*, and you'd certainly not lose money on it. And then, there'd be a bit of honor in doing that. Among your numerous relations you could find an educated writer who would do you a good and *literal* translation for an *honest* and moderate price, but much higher than Lacroix pays his experts. Get your translation underway promptly and you'll kill Lacroix's operation.

I don't need to add that this *in no way concerns me*. I've devoted a lot of time to Edgar Poe, because he resembles me a little, but I'm not a translator. Perhaps you're on good terms with Mlle Judith? in which case my idea is destroyed.

I found the *Belgian* procedure a little too discourteous and I thought it would be a good idea to indicate to you a trick in which there may be a good and *noble* affair. Publish *Histoires grotesques et sérieuses* at the latest possible date. I'm penniless and very eager to draw the last rehashes from the sack.

As you see, I'm a good hater, to use Byron's term—moreover, I believe that it is hatred that has enabled me to write a good book on Belgium. Have you read the infamous article by *Eraste* against Heinrich Heine and the satanic poets? I'm in the process of writing a reply.[10]

Thank me by your acts, since you never reply.

172   To Mme Paul Meurice

18 February 1865

Your letters, dear lady, are always full of kindness but the pleasure that kindness gives me doesn't blind me to your gift for satire, which, moreover, I've always suspected. I was especially moved by what you said of Meurice's feelings in regard to me. Thank him for me.

Manet wrote me recently about the *Melmoth* business. I was irritated for two reasons. First, because I've always been *penetrated* by the bizarre feeling that beautiful things should be kept hidden, and enjoyed only in

10. "Eraste" was Jules Janin, whose article appeared in *L'Indépendance belge* of 12 February. Lévy had published Heine's works.

an aristocratic manner, and second because I remember very clearly discussing eight months ago with Verboeckhoven the question of good books in need of resuscitating. He didn't know Maturin and I explained to him who he was. He said to me: "I'll discuss it with Lacroix." But I didn't offer my services as a translator. I'm afraid of such tasks. I lost a great deal of time in translating Edgar Poe and the great benefit it brought me was to make some kindly souls say I'd borrowed *my* poems from Poe—poems I'd written 10 years before I knew Poe's works.

I consider translations as a lazy man's way of making money. The way I'm talking about the affair doesn't imply a contradiction with the way you related it. The only thing is that all unawares I lined Mlle Judith's pockets. I didn't offer my services, but when those gentlemen decided to publish Maturin, courtesy should have led them to offer the work to the person who had suggested it to them. So I wrote to two publishers in Paris, Michel Lévy and Julien Lemer, to advise them to get the translation done quickly. But I didn't offer my services to them, either. I admit I'd feel a certain pleasure in playing a nasty trick on M. Lacroix, *whom, moreover, I do not know. I've never spoken to him and never greeted him.*

Now I'll answer some of the ideas you've expressed to me so graciously. First, Meurice is wrong to think of Maturin as a writer who is hard to understand. His English is as simple, as limpid, as clear as can be. If there is a difficulty, it lies not in understanding but in expressing. There is in this writer a strangeness and an excessive violence of feeling, and then he's in the habit of using prodigious metaphors; in brief, it's a strange style, the style of another age. He's an *old Romantic* and to interpret him well you have to be an *old Romantic.*

The idea of my collaborating with Mlle Judith is crazy.

As for a critical and biographical study, even supposing those gentlemen agreed to it, I can see a further problem. In such a study you'd have to explain what Maturin is, what rank he occupies in the history of modern literature, what satanic literature is, how he stands in relation to Byron, etc. etc. —Well you can see what a fine figure such a preface would cut if the translation didn't give a sufficiently high idea of the author thus praised! —I'm willing to believe that Mlle Judith's translation will be good but I know that the translations Lacroix commissions are, generally speaking, execrable. I've cast my eyes over a few of them. It's done on a *budget* and by people who, although their job should require a knowledge of two languages, don't even know one. (Take for instance Kinglake's *History of the Crimean War.* The mistranslations stick out even without the reader's having recourse to the original.) It might perhaps be a good idea for you to look at the letter I wrote Meurice. He'll find it quite natural that Manet and you let me know what is happening. In any case, many thanks to him for the interest he showed toward me in this affair.

I don't at all share your severe views on women who wear low-cut dresses. It's very pleasant for those men who have no wife to lose, or who are placed outside human interests, and who are seeking merely a spectacle. I even think that it's pleasant for those who would be better advised to hide their women away. It makes them proud.

Don't ever talk to me about MM St . . .[11] They are moreover enviable people, particularly Arthur, who thinks that all women throw themselves at him. But there's nothing *original* in that, at least *not in this country*. Every Belgian is convinced of the same thing, where he himself is concerned.

POSTSCRIPT: Like you, I reproach all those brutal men who flee from women, but it must be said in their defence that women are much less amiable than they were in the past.

173   To MICHEL LÉVY

9 March 1865

My dear Michel,

I've been so ill these last few days that I couldn't find the heart to answer any letters. Moreover your letter of 21 February didn't demand an immediate reply. You were advising me that you were going to put on sale the tales of the grotesque and serious. Very good. It's your book. You're the master and I'm the one to thank *you* for all the kindness you've shown me. —Only, if by any chance the book hasn't yet gone on sale and if Julien Lemer, whom I'm putting in charge of my literary affairs, had found publishers for the fragments (*Marie Roget* and *Habitations imaginaires*[12]) and these pieces were on the point of being published, wouldn't you wait just a little? —So be good enough to check on that with Julien Lemer.

My dear friend, in no way did I offer to translate *Melmoth* for you myself. *I told you it was just an idea I was suggesting to you.* You'll easily find an honest translator. I confess that it was the bad mood MM. Verboeckhoven's and Lacroix's indelicacy put me in that led me to mention the matter to you, and particularly the conviction that this fine work would be spoiled, messed up, botched. Moreover, I might perhaps go

11. The Stevens brothers.
12. That is, "The Domain of Arnheim," "Landor's Cottage," and "The Philosophy of Furniture."

back on what I said. I'm going to write to Julien Lemer about it. I'm convinced that a simple notice: Maturin's *Melmoth*, translated by M. Charles Baudelaire with a preface by M. Flaubert, or M. d'Aurevilly (who, like me, are old Romantics) would suffice to scupper Lacroix's speculation. I've worked out that it would need only two months' regular work to translate the entire novel. You could confidently do a first run of 10,000 copies. — I know what I'm saying. I've just read the detestable translation of 1820 and beneath the French text I could guess in all cases what the original had been. But as you tell me, none of that concerns you. But if you see Lemer, tell him what I've said to you. [. . .] I finished my answer to Janin (long ago)[13] regarding the article on Heine and the youth of the poets. Then, once it was done, and pleased at having done it, I kept it—I didn't send it to any paper. I also refuted the preface to *Julius Caesar* but then kept it. I've begun and am continuing with a little study on Chateaubriand considered as the leader of *Dandyism* and the *world of ideas*, in which I'll avenge this great man for the insults of the whole pack of moderns. But I won't send that to the newspapers either. I'm sick of the columnists, the ignorant, the penpushers, chief editors and all their *pendantry*. Footsloggers don't like pathbreakers. It's my sympathy for d'Aurevilly no doubt that inspires this detestable pun.

I'll just keep these pieces to add them to my book: *My Contemporaries*. Lemer will place it with whatever editor he chooses, since M. Michel Lévy claims that the critical works of M. Charles Baudelaire aren't sufficiently interesting.

174   TO CHARLES-AUGUSTIN SAINTE-BEUVE
                                   30 March and 4 May 1865
My dear friend,

Thank you for your excellent letter—could you be capable of writing any that weren't excellent? When you call me "My dear child," I'm simultaneously touched and amused. Despite my long white hair which makes me look like an academician (*abroad*) I'm much in need of someone who loves me enough to call me his child, but I can't help thinking of that burgher aged 120 who, when speaking to an 80-year-old burgher said to him: "Young man, be quiet!" (In parentheses, and just between the two of us, if I wrote a tragedy I'd be afraid of slipping in expressions like that and of hitting a target different from the one I'd aimed at.) But I note that in your letter there is no allusion to the copy of *Histoires grotesques et sérieuses* that I asked Michel Lévy to send you. I've every right

13. The response to Janin's letter on Heine.

to conclude that this publisher, who belongs to the race that crucified our Lord, was capable, very naturally, of economizing on a copy at your expense. Moreover, I swear that I've no intention of extracting from you any *advertisement* for my book. My only aim, since I know how well you're able to distribute your time, was to give you a chance to enjoy once again an astonishing subtlety of logic and sentiment. There are people who will find this fifth volume inferior to the preceding ones but I don't care in the least about that.

We're not as down in the dumps as you think, Malassis and I. We've learned to do without everything in a country where there is nothing and we've learned that certain pleasures (those of conversation for instance) increase in inverse proportion to certain needs. Talking of Malassis, I'll admit to you that I'm amazed at his courage, his activity, and his incorrigible gaiety. He's acquired astonishing erudition where books and prints are concerned. Everything amuses and instructs him. One of our great pleasures consists in his putting his mind to playing the atheist while I do my best to be a Jesuit. You know I can be pious by contradiction (*especially here*), just as to become impious I only need to come in contact with a foul *curé* (foul in body and soul). As for the publication of a few jokey books, which he took pleasure in correcting with the same piety that he would have placed at the service of Bossuet or Loyola, I even drew a tiny, tiny, unexpected profit from it, for I gained a clear understanding of the French Revolution. When these people enjoy a certain kind of pleasure it's a good diagnostic for revolution.

Alexandre Dumas has just left us. That good chap put himself on show with his usual candor. While lining up around him to get a handshake, the Belgians mocked him. That's base. A man can earn respect for his *vitality*, a negro vitality admittedly. But I think that many others as well as I, those who love serious things, were carried away by *The Lady of Monsoreau* [*La Dame de Monsoreau*] and *Balsamo*.

As I'm very eager to return to France, I wrote to Julien Lemer to put him in charge of my affairs. I'd like to publish a three- or four-volume collection of the best of my articles on Stimulants, on painters and poets, adding to them a series of thoughts on Belgium. If, in one of your rare walks, you're going along the Boulevard de Gand, whip up his goodwill for me, and exaggerate your opinion of me.

I must confess that three important fragments are missing—one on *Didactic Painting* (Cornelius, Kaulbach, Chenavard, Alfred Rethel)—another, *Biography of the Flowers of Evil*—and finally one on Chateaubriand and his family. You know that my passion for this old Dandy is beyond reform. In all, not much work, ten days, perhaps. I've a treasure trove of notes on these topics.

Forgive me if I'm touching on a delicate question. My excuse is my longing to see you happy (supposing certain things would make you happy) and to see everyone treat you as you deserve. I hear lots of people saying: "Gracious! Sainte-Beuve isn't a senator yet?" Many years ago I said to Eugène Delacroix, with whom I used to speak completely frankly, that many young people would prefer to see him as a pariah and a rebel. (I was alluding to his obstinate persistence in presenting himself at the Institute.) He answered: "My dear sir, if my right arm were struck with paralysis, membership of the Institute would give me the right to teach, and providing I were still well enough the Institute would serve to pay for my coffee and cigars." In a word, I think that many minds as well as my own have felt like accusing Napoleon's government of a degree of ingratitude. Forgive me, won't you, for violating the limits of discretion. You know how fond of you I am, and besides I'm chattering away like someone who rarely has the chance to talk.

I've just read Emile Ollivier's long speech.[14] It's very odd. It seems to me that he's talking like a man with a great secret up his sleeve. Have you read Janin's dreadful review attacking the melancholy and mocking poets (about Heinrich Heine)? And he cites Viennet as one of France's great poets! And two weeks later an article in favor of Cicero. Does he take Cicero for an Orleanist or an Academician? M. de Sacy says, "Cicero is our very own Caesar!" Yes indeed.

Affectionately,

C. B.

Without any transition let me say I've just found an admirable, melancholy ode by Shelley, composed on the shores of the gulf of Naples, and ending thus: "I know I am one of those whom men love not, but I'm one of those they remember."[15] Bravo! There's poetry for you!

4 May 1865

My dear Sainte-Beuve,

As I picked up my pen to write a few words of congratulations on your nomination,[16] I came across a letter I wrote you on 30 March and that wasn't posted, probably through an error on my part or on that of the hotel staff. On rereading it I find it childish, boyish. But I'll send it to you anyway. If it makes you laugh I won't say "too bad" but "all to the

---

14. Ollivier, a member of the Chamber of Deputies, had delivered an important speech on the freedoms the government should grant.

15. "Stanzas Written in Dejection, Near Naples." The exact words are: "For I am one / Whom men love not, —and yet regret."

16. Sainte-Beuve had just been nominated senator.

good." Knowing your indulgence I'm not at all afraid to show myself to you just as I am.

To the section dealing with Lemer, I'll add that I've finished the pieces mentioned (apart from the book on Belgium, which I don't have the courage to finish here) and that, as I'm obliged to go to Honfleur to get all the other bits and pieces to make up the books I'd announced to Lemer, I'll probably go through Paris on 15 May to shake him up a little. If you happen to see him, you can let him know I'm coming.

As for Malassis, that terrible business of his happens on 12 May.[17] He's convinced he'll be given a 5-year sentence. What's serious is that that means he'll have to stay out of France for 5 years. The fact that that will briefly cut off his livelihood doesn't seem to me such a bad thing. He'll be forced to do something different. It's counting too much on universal intelligence to flaunt the obligatory public modesty. As for me, and I'm no prude, I've never owned one of those imbecilic books, not even one printed in fine lettering and with beautiful engravings.

Alas! The prose poems, for which you yet again sent off words of encouragement recently, are greatly delayed. I'm always taking on difficult tasks. One hundred laborious little nothings that demand constant good humor (good humor is essential even if you're going to treat sad subjects) and a bizarre elation that demands spectacles, crowds, music, even streetlights, that's what I aimed to write! I'm only up to number 60 and can't go any further. I need that famous *bath of the multitude*[18]—an expression the incorrectness of which rightly shocked you.

Monselet has come here. I read your article. I admired your suppleness and your aptitude for entering into the heart of each individual talent, but that particular talent lacks something I can't define. Monselet went to Antwerp, where there are some splendid things, particularly examples of that monstrous Jesuit style I like so much and which I'd scarcely known except in the chapel of the College at Lyon which is made of marble of various different colors. Antwerp has a very special kind of museum, full of unexpected items, unexpected even for those capable of assigning the Flemish school its true place. Summing up, I'd say the town has a great, solemn air to it, the air of a former capital city, intensified by the presence of a wide river. I think that good old Monselet saw none of that. He only saw the great fry-up he went to eat on the other side of the Escaut. He is moreover a charming man.

I really congratulate you from the bottom of my heart. You're now

17. Malassis was found guilty of publishing political and pornographic works in Brussels and sending them to Paris. He was given a one-year prison sentence and a fine.
18. Baudelaire used this phrase in "The Crowds."

(officially) the equal of many mediocrities. What does that matter to me? It was what you wanted, isn't it? Perhaps what you needed? You're happy, so I'm glad.

175   To Edouard Manet

11 May 1865

Dear friend,

Thanks for your good letter, brought to me by M. Chorner this morning, together with the piece of music. For some time I've intended to go through Paris twice, once on my way to Honfleur, once coming back, and I'd admitted as much to that madman Rops, swearing him to secrecy, for I'd barely have the time to greet two or three friends; but according to M. Chorner, Rops mentioned it to several people, as a natural result of which lots of people now think I'm in Paris and consider me a frightful ingrate.

If you see Rops, don't attach too much importance to certain violently provincial traits of behavior. Rops likes you, he's understood what value to place on your intelligence, and he's often confided to me certain observations he's made about people who hate you (for it appears that you have the honor of inspiring hatred in some people). Rops is *the only true artist* (in the sense *I*, and I entirely alone perhaps, give the *artist*) that I've found in Belgium.

So I must talk to you about yourself again. I must set myself to show you your own worth. What you demand is really crazy. People tease you; their jokes irritate you; no one knows your real worth. Do you think you're the only man in that position? Do you have more genius than Chateaubriand and Wagner? But they were jeered at, weren't they? It didn't kill them. And to avoid turning your head, I'll add that those men were models, each in his own way, and in a very rich world, whereas you, *you're only the first in the decline of your art*. I hope you won't bear me a grudge for my lack of formality. You know my friendship for you.

I wanted to get M. Chorner's *personal* impression, at least to the extent that a Belgian can be considered a *person*. I have to say he was kind and what he told me corresponds to what I know of you and what several intelligent people say of you: *"He has faults and weaknesses, a lack of aplomb, but he also has an irresistible charm."* I know all that. I was one of the first to realize that. He added that the painting which depicts a naked woman, with the negress and the cat (*is* it really a cat?),[19] was far better than the religious painting.

19. The reference is to Manet's painting *Olympia*, which does indeed contain a cat.

As for Lemer, there's nothing new. I think I'll go myself and shake him up. As for completing *Poor Belgium!*, I'm incapable of doing it. I'm weakened, I'm dead. I've a pile of prose poems to spread through two or three reviews. But I can't get any further. I'm suffering from a disease I haven't contracted, as I did when I was a lad and lived at the ends of the world. And yet I'm not patriotic.

176   TO CAROLINE AUPICK

30 May 1865

My dear good Mother,

There are no changes in my plans. Moreover, it's absolutely essential that I talk to several people in Paris and I also have to go through all my papers at Honfleur. I'll leave very soon. Only the proprietress of my hotel promised me for ten days that she'd bring someone who can mend my linen and the person I eventually found hasn't yet finished her work. And, too, I've suddenly started suffering again from neuralgia (that's nothing) and pains in the stomach. I dosed myself like a horse, and am pretty weakened by a series of purges. I'm spending my time slowly building up my packet of prose poems because while I'm waiting for my affairs to be arranged I'd be quite pleased to pick up in Paris some small contributions for unpublished work.

My dear mother, you write things that bring the tears to my eyes. So I'll find that you're *very old, very old indeed*. What does that matter to me? I know I'll never be bored when I'm with you. I'll only make the cruel reflection that I've been mad not to spend these last years with you. I've criminally deprived myself of those last years.

Mme Bâton's voyage both pleases and torments me. It pleases me because it will be a distraction for you but it torments me because of the fears you mentioned to me. But really that woman can't be mad or indiscreet enough to demand from an old friend that she be perpetually on the move beyond her strength.

If I attain my goal of settling down at Honfleur at the end of June, I swear to you I won't budge for at least 6 months, not even for little business trips. I hug you and beg you to forgive me for all my faults, all my weaknesses, all my laziness. I'm not mad, I'm not ungrateful. I'm weak and consumed with remorse.

POSTSCRIPT: You mustn't torment yourself as you usually do about the indisposition I mentioned to you. It's a great nuisance but that's all. And this time the mobile neuralgia fixed itself neither in my head nor in my heart. Those are the most unbearable cases. Your letter of Saturday 27 didn't arrive until yesterday, Monday 29.

9 August 1865

My dear friend,

It was only this morning, Wednesday 9 August, that I received your letter dated 7 and postmarked 8 August. You'll receive this letter tomorrow morning, Thursday 10. Will that leave you time to make use of a few hints about *The Flowers of Evil*, hints I consider to be not unimportant?

Firstly, let me thank you for all the care you're taking and above all for your letter of this morning. To give you an idea of certain weaknesses in my nature, let me tell you only that seeing nothing come from you *I'd imagined that henceforth none of my books would sell*, and that therefore it was useless to complete *Spleen* and *Belgium*. Utter discouragement. Your letter did me a lot of good and I've returned to *Spleen*, which will certainly be finished at the end of the month.

So as to avoid neglecting any means of getting a bit of money, we'll give, or I'll give, the remaining pieces to Charpentier or the *Revue française*. For the need of money is making itself cruelly felt and I thought the matter could be resolved in two weeks. Well, I want to eat into as little as possible of the sum you'll get from the printer—from which sum I'll have to extract first the 1,200 francs for Hetzel and 500 for Manet—even before paying my debts in Brussels.

I forgot to tell Hetzel that the Damocles' sword of Malassis no longer existed and that he needn't fear a trial anymore. There will still be time to tell him when *The Flowers of Evil* and *Spleen* are sold.

Now, I'm coming to your letter. For the moment, I couldn't care less about the fate of *Poor Belgium!* (which I think I'll call *A Ridiculous Capital*). Sixteen months ago, I was saying to M. Dentu that I was going to leave for Belgium and that I might bring back a book. He then suggested to me that he'd buy it. On the other hand, when I was in Paris recently Massenet de Marancour told me that M. Faure would willingly take it. I answered that I'd put all my affairs in the hands of Julien Lemer and that I had no right to intervene directly. Have you seen Marancour?

As for abandoning this book under the pretext that I've pushed it aside today—well, that's absurd. I've already worked on it too much not to finish is. Moreover, I've some scores to settle with this unmentionable tribe. M. Garnier's repugnance made me laugh and made me think of what Alphonse Karr calls the Tyranny of the Weak. Belgium is inviolable. I know that. But I don't care. I think it would be good to speak to the publisher about the order in which he'll print things. This is how I think he should proceed:

First and foremost, *The Flowers of Evil*, augmented by several poems—and several articles and letters concerning the first and second editions (522 names). All that would be put at the end, as Sainte-Beuve did in *Joseph Delorme*. All that is partly with my mother, partly with Malassis, and partly with M. Ancelle. I'll certainly find a lot of those items. Note that the book is dedicated to Théophile Gautier and that the preface, set beside the dedication, will create an extraordinary effect.

I *know* that M. Eugène Crépet has no rights to the extracts that can be taken from his *Anthology* which he later sold to Hachette. *The Flowers of Evil* is the most urgent publication because, especially over the last two years, it has been in demand everywhere and in sales it's even fetching high prices.

If the publisher wants to make a deluxe edition later, a big in-octavo or a quarto, he'll only have to buy back from Poupart-Davyl the forms for the *fleurons*, the ornamental letters, and the *culs de lampe* prepared in Malassis's day. All that's needed now is a portrait and a frontispiece in the same style, the drawings for which are with Bracquemond.

So, first: 1. *The Flowers of Evil*

2. *The Spleen of Paris* (which acts as a counterpart to the poems.)

3. *Artificial Paradises* (a little known work)

4. Contemporaries, Painters, and Poets (on which I'm counting a lot and in this way they'll be bolstered up by three amusing books.)

Since you sometimes go to the Baden cafe in the evenings, give my regards to Manet—and tell him I'm relying on his not going to Spain without letting me know. I'm going to write a few words to Sainte-Beuve. I can see, my dear friend, that I'm going to give you a lot of work and I think it would be inappropriate to accept, even from you, an unpaid devotion.

POSTSCRIPT: I'm going to get back to work on *Spleen* and neglect *Belgium* for the time being. I'll send you *The Flowers of Evil* at the same time as I send the relevant articles.

178   To Catulle Mendès

3 September 1865

My dear Mendès,

Thanks for your letter [20] and your kind regards. I could perhaps be of assistance to you one of these days by giving a reading of English poems, or with a critical study of my *Flowers of Evil*. In the past I had an idea similar to yours, which was a series of recitations (interspersed with critical commentaries) creating a kind of perspective of French poetry—or

20. Mendès's letter of 22 August requested Baudelaire's aid in putting on a series of poetry readings, to include æsthetic studies and translations of foreign poetry, and readings by poets of their own works (*Lettres à Charles Baudelaire*, p. 243).

a family tree. There are such beautiful things—and they're so little known. The great danger of your enterprise is that it could turn into a fair, an exhibition of the weak, the vain, and the mediocre. Five or six poets each evening! Great heavens! In *fertile* centuries there are perhaps 10.

It brings to mind the end of an article in a Belgian paper about the (civil) burial of Armellini.

—Minute description of the catafalque.

—And then: "Behind there followed *a numberless multitude of free-thinkers.*" Well, how many have there been in historical times? Joking aside, I wish you good luck and ask you to convey my friendliest greetings to Leconte de Lisle and to the good Philoxène Boyer, whom I haven't seen for years and of whom I often think. He could perhaps *do things for you*. All yours. This is a country beloved of neuralgia. That's why I'm so late in answering.

Note: "and then two or three young people *like me.*" That, my dear friend, is an affection of modesty that shocks me. You know very well that I've read all your poems and I could astonish you by reciting some of them—that I've read only once.

179   To Charles-Augustin Sainte-Beuve

3 September 1865

My dear friend,

It would be very kind and friendly of you to take five minutes from your daily round to write me a few lines! I came back here (to Brussels) on 15 July. *There's been nothing new in the Lemer-Garnier business* since 9 August, when I received a letter from Lemer telling me he'd seen Hippolyte Garnier three times and that he hoped to conclude matters before the 12th, as Garnier had to set out on his travels again on that date. —Since then, complete silence. Lemer is too zealous a disciple of Pythagoras.[21] And, too, he doesn't know what the nerves of exiled people are like when they are cut off from news and communications. (Has the matter fallen through? Or has it been put off until Garnier's return, and is the latter still away? It's impossible to guess what is going on in all this.)

But what would help me forward a great deal in my work and conjectures would be to know *if you'd been consulted.*[22] Tell me, I beg you, that's all I'm asking. If you've been consulted that would prove to me that the affair has worked. But if, knowing me as you do, you want to attack me

21. The followers of Pythagoras took an oath of silence.

22. Sainte-Beuve replied that he had been consulted but that the Garnier brothers might have been alarmed at the thought of publishing the complete works, as they were "great skeptics when they couldn't see a clear profit right from the start" (*Lettres à Charles Baudelaire*, p. 344).

for my weakness and discouragement, go ahead and do so. The attacks you make would bring me pleasure and would at least show me that you're in good health.

If I were to fill 10 pages with my impressions caused by the last volume you gave me I'm sure I'd amuse you. I read it slowly for reading in the train hurts my eyes and in this foul climate I'm consumed with neuralgia. I've now met that M. Deleyre but you let me know him so well that I feel I've known several Deleyres. He's not an individual anymore but a type. Your enumeration of the army of tattletales and ultras under the Restoration made me laugh like a maniac, and I hardly ever laugh here.

But in general what most struck me in your book is the tone of justice and equity, a kind of philosophical good humor that lets you see what is good even in things you don't like. I could never have that talent. Talking of Rodin [23] and works that voice the popular hatred for the Congregation, you've forgotten *The World As It Really Is* [*Le Monde tel qu'il est*] by de Custine, which preceded E. Sue's books by many years. It's a book that I assure you struck me as very surprising, a book Balzac found too misanthropic and at which he leveled the same accusation that was later to be leveled at *The Human Comedy*. I'm alluding to an unpublished article by Balzac that Dutacq rediscovered. Your work on Lacordaire is illuminating. Your studies contain a mass of little details that are *very weighty*, by which I mean rich in suggestion, and it's a pleasure to seek out their meaning. I'm well aware of Father Lacordaire's weak points but I still love the great rhetoricians, in the same way I love painting and music. You need have no worries on that score. I'll be like all men in that my sensuality will diminish with time.

I reread the article on *Salammbô*, and the reply. Our excellent friend has good reason to defend his dream in all gravity. You were right to show him laughingly that it's sometimes not very clever to be too serious, but perhaps in certain places you laughed too much.

You can see how bored I am since I chatter on to such an extent that I'm even talking to *you* about your own books.

Forgive me and love me.

23. A character in Sue's novel *The Wandering Jew*.

1 October 1865

My dear friend,

It would be very kind of you if you sent me a note telling me the price of a copy of *Justine* and where I can find it, *immediately*; and telling me the price of the *Aphrodites*, of the *Devil in The Flesh*[24] [*Diable au corps*], and what, in your opinion, are the *Moral and Literary Characteristics* of other bits of trash, like those Mirabeau and Rétif produced.[25] What in the world does C. Baudelaire, esquire, want with a packet of filth? C. Baudelaire, esquire, has enough intelligence to study crime in his own heart. This note is intended for a great man[26] who thinks he can study it only in others.

I received a strange letter from Paris. It seems I staged *The Inimicable Brothers* at the house of Garnier. Meaning that Auguste is against me and Hippolyte is for me. Meanwhile I lack everything and I'm getting black looks here. A police officer came this morning to tell me I'd been in Brussels for a very long time and that he requested me to have sent from Paris an extract from my birth certificate.

Was that a sign of ill will or simply the result of some regulation or other? Thanks to Lemer's slowness, when the matter is finally sewn up I'll have spent everything in advance.

All yours,

C. B.

POSTSCRIPT: Arthur thinks it highly advisable to keep a watch on foreigners.

181   To Edouard Manet

28 October 1865

My dear friend,

The first lines of your letter sent shivers down my spine.[27] There aren't ten people in France—no, certainly not as many as ten—about whom I could say as much. The enforced slowness with which Lemer is acting (for I've really nothing to blame him for) does indeed make me suffer a great deal. I can see myself going through the 4,000 francs promised before I receive them. And you know I had the intention of taking out a sum for

24. *Justine* is Sade's novel, the other two, equally salacious, are by Nerciat.

25. Mirabeau was the author of a work entitled *Hic and Hec or the Art of Varying the Pleasures of Love*. Rétif wrote a series of novels about peasants corrupted by city life.

26. Sainte-Beuve had requested this information from Baudelaire.

27. Manet had contracted the "reigning epidemic," as he put it (*Lettres à Charles Baudelaire*, p. 237), cholera.

Hetzel and a sum for you. It should have been finalized on July 15, the day I returned to Belgium. Then it was to have been finalized on 12 August. Hippolyte Garnier set out for his country house and his annual holiday before matters were concluded. On 3 October, Lemer sent me a letter of explanation from which it transpires: 1, that Hippolyte Garnier left before the matter was concluded; 2, that they were awaiting Garnier's return on 25 October; 3, that Hippolyte was for me but Auguste against me; 4, that the book on Belgium was excluded from the bargain.

I'm going to send Lemer a table of contents, *very well set out and readily intelligible* and I'll beg him to find a deal *immediately, immediately* for the book on Belgium. If I'm keeping him waiting a little it's because I'm suffering again from my horrible bouts of neuralgia. That curse increases with age. Before, I experienced it only in my arms and legs. Now it's sometimes in my chest and head as well. What's strange in my case (my *literary* case) is that people continue to ask for my books in shops although I'm not publishing anything and I've let years pass between editions. How businessmen must despise me! And Victor Hugo! You say he can't do without *me*. He's been wooing me a little. But he woos everyone and treats all and sundry as *Poets*. My dear friend, your sentence has a whiff of the Stevens letters. Three spies in human form who rival the Havas letters. [Victor Hugo sends Baudelaire his latest published work. Baudelaire mentions this in the following terms: He wrote on the volume: "To Charles Baudelaire, *jungamus dextras*"] [28] I believe that means more than "Let's shake each other by the hand." I recognize the suggestions in Hugo's Latin. It also means: "Let's join hands, TO SAVE THE HUMAN RACE"—but I don't give a fiddle for the human race, and he hasn't even noticed.

You understand, my dear Manet, that I'm writing to you in *secret*, where many things are concerned—so if you see Mme Meurice, there's no point in hurting her convictions. That excellent woman, who in the past would have taken a pleasure in life, has fallen, as you know, into democracy, like a butterfly into gelatin. I likewise recommend you, if you see Lemer, not to tell him anything of my letter except the bits you think fit to pass on. It seems that M. Bracquemond, who came to Brussels, didn't think it worth coming to see me. He's putting on a sale of his lithographs in January. I very much want four or five Devérias, which he has. Sale, exchange, gift—whatever he chooses.

Don't forget to give your mother and your wife my most affectionate regards.

28. The autograph of this letter had not been found. The original publisher cut it after "Havas" and replaced the following passage with the analysis given in brackets.

13 November 1865

My dear Champfleury,

I beg your pardon for taking so long to thank you for your second volume on *Caricature*. There is a certain state of mind, vaporous and somber, that you can call, if you will, laziness or melancholy and which is the same as the weariness that results from an overviolent burst of activity. And that hateful state of mind makes us fail to carry out all our duties, even those that would be a pleasure.

I can't give you a detailed account of my impressions on reading your book. I found in it your three great qualities: sensitivity, good humor, and the spirit of justice. But—and this may not be without importance for you—this volume aroused in me a very strange sensation—it awakened in me the memory of a host of facts, anecdotes, amusements, pleasures, and impressions I'd all but forgotten. It allowed me to live again in days already long past. It renovated a painting that had become a little tarnished in my mind.

Thank you for everything in your volume that was personally agreeable to me. But, frankly, you praised and quoted me rather too much.

You often walk down the *Boulevard des Italiens*. If you meet Lemer, let him know my state of mind. Tell him I imagine—that I'll never be able to get anything published again—that I'll never be able to earn a cent again—that I'll never see my mother and friends again—and finally that if he has disastrous news for me he should announce it rather than leaving me in uncertainty.

If you see Uncle Beuve's amiable secretary, get him to send the articles on Proudhon. I know you're no longer on good terms with the Old Rascal [29] but if his article on the *Songs of the Streets and the Woods* [*Chansons des rues et des bois*] has appeared I'd be much obliged if you'd send it to me.

You can see I write like a man abandoned by everyone.

183   To Caroline Aupick

22 December 1865

My dear good little mother,

I should have answered you immediately, as you begged me to, but I stupidly procrastinated for three or four days and then was seized by a severe neuralgia or rheumatic attack in my head, like the bout I had last year, but of longer duration, for I've now been in agony for *fourteen* days.

---

29. Nickname for Barbey d'Aurevilly, a critic and prose writer.

It's true that there are moments of respite, the proof being that I'm now writing to you, but I'm never sure of a break, of even two hours. I've taken purgatives; I've wrapped my head in linen soaked in sedative water. That eased me momentarily, but the pain just won't go away. I'm no longer master of my time. That's when one regrets not working when one was healthy. ·

The word *income* was calculated to strike you, wasn't it? It's not exactly accurate but what I have in mind is very like an *income*. There are books that have a brief popularity and others that are always in demand. My translation of Poe, the rights to which I signed away for 2,000 francs two years ago, brought in, come rain, come shine, 500 or 600 francs. If, over the last nine years, I'd given careful attention to *The Flowers of Evil* there would have been at least 9 new editions, if not more, and each time I would have been paid copyright. Among the works Lemer is undertaking to sell there are, I think, only three that can hope for, if not continuous sales, at least several impressions, and those are *The Flowers of Evil*, *The Spleen of Paris*, and *Artificial Paradises*. My critical articles, by and large, sell slowly and are not often reprinted. You've fully understood now that when a writer remains the master of his property and has a certain number of works that sell well, he possesses a kind of steady income. To clarify matters briefly, imagine that the law allowed an indefinite transfer of literary property and that Racine's heirs had drawn since his death on the republishing rights of his tragedies, can you imagine the enormous sums they'd have been paid, even if we suppose the copyright payments to be excessively small? To have ownership of your literary property (if some of the works are the sort that go on selling for a long time) amounts to being almost rich.

Just now an imbecile took it into his head to have the awful idea of visiting me. After his departure my head was seized again with the gallops of neuralgia. I'll have to interrupt this letter. There are pills for neuralgia, consisting, I think, of quinine, codeine, and morphine. The horror that I've long felt about taking opium has prevented me from using them. But if this goes on I'll try them in two or three days' time.

Saturday 23 December

Where the jinx I complain of is concerned (and I'll revenge myself for it if possible) I cannot share your opinion, my dear little mother, despite all the deference I feel for you. I know my vices, my errors, my weaknesses, as well as you do. I'd willingly magnify my wrongs and despite all that I maintain that Paris has never been just toward me; that I've never been paid either in esteem or in money WHAT IS OWED ME. And the best proof that there is a kind of jinx on me is that in many circumstances my mother herself turns against me. In three and a half months I'll turn 45.

It's too late for me to make even a small fortune, especially given my unpleasing and unpopular talent. It may be too late for me even to be able to pay my debts and safeguard enough to support an independent and honorable old age. But if I can ever regain the freshness and energy I've sometimes enjoyed I'll assuage my wrath in horrible books. I'd like to set the entire human race against me. That offers a pleasure that could console me for everything. Meanwhile my books lie dormant, sources of income that have momentarily been lost. And, too, people are forgetting me.

A young man who's one of my friends and who, on his way from Paris, came through Brussels, told me he'd met Lemer coming out of the Garnier brothers' press and still asserting that the affair would go forward. It's not 4,000 francs he's talking about now but 5,000 or 6,000. But what a mystery there is in all these delays! In the end I'll go to Paris myself once the hurly-burly of New Year has died down and find out for myself what all this is about and then I'll certainly go to Honfleur.

Lemer sends me word that he'd very much like to see the plan and fragments of my book on Belgium. Belgium is now in fashion because of the death of that old fool of a king, and through a host of minor circumstances. I suspect Lemer would like to use it for his own purposes. But even if the book were completely finished, 800 francs, and that's all he can offer me, couldn't get me out of my difficulties and for reasons you'll have no trouble guessing I can't allow the book to be printed and published until I'm *out of here*. So it's essential to go back to the Garnier business, since he wants to persist with it. But 6 months lost! And why?

Finally, my dear mother, I'm dying of boredom—my great entertainment is thinking of you. My thoughts are always turning to you. I see you in your bedroom or living room working, walking, moving about, complaining and reproaching me from afar. And then I see again my whole childhood spent with you, and rue Hautefeuille and rue Saint-André-des-arts, but from time to time I wake from my reveries and say to myself with a kind of terror: "The important thing is to acquire the habit of working and making that disagreeable companion my sole pleasure. For the time will come when I'll have no other."

It wearies you, doesn't it, to write to me? You revealed that in your last letter. Write me a couple of lines from time to time, to tell me you're well if that is indeed the case. For I want the truth above all.

I'd very much like to have a portrait of you. That idea has *taken hold of me*. There's an excellent photographer at Le Havre. But I'm very much afraid that it won't be possible now. *I'd have to be present*. You know nothing about it and all photographers, even those who are first-rate, have ridiculous manias. They think a good picture is one where all the warts, wrinkles, faults, all the coarse features of a face are rendered visible in a highly exaggerated form. The HARDER the image is the happier they are. Moreover, I'd like the face to be at least one or two inches in dimension. There's almost nowhere but Paris where people know how to carry out my wishes and make an exact portrait, but one that has the soft lines of a drawing. But we'll give the question some thought, won't we?

Some time ago I got a couple of little things that I hope will please you. As soon as I have enough money to pay package and carriage I'll send them to you. If you don't like them, tell me frankly, but you'll accept the intention of a son who would be very happy to give you presents *every day* and who would do his utmost to obtain your pardon for all the grief he's caused you. Write and let me know how you are.

This letter will leave this morning. You'll have it Sunday morning if they sort at Honfleur on a Sunday.

184   TO NARCISSE ANCELLE

26 December 1865

My dear friend,

Thank you. I went out this morning to go to the post office and to find someone to pack the things I want to send my mother. My head feels a little strange, as though there's a fog in it, and I can't concentrate. That's connected with a long series of crises and also the use of opium, digitalis, belladonna, and quinine. —A doctor whom I summoned didn't know that in the past I'd used opium over a long period. That's why he was careful with me and that's why I was forced to double and quadruple the doses. I managed to put off the hours of attacks: that was a great benefit. But I'm very weary.

Thanks, therefore, for the 100 francs. But as for the watch, you're wrong in thinking it's not urgent. I first pawned it in September '63. The latest they'd hold it was October '64. You renewed the loan—final date November '65. Well, we're now at the end of December so *the legal period is over*. If anything goes wrong (for once the 13th month has passed the pawn shop considers the objects belong to them), we'll have to consult the sales registers (a great bore) and find the name of the buyer and then buy it back from him *at the price he asks, even assuming he still has it*. And think, too, how wearying it is for me to have to listen out for the vague ringing of the town clocks, as I sit in my accursed bedroom.

I must talk a bit to you again about Lemer. All these delays are highly mysterious to me. Are they the result of a weakening of willpower, or a fault in Lemer's character, or perhaps they're the sign of an excessive prudence on the part of this good chap, who has written to me two or three times saying: "Patience! Patience!" and who, having *refused any salary from me, still hopes the Garnier brothers will pay him, as he's brought them a first-rate affair.* What I'm saying is subtle, but not lacking in sense.

As a result of the Malassis business, you had occasion to see Lemer six months ago, and he knows you are a friend of the family and that you sometimes have money to give me. I see, therefore, no harm in your calling on him and with your usual tact, gently, delicately, without hurting him, talking to him about my worries and the obstacles he's encountering in carrying out *his promises.*

If you do, bear 4 points in mind:

1. If I didn't obey the invitation he conveyed to me through a mutual friend, Commander Lejosne (to send him a *plan and sections* of the book on Belgium) it's because I've been gravely ill, particularly since the visit of M. Massenet de Marancour.

2. My problems and worries. The small sums you've been able to send me don't come up to my expenses. So I'm obliged to go into ever-increasing debt.

3. My real need to see my mother and my home once more.

Finally, 4. The danger there is in *letting the public forget me* and in *letting my books sleep.* That's what torments me most.

Now the great comedy of the Belgian Mourning Period is over, the bitter articles about Leopold I are beginning. He really was *a wretched rascal.* Believe me! I've read the French papers. In general they're *inept*; apart from an article in *La Patrie* signed *Casimir Delamarre,* the French have no understanding of the Belgian question.

Read an article in *Le Figaro* on Leopold—a good article signed by Yvan Woestyne—which means *Van de Woestyne*—a Belgian artillery officer I knew in Paris. The Belgian officers treat him as a scoundrel, need I add.

Sainte-Beuve's articles, 3 or 4 of them, have appeared in the *Revue contemporaine*—they are miracles of intelligence and suppleness.

All your liberals will be *damned.*

Write to me *as soon as possible.* A thousand thanks.

185 TO CHARLES-AUGUSTIN SAINTE-BEUVE

2 January 1866

My good friend,

I've just seen that for the first time in your life you've given your physical being to the public. I allude to a portrait of you, published by *L'Illustration.* It really *is* you! That friendly, teasing expression, slightly concentrated, and even the little round cap didn't hide away. Shall I tell you I'm so bored that that simple picture did my heart good? That statement seems impertinent. It merely means that, abandoned as I am by some old Paris friends (among them Lemer), your picture is all that's needed to cheer me up in my boredom. What wouldn't I do to get to rue du Mont Parnasse in five minutes, to spend an hour chatting with you about your articles on Proudhon—chatting with you, who know how to listen even to people who are younger than you?

Do believe me when I say I don't find the reaction in his favor unwarranted. I've read a lot of his writings and I've known him a little as a person. As a writer he was a *good old bugger* but he never was and never would have been, even on paper, a *Dandy*! And that's something I'll never forgive him for. That's what I'll say, even if it means arousing the ill humor of all those great right-thinking idiots in *L'Univers*.

I'm not going to say anything about your work. You seem even more like a confessor and a midwife for souls. I think the same was said of Socrates. But mylords Baillanger and Lelut[30] have declared on their word of honor that he was mad.

A new year is beginning and no doubt it will be as dull, as stupid, as criminal as the ones that have preceded it. What good wishes can I make for you? You're virtuous and amiable, and (this is an extraordinary thing!) people are beginning to pay you your just deserts! (There are only two people I can chat to about you here, but in very different ways—Malassis and Mme Hugo.[31])

When I came back to Brussels in July, I thought that a French writer couldn't fail to visit Victor Hugo. This feeling, stemming from an innate politeness, precipitated me into the most baroque of adventures. I'll tell you about it if I ever see you again. For I sometimes feel that although I'm only 6 hours away from my friends, I'll never see them again. Mme Hugo alone, despite her sons, takes pleasure in hearing your name and your praise. The expression "great poet" doesn't arouse her astonishment. To tell the truth, in that regard, not enough light has yet been cast. It may well be I who'll help most to shed it—if anyone will print a line from my pen.

I'm chattering far too much, like a nervous man who is bored. Don't answer this if you haven't 5 minutes' leisure. [. . .]

---

30. Specialists in diseases of the mind, referred to in Baudelaire's prose poem "Let's Beat Up the Poor!"

31. Sainte-Beuve's novel, *Pleasure* (*Volupté*), is a literary transposition of his affair with Mme Hugo.

186 To Catulle Mendès

19 January 1866

My dear Mendès,

It's very good and you know I'm entirely at your disposal. I'll even go so far as to say I wouldn't spurn the 100 francs.[32] For I must go to Paris in the very near future and I haven't a cent. Is it credible that a distance of 7 hours would make our friends forget us so much? But we'll have to see what's possible.

1. I'm in the same position as you. I've just been frightfully ill, a lot of my pieces are overdue, and I don't know that I can prepare something for you right away.

2. Second, tell me if you forbid me to reproduce in a further edition of the *Flowers* whatever poems I choose to extract from *Le Boulevard*, the *Revue nouvelle*, and the *Revue fantaisiste*. If you did forbid me, that would raise obstacles.

3. I intend to revise those poems a bit, on the proofs, of course.

4. I'll have sent to you in the near future a little volume of mine and you can take from it what you will. That volume was done without my intervention; you'll find in it little pieces unknown to you and even buffooneries. Unfortunately it contains the six poems that were condemned in *The Flowers of Evil*, as a result of which it wouldn't be possible to sell it or send it to the papers. I didn't get angry, but I'll be careful to see that that pamphlet doesn't fall into any but friendly hands.

5. As for the general title, invent one.

Remember me warmly to Banville, Asselineau, Philoxène, Leconte de Lisle. —I'm fairly curious to know the identity of the audacious, absurd, inept, antiprogressive and divine mortal who dared to think that there would be readers for whom poetry, albeit excellent, I always imagine poetry to be excellent, could be a pleasure. It would seem that the absurd is still alive and well. I thought I was the only one of that type left.

I recently received a letter from Sainte-Beuve telling me of a journal I hadn't known of, *L'Art*. What manner of beast is this? All yours.

And as I imagine that like all *sensitive* people you can suffer only through the blood, the bile, and the nerves, I recommend to you quinine, Vichy water, digitalis, belladonna, and opium.

POSTSCRIPT: Don't forget to *take* a packet from Philoxène. *He has some magnificent things.* But through a strange weakness, which is moreover in harmony with all his personal *baroquerie*, perhaps as a result of

32. The lecture project having been rejected by the government, Mendès founded a periodical, *Le Parnasse contemporain*, for each issue of which the author would receive 100 francs.

241

particular ideas on the value of virginity, he doesn't want his poems published. He hides them, exactly as another man might reveal his. You'll have to rape him.

187   To Narcisse Ancelle

30 January 1866

A thousand thanks for all your zeal. You're making a much better job of it than I thought you would. I first read your letter to M. Lécrivain which will be posted today and which you should probably receive on the *second* or the *third*. Here, more or less, is the result of our conversation and consequently the subject of your future conversation.

1. The future arrangements you mention, are they a *reality*, at least a reality that's underway, or are they *an account of Lemer's hopes?* (Lécrivain, *who was associated with Lemer in the past*, would perhaps have pushed him on that question.)

2. I find the print runs are *too low*. Lécrivain says it's not very important and that the Garnier brothers will soon realize the value of my books.

3. What's the meaning of *this three-year delay?* And if, in 6 months, one of the 5 print runs has sold out, won't they have to pay me new author's rights, at the rate agreed? Lécrivain claims that that goes without saying.

4. I want to correct the proofs. I won't let a single line of my writing be printed without having read it at least twice.

5. Get someone to tell you what the double *mains de passe* are:[33] I'm claiming that some of these should be set aside for friends and journals.

6. Let MM. Garnier know that if I accept conditions I consider miserly, it's because I want *my works* to be protected henceforth by a *solid publishing house* and that I hope that's a reason for my whole *future* to be attached to that company. The Garnier brothers have no idea what the *Spleen of Paris* is; —that Sainte-Beuve, at the time of my farcical but deeply intentional candidature to the Academy, wrote in the *Constitutionnel* that some of these fragments were *masterpieces*. These are not my words. The article could be located.

The Garnier brothers are unaware of the value of the vindicating articles on the *Flowers of Evil*. (These are articles by Sainte-Beuve, Custine, Gautier, d'Aurevilly, etc.) Someone will have to talk to them about this. But M. Lécrivain claims that with people as cunning as the Garniers one mustn't appear to be in too much of a hurry. And, too, remember that if the two Garnier brothers have equal shares in the

33. Extra pages run off to replace faulty pages.

property, they are very unequal in intelligence and function. Hippolyte is the intelligence behind the operation.

All these points, without exception, are equally valuable. Lécrivain will also talk to you about *Belgium en déshabillé*. All the stories Lemer told you about this are *radically absurd*. It's true that no newspapers, no *review* even, can take the whole of this book, only perhaps a few descriptive fragments. It must come out, fresh and in its entirety, through a publisher. —There can be no publisher so stupid he can't follow the detailed program I sent you. There can be no publisher so stupid he can't understand that the condition I'm imposing (payment for the book quarter by quarter) is the best guarantee of my activity. (That's to allow me to finish the volume in France.)

I willingly accept M. Nisard's help. (Lécrivain doesn't agree with this.) I thank him for it in advance. Had M. Nisard read my program more attentively, he would have seen a line that corresponds to his thought: that Belgian impiety is a counterfeit, resulting from the teaching of French refugees. As for the dishonest and injurious lines he attaches to M. Hugo's name, my own thoughts go even further than his. But I can't express them.

Remember that *Belgium en déshabillé* is a very grave, very severe sketch, severe in its suggestions, under a frivolous appearance, at times excessively frivolous. This accords with your reproaches about the "shitty stick"[34] and other expressions made in strictest confidence. I'm convinced the publisher to whom you show this abstract of the work won't be misled.

I'm now feeling in better heart. I'm going to *rework Spleen*, and also rework *My contemporaries* (relying solely on memory, alas! for the manuscript is with Lemer). I'll have finished on 20 February if my fainting fits and vomiting don't come back. All I need, therefore, is that *all the clauses be voided by 20 February*.

As for your final piece of advice, I can't follow it. I'll never find the courage, first, to tell the proprietress of my hotel that I'm leaving without paying her, and second to steal again from my mother, whose goodness I've shamefully abused.

It's six o'clock. I don't have time to thank you as my heart desires.

POSTSCRIPT: Reread this letter *together with M. Lécrivain and discuss together the value of each part of it* (except the confidential passages on my poverty).

34. This expression appears in the argument of chapter 21, on annexation, in the notes for *Poor Belgium!*

15 January 1866

My dear friend,

I can't thank you too warmly for your good letters. It's really all the finer on your part in that I know how very busy you are. If I'm sometimes very tardy in replying it's because my state of health is destroying my willpower and even forces me to take to my bed for several days at a stretch. —I'll follow up your advice and go to Paris to see the Garnier brothers myself. In that case I may commit the indiscretion of asking for your aid again. But when will that be? For 6 weeks I've been plunged in pharmacy. That I have to give up beer is fine. Tea and coffee—giving them up is more serious, but acceptable. Wine? Now that really is cruel. But along comes an even harsher animal who says I mustn't read or study. It's a funny sort of medicine that suppresses one's principal function. The only consolation another medic gives me is that of telling me I'm *hysterical*. Do you share my admiration at the elastic use of these great words, carefully chosen to veil our total ignorance?

I tried to bury myself again in *Spleen* (prose poems) for it wasn't finished. At last I hope that one of these days I'll be able to show a new Joseph Delorme fixing his rhapsodic poetry on everything that occurs during his wanderings and drawing from each object an unpleasant moral lesson.[35] But these little things, when one wants to express them with both penetration and lightness of touch, are so difficult to perform!

Joseph Delorme came quite naturally to my pen. I started reading your works again from scratch. I saw with pleasure that each time I turned the page I recognized lines that were former friends. It seems that when I was a lad I didn't have such bad taste. (The same thing happened to me in December with regard to Lucan. The *Pharsalis*, always sparkling, melancholy, heart-rending, stoical, consoled me for my neuralgias. That pleasure led me to think that in reality we've changed very little. By that I mean that there is within us something that remains constant.)

Because you confessed to me that it doesn't displease you to hear your works discussed, I'm really tempted to confide in you 30 pages on that head, but I think I'd be better employed writing them out first in good French for myself and then sending them to a newspaper, if there still exists a newspaper in which one can talk of poetry. Nevertheless here are a few suggestions about the book that come to me at random:

I understood far better than previously *The Consolations* [*Les Consolations*] and the *Thoughts of August* [*Pensées d'août*] I noted the following pieces as the most striking: *Sonnet to Mme G*, p. 225 (So you know Mme

35. The reference is to Sainte-Beuve's collection of poems.

Grimblot, that tall, elegant redhead for whom the word "mercurial" was created—and who had that harsh voice, or rather that deep and likable voice possessed by a few Parisian actresses? I've often had the pleasure of hearing Mme de Mirbel lecturing her and *that was extremely funny.* — After all, I may perhaps be mistaken; it may be another Mme G. Those collections of poetry are not only poetry and psychology, they're annals as well.) You Rebel {*Tu te révoltes*} (p. 192), In This Gig [*Dans ce cabriolet*} (p. 193), Returning from the Procession [*En revenant du convoi*} (p. 227), There She Is [*La voilà* } (p. 119).

On p. 235 I was a little shocked to see you desiring the approbation of MM. Thiers, Berryer, Thierry, Villemain.[36] Do these people really feel *the lightning bolt or the enchantment of a work of art?* And too, are you really so afraid of being appreciated that you've accumulated such a lot of justifying documents? If I'm to admire you, do I need the permission of M. de Béranger?

Tarnation! I was about to forget *The Organ Grinder* [*Le Joueur d'orgue*] (p. 242). I understood far better than before the aim and artistry of such tales as *Doudon, Marèze, Ramon, M. Jean*, etc. The expression "analytic elegy" applies to you far better than to André Chénier. There is one more poem I consider marvelous, which is the recital of a funeral watch over an unknown body. This poem is addressed to Victor Hugo on the occasion of his son's birth. What I call the decor (the countryside or the furnishings) is always perfect. In certain places in *Joseph Delorme* I find a few too many *lutes, lyres, harps, and Jehovahs.* That clashes with the Parisian poems. Moreover, you'd come with the aim of destroying all that. In truth, forgive me! I'M WANDERING. I've never dared say so much to you. I've rediscovered poems that I knew by heart (why does one find such pleasure in rereading in printed letters poems one's memory could easily recite?) "On the Ile Saint-Louis" ["Dans l'île Saint-Louis"] (*Consolations*) "The Hollow in the Valley" ["Le Creux de la vallée"] (p. 113). Now that's vintage Delorme! And *Rose* (charming) (p. 127), "Stanzas of Kirk White" ["Stances de Kirk White"] (p. 139), "The Plain" ["La Plaine"] (a beautiful autumn countryside, p. 138). Gracious! I must stop. It looks as though I'm paying you compliments and I've no right to do that. That's impertinent of me.

5 February

My dear friend,

This letter was interrupted for a long period. I've been seized again by vertigo and trembling fits. Then I learned that you yourself were ill or

36. The reference is to the long poem "To M. Villemain" in *Thoughts of August*.

had been ill. That worried me and it worried Malassis, too. It seems there was some talk of an operation. What's it all about? What stage are you at?

No polite expressions when you write to me. But I beg you, charge your *fidus Troubatès*[37] with writing me *a few lines on your health*. Tell him, too, if he can spare a few minutes for these nothings, that it would be most kind of him to find that edition of a new journal, *L'Art*, and to give me information about another periodical, in verse, *Parnasse* (with an adjective after the noun).[38] Malassis could find nothing more on *Voisenon*. I think he was a little confused by the brief sermon you gave him. He had indeed had a bizarre idea (without realizing it). Knowing that you never go on attacking for any length of time those you are fond of, I laughed a great deal about it. As regards friendship and friends denied, do you know that the splendid line:

Is like a child who has died within us before its time

(line 12, p. 195, volume 2)
has been translated into prose—and very well indeed—in a short story by Paul de Molènes, "The Pastry Cook" ["La Pâtissière"], I think it's called, a story of the love of *a perfect light-horse officer* (to use Molène's style) for a pastry cook. The image is transferred from friendship to love. Perhaps he was unaware he was copying you.

But you're ill and it's possible I'm wearying you.

189   TO CHARLES ASSELINEAU

[5 February 1866]
It's not an easy matter for me to write. If you have some good advice for me, that would bring me pleasure. I've been ill for almost all the last 20 months . . . In February last year, a violent neuralgia in my head, or an acute, piercing rheumatism. It lasted two weeks, more or less. Perhaps it's some other illness? A return of the same affliction in December. In January, a further incident: one evening, when I'd had nothing to eat, I began to roll about and have convulsions as if I were drunk, seizing onto furniture and dragging it with me. I was vomiting bile or white foam. This is invariably the pattern: I'm perfectly well, I've eaten nothing, and suddenly, without warning or apparent cause, I feel confused, distracted, stupefied. And then an atrocious pain in the head. I can't possibly prevent myself falling over, unless I'm lying on my back. Then I suffer from a cold sweat, vomiting, and a long stupor. For my neuralgia they made me

37. Troubat was Sainte-Beuve's secretary.
38. *Le Parnasse contemporain*.

take pills consisting of quinine, digitalis, belladonna, and morphine. Then they applied sedative water and turpentine which were, moreover, useless, or at least that's my opinion. For my vertigo, Vichy water, valerian, ether, Pullna water. —The illness continued. Now I'm taking pills which I remember contain valerian, or zinc oxide, asafoetida, etc., etc. Is that an anticonvulsant? The illness persists. And the doctor pronounced the word *hysteria*. To put it in the vernacular: I'm going round the bend. He wants me to walk around a great deal. That's absurd. Not only am I so timid and clumsy that the street is unbearable, but it's impossible to walk around here, because of the state of the roads, particularly in this weather. This is the first time I've yielded to the pleasure of complaining. Do you know this kind of infirmity? Have you seen it before?

Thanks again for your good letter. Give me the entertainment of a reply. Shake hands for me with Banville, Manet, Champfleury—if you see them.

190   To Caroline Aupick

6 February 1866

My dear good mother,

Although I think of you all the time, I could say every minute, I scarcely give you any proof of it. But that's because it's very hard for me to write. You tell me wisely that we're always wrong to frighten our friends. So I'm unwilling to frighten you. First, I'm not ill at all, except during my attacks. But as I'm not pleased with my doctor, who always looks unsure, I beg you to read this note to your friend M. Lacroix, that is, if you're well enough to bother. He may perhaps burst out laughing. My doctor didn't take the matter seriously, either, until I had an attack under his very eyes. Moreover, it's pretty stupid to spend one's life lying down, and not being able to work. Now I'm an *oyster*. Perhaps M. Lacroix is familiar with this kind of sickness?

(My debts, my incapacity for work, the Conseil Judiciaire, your health, the Garnier business, all that bustles about in my brain and my immobility makes it all worse.)

And then, above all, how are you? Your legs? Your spine and the turpentine? Ancelle, as you know, went and threw himself rather thoughtlessly into the Garnier affair, without notes, without documents, knowing nothing at all of the habits of the house. Scold him? It wasn't possible for his intentions were good. I insisted that he go to Lemer to obtain documents. (He saw only the bad Garnier) and then I'm directing him by letters (what a bore!). Finally, one of my friends, a Frenchman, went to Paris and will teach him a few points about publishers.

I ask nothing better than to see your cousins. But when? Give them my affectionate greetings. I repeat I'm not suffering at all. But my powerlessness exasperates me. I feel that *it's not important*, however disagreeable it may be. If I could walk a few leagues under the sun around Paris I'd be cured, or so it seems to me. But when?

I love you very much. Write me a few lines if you can.

191   TO EDOUARD DENTU

18 February 1866

Dear Sir,

Two years ago, you told me that if I ever wrote something on Belgium I should let you know. It may be that what you had in mind then was a description of monuments. The *bride* is perhaps *too beautiful* for you now. What I have is a sketch of local customs that includes *everything*, or *almost everything*, not counting the descriptions, above all concerning certain towns where the imbecilic guides are so set in their ways that they are incapable of seeing anything.

One of my old friends, M. Ancelle, will give you, or have sent to you, a very detailed plan of the work (one volume of 10 sheets at the least 320 or 360 or 400 pages). *It's a plan designed to be read by a publisher*, not a list of contents. Belgium is somewhat in fashion at present thanks to French stupidity. The time has come for the truth to be told about *Belgium*, as about *America*, that other Eldorado of the French rabble—and the time has also come to undertake the defence of a truly French ideal.

The book (or rather my notes) is so copious that I'll be forced to cut bits out—but there's no great harm in that. There are redundancies. Think of the state in which Proudhon left his manuscripts. It can all be put into a presentable state within a month. But I've sworn not to write another line without the guarantee of a contract. I don't want any money immediately but I do want a series of partial payments each time I deliver a section of the manuscript. This arrangement is an excellent way of speeding the completion of a book, and the contract will be nullified if I don't deliver the work in its entirety or if I die, etc., etc. And in that case I could even, at a pinch, guarantee the repayment of the partial payments.

I'm currently master of all my books, without exception. I would *perhaps* have liked to offer you more, but one of my friends, whom I've put in charge of my affairs, has initiated an arrangement with someone and loyalty behooves me to wait either for a solution or for a refusal.[39]

39. This letter was included in one to Ancelle, but since on 21 February Baudelaire requested Ancelle not to interfere in his literary affairs, Ancelle did not deliver it.

21 February 1866

At last, my dear mother, a letter that does me good. You tell me you've now recovered from everything that alarmed you, and all at once. That's wonderful. But you'll have to write and tell me again several times, you must confirm it and with details. I hope and pray that it will last!

As for me, *I'm well*, apart from several recurrences of fever and a permanent background of neuralgia as in December. I'm weak, I'm stiff, I'm timid and clumsy, but that's all.

Yes, I've heard the bad news.[40] I've just written to Ancelle begging him not to get involved in anything. But rest assured I put that delicately. He finds the time to write to you far too often, and not often enough to me. The Garnier brothers wrote him a letter that he sent on to me and which is full of errors and stupidity. It's clear that Lemer presented the matter as clumsily as possible. Lécrivain, to whom I showed Ancelle's letter and that of the Garnier brothers—and who had been convinced of success beforehand—declared to me: "It's possible that Lemer meant to be very clumsy, to make the affair fall through and to force you to address him directly." That would have been very evil. — Ancelle obviously can't behave with tact and skill in matters completely new to him. I'm distressed that he threw himself into the Dentu business as thoughtlessly as he did with the Garnier brothers. It's absolutely essential that I stop him. That's going to mean yet another publisher *closed* for me and this will be grave because he will obviously let Dentu know about the *failure* with the Garnier brothers and repeat, as if it were gospel, all the false objections raised by the Garnier brothers. Dentu will then repeat them to others and so it will go on.

(I *beg* you, do you understand me? I *beg* you, I *adjure* you not to write to Ancelle. You waste a lot of paper in conjectures about matters you don't understand at all.)

I'll stick to my plan of presenting the matter in its entirety. Lemer was right when he said to me: "Don't separate *The Flowers* and *The Spleen of Paris* from the rest." It seems that Lemer consulted Lécrivain a great deal about what he saw as the commercial value of the whole affair. Isn't that odd! And isn't it suspicious? When I can I'll go to Paris. Yes, I know the story of Deschanel's ridiculous lecture.[41] The chronicler in *Le Temps* indicated it in a jocular and charming way. But a letter from Ancelle served as an excellent commentary. I believe that the good man shares Deschanel's

---

40. The Garnier brothers has refused to offer Baudelaire a contract, at least until he returned from Belgium.

41. Deschanel gave a public lecture on Baudelaire's poetry, which Ancelle attended, arousing the mockery of the poet, who described Deschanel as a "Professor for young ladies," a "little vulgarizer of vulgar things."

opinion. Note well that it's very likely that the people who applauded the poems found that book monstrous and mad nine years ago. It's said (and I believe it today) that the other nations are even stupider than the French. In that case, I must either return to live in France, despite that country's stupidity, or go to the other world. I propose to thank Deschanel when I see him. I bet he won't realize I'm mocking him.

I hug you and beg you never to let a long time go by without telling me about yourself.

193 To Jules Troubat

5 March 1866

My dear Troubat,

I think I forgot to thank you for your letter of 20 February. I received from M. Lemerre two of the three numbers of *L'Art* containing the articles concerning me. The fact that he forgot the first number isn't so serious that you should go to any trouble about it. I've read through the two numbers.[42] Those young people certainly don't lack talent, but what a lot of folly! What a number of inaccuracies! What exaggeration! What a lack of precision! To tell the truth they put the wind up me. I like nothing better than being alone.

I'm persisting in my idea of publishing my 6 volumes as a whole. I'll follow Sainte-Beuve's advice and go to Paris myself in three weeks' time, to try my luck. I may see that M. Lemerre but in speaking to him I'll use a great deal of discretion and I'll only mention a few DELICIOUS LITTLE PAMPHLETS, the main extracts from three volumes of various critical articles, pamphlets that I imagine presented along the lines of the *Original Library*.[43]

But in my view, that's merely a horrible makeshift in case I'm unable to insist on those articles being taken together with *The Flowers of Evil*, *Spleen*, and *Belgium en déshabillé*. Oh! that *Spleen*! What rage and what labor it's caused me. And I'm still not satisfied with certain bits of it.

I told you about the Lemer-Garnier disaster. M. Lécrivain, who saw Lemer on his last trip to Paris, is convinced Lemer presented the matter to Garnier as clumsily a possible, but with malice aforethought, to force me to take refuge in him. I don't like those overly profound thoughts. But Lemer has become suspect in my eyes.

It would be very kind of you to find me the address of Léon de

42. Verlaine's study of Baudelaire appeared in *L'Art* on 16 and 30 November and 23 December 1865.
43. This was a collection edited by René Pinceboude.

250

Marancour—you'll find it through Achille Faure, whose address is likewise unknown to me. I'm thinking of Dentu, of Faure, and perhaps even of making up to that *monster Lévy* again. But I've become clumsier and stupider than I've ever been. I was very happy to hear of Sainte-Beuve's recovery. I've only felt that sort of emotion about someone else's health in the case of E. Delacroix, who, however, was a great egoist. But affection in my case is closely connected with my mind. I very much hope that when I'm in Paris we'll dine with him one evening, that is, with Sainte-Beuve.

POSTSCRIPT: I'll bring you a little item whose only value lies in its rarity.

194   TO CAROLINE AUPICK

5 March 1866

My dear Mother,

As I know that the slightest bagatelles concerning me are capable of amusing you, I'm sending you this article in three numbers (I've only got two of them, I didn't receive the first), which came out a long time ago. These young people have talent—but what sillinesses! what exaggerations! what youthful infatuation! For several years now, I've been noticing here and there imitations and tendencies that alarm me. I know of nothing more compromising than imitations and I like nothing better than to be left alone. But that's not possible. It seems there is in existence a *Baudelaire school*.

You wrote me a lot of extravagant things, my dear mother, and your reproaches over my imprudence offer me no consolation. I've been duped, duped by Belgium, and then duped by Lemer. I've been deprived of your company two years longer than I'd thought after having already been deprived of it for such a long time. I'll now have to get by on my own and repair all the mess. You could quite rightly abandon me to my fate without adding reproaches.

But even reproaches are preferable to nothing at all. For your silence is always what alarms me most. Since you make no mention of your health I'm assuming it's good—*I'm right, am I not?*

I'm going to spend two weeks working actively on my *Spleen of Paris* and a few bits and pieces. When all that's done (except for *Belgium*) I'm going to Paris to try my luck myself. Obviously I'll be forced to return to Brussels but if I succeed in Paris, if I succeed in arranging the sale, I'll return to Belgium only for a few days. It's essential that I carry out a few errands, that I pay my bills, and that I pack up.

Do you really believe I take pleasure in living in a place populated by fools and enemies, where I've seen several French people suffering from the same illness as mine, and where I believe the mind deteriorates as the body does, not to mention the fact that *people are beginning to forget me* and that I'm unwillingly *breaking all my ties with people in France?* My installation at Honfleur has always been the dearest of my dreams. I learned that Sainte-Beuve had been very ill. He's written to me saying he's now very well. In his capacity as a former medical student, he took it into his head, despite everyone's advice, despite the dangers increased by his age, to insist that a painful operation be performed on him. But the thing was a success.

For several days now I've been suppressing my morning wine. I've taken cold meat and tea, in the English manner. The great advantage is that one can settle down to work immediately and continue for a long time. But that little intoxication the tea procures congests me a little, rather in the way one's head sometimes feels congested after eating an ice. Well, I've an extreme fear of all headaches. That M. Lécrivain (who went to see Lemer and has returned here) has just been seized by neuralgia again, by bilious attacks and cold sweats. Well, that man, who's a colossus of strength, is in a far worse state than I've been in.

POSTSCRIPT: I haven't heard a word from Ancelle for a long time. If I've offended him *it wasn't through a lack of precautions.* I'll see him in Paris.

195   TO CATULLE MENDÈS

29 March 1866

My dear friend,

My deepest thanks. Everything you tell me is pleasing and I'm content with your title. I'd already received yesterday from a printer called Toinon, with one foot in Saint-Germain and one in Paris, who returned yesterday evening to his Paris office, the proofs corrected partly by me and partly by Millot because, as I'm very ill, my handwriting is indecipherable. You'll receive this letter tomorrow morning, which is Friday, and I'd be very grateful to you if you'd run your eye over our corrections.[44]

POSTSCRIPT: It's *Sad Madrigal* and not *The Madrigal*. It's *Epigraph for a Condemned Book* and not *Epigraph for a Book*; *To a Malabaraise Woman* and not *To a Malabraise Woman.*

The last line of the poem entitled *Very Far from Here* should be preceded by a hyphen (-) to give this line a certain isolation—to set it apart from the rest. [. . .]

44. The reference is to the poems Baudelaire had provided for the fifth number of the *Parnasse contemporain*.

New Flowers of Evil should be written in such a way that *Flowers of Evil* is a title distinct from the word NEW.

196   TO CAROLINE AUPICK

30 March 1866

My dear Mother,

The reply sent on Monday reached you on Tuesday evening. Wednesday, Thursday, and today Friday you could have given me news of yourself, and if you didn't do so, it must be that you imagine I'm concerned only with myself.

It's absolutely essential that you give me your news. I received a letter from Ancelle telling me he'd come soon. That's useless, or at least premature.

—first, because I'm not in a condition to move;[45]

—second, because I'm in debt;

—third, because I have six towns to visit, say, two weeks' worth. I don't want to lose the fruit of a long period of work. I feel his main desire is to please and obey you. That's why I'm writing to you about it. Moreover, I'd like to return as soon as possible. Write me a long, detailed letter about yourself. I embrace you with all my heart.

Charles.

45. The stroke that partially paralyzed Baudelaire and rendered him all but speechless occurred that day or the day after.

Index of Works by Baudelaire

Works planned by Baudelaire but never completed
are preceded by an asterisk.

General Index

Abbatucci, Jacques-Pierre-Charles (minister of justice in 1857), 99
d'Abrantès, duchesse (writer of *Mémoires*), 13
Amic, Auguste (director of the Society of United Workers), 46–47
Amyot (bookseller), 214
Ancelle, Narcisse, xiii, xiv, xv, xxiii, xxvii, 25, 26, 27–29, 30, 31, 32, 33, 38, 39, 40, 45, 48, 50, 51, 56, 57, 69, 74, 75, 76, 77, 78, 79, 86, 97, 110, 111, 112, 140, 171, 194, 195, 207–9, 209–10, 218–19, 230, 238–39, 242–43, 247, 248, 249, 252–53
The Angelus (*L'Angélus*; painting by Legros), 131
Aphrodites (by Nerciat), 233
Argenson, Marc-René de Voyer, marquis (politician), 37
Armellini (Italian politician, exiled to Belgium), 231
Arondel, Antoine-Jean-Marie (owner of art shop), 68, 158–59
L'Art (periodical), 241, 246, 250
L'Artiste (periodical), xxix, xxx, xxxi, 23, 94, 124, 126, 134, 139, 155, 160, 163, 180, 181, 189
Asselineau, Charles (close friend of Baudelaire, critic and short story writer), xxiii, 81–83, 90, 125, 144, 188, 241, 246–47
L'Assemblée nationale (newspaper), 85
Astruc, Zacharie (art critic), 143
L'Athenaeum (periodical), 83
Augustine, Saint, 158
d'Aumale, duc (fourth son of Louis-Philippe, historian), 15
Aupick, Caroline, xi, xii, xiii, xiv, xviii, xix, xx, xxi, xxii–xxiii, xxvii, 3, 4, 5, 8–15, 16, 17, 18, 19, 21, 23, 24–26, 27, 28, 29, 30–34, 38, 39, 45, 47–51, 54–57, 66, 68–69, 74–79,

85, 86–89, 95–98, 99–100, 104–5, 106–14, 120, 127, 136–37, 138, 140, 143, 158–61, 164–73, 177–79, 186–87, 189–90, 191–92, 194–96, 198–99, 200–2, 204–6, 209, 210, 228, 230, 235–38, 239, 243, 247, 249–50, 251–53
Aupick, Jacques, xi, xii, xiii, xxvii, xxviii, 5, 8–9, 10, 11, 12, 13, 14, 15–17, 18–19, 21, 22–23, 28, 49, 68, 95, 96, 97–98, 110, 114, 170
d'Aurevilly. *See* Barbey d'Aurevilly
Autard de Bragard (M. and Mme), 22–23
Aymard, General, 6

Babou, Hippolyte (critic and novelist), 123, 125
Baillarger (mental specialist), 240
Balsamo (play by Dumas père), 224
Balzac, Guez de (seventeenth-century writer), 153
Balzac, Honoré de, xi, xxi, 40, 41, 70, 106, 108, 121, 153, 219, 232
Balzac, Mme de, 40
Banville, Théodore de (poet and playwright), xiv, 28–29, 53, 95, 184, 185, 187, 188, 199, 241, 247
Barbara, Charles (novelist and short story writer), 53
Barbey d'Aurevilly, Jules (critic and writer), 85, 95, 99, 127, 147, 190, 223, 235, 242
Barbier, Auguste (poet), 139, 152, 185
Bartolini, Lorenzo (sculptor), 217
Bâton, Mme, 228
Baudelaire, Caroline. *See* Aupick, Caroline
Baudelaire, Claude-Alphonse (half-brother of Charles), xxvii, 3, 4, 5, 6, 7, 21–22, 27, 28, 78–79, 160, 177
Baudelaire, Félicité (wife of Claude-Alphonse), 5, 22

Lemer, Julien (*continued*)
229–30, 231, 233, 234, 235, 236,
237, 238–39, 240, 242, 243, 247,
249, 250, 251, 252
Lemercier (banker), 162–63
Lemerre, Alphonse (publisher), 250
Lenglet, M. and Mme Amand (friends of
family), 40
Lenormant, Mlle (fortuneteller), 183
Leopold I (king of the Belgians), xv, 219,
237, 239
Lepage (owner of the Hôtel du Maroc), 68
Le Poitevin Saint-Alme (editor of *Le
Corsaire-Satan*; his name is sometimes
spelled Lepoitevin), xiv, 29
Leroy, Charles-Georges (eighteenth-
century writer), 192
Letters on the Animals (by Leroy), 191–92
Levaillant, Jean-Jacques (?) (cousin of
C.B.; he had three cousins with this
surname), 16
Le Vavasseur, Gustave (surname some-
times spelled as one word; poet ad-
mired by Baudelaire for his technical
virtuosity), 29, 139
Lévy, Michel (founder of one of the largest
publishing houses in France), xx,
xxviii, xxxi, xxxii, 76, 83, 86, 87, 89,
91, 107, 120, 138, 149, 153, 156,
191, 195, 198, 200, 201, 208, 211,
214, 219–20, 221, 222–23, 224, 251
Lewis, R., xxvi
Limayrac, Paulin (editor of the newspaper
Le Pays), 133
Lloyd, Rosemary, 87
Loève-Veimars (translator, best known for
his translations of Hoffman), 115
Lohengrin (by Wagner), 146
Longfellow, Henry Wadsworth, 161
Love (by Michelet), 120
Lough, J. and M., xxv
Louis-Napoleon. *See* Napoleon III
Louis-Philippe (king of France 1830–
48), 6, 15, 210, 214
Loyola, Ignatius of (founder of the Jesuit
order), 224
Lucan (Latin author), 244

Machiavelli, Niccolò, 153
Madame Bovary (by Flaubert), xi, xxviii,
102, 105, 114

Mademoiselle Mariette (by Champfleury),
xiv, 53, 60
Madier de Montjau (politician), xv, 38
Maistre, Joseph de (Christian philoso-
pher), 80, 132
Maître Favilla (by George Sand), 72–74
Maja desnuda; *Maja vestida* (paintings by
Goya), 128, 132
Malitourne, P., 188
Manet, Edouard, xviii, xx, 197, 203,
204, 217, 220, 222, 227–28, 229,
230, 233–34, 247
Mansell Jones, P., xxv
Marancour, Léon Massenet de (novelist,
dramatist, and political writer), 229–
30, 250–51
Marie (?), 43–45
Marin, Hippolyte (lawyer), 171
Mars, Victor de (secretary of the *Revue des
deux mondes*), 71–72
Massoni, General Charles, 11, 19
Mathilde, Princess, 99
Maturin, R. C. (novelist; best known for
Melmoth the Wanderer), xx, 137, 219,
220, 221, 222–23
Mayne, Jonathan, xxv
Mazzini, Giuseppe (Italian politician),
158
Melmoth the Wanderer (by Maturin), xx,
219, 220, 221, 222–23
Mendès, Catulle (writer, founder of the
Revue fantaisiste), xx, 230, 241–42,
252–53
Mercadet (by Balzac), 41
Le Mercure de France (periodical), xii
Mérimée, Prosper (writer and diplomat),
99, 113, 179
Méryon, Charles (artist, admired by
Gautier and C.B.), xvii, 141–42, 144
Le Messager de l'assemblée (newspaper),
xxviii
Meurice, Eléonore (wife of Paul Meurice),
212, 215–18, 220–22, 234
Meurice, Paul (dramatist and disciple of
Hugo), 134, 137, 147, 212, 217,
220–22
Meyerbeer, Giacomo, 56
Michelet, Jules (writer and historian),
120, 142
Millot, Gustave (republican journalist),
252